THE ELIZABETHAN PLAYER

THE ELIZABETHAN PLAYER

PLAYER

Contemporary stage representation

David Mann

London and New York

First published 1991
by Routledge
11 New Fetter Lane, London EC4P 4EE
Simultaneously published in the USA and Canada
by Routledge
a division of Routledge, Chapman and Hall, Inc.
29 West 35th Street, New York, NY 10001
© 1991 David Mann
Typeset in 10/12pt Bembo by Witwell Ltd, Southport.
Printed in Great Britain by TJ Press (Padstow) Ltd, Padstow, Cornwall

British Library Cataloguing in Publication Data
Mann, David
The Elizabethan player : contemporary stage
representation.
1. Drama in English, 1558–1625 – Critical studies
I. Title
822.309
ISBN 0–415–04896–6

Library of Congress Cataloging in Publication Data
Mann, David, 1941–
The Elizabethan player : contemporary stage representations /
David Mann.
Includes bibliographical references.
ISBN 0–415–04896–6
1. English drama—Early modern and Elizabethan, 1500–1600—History
and criticism. 2. English drama—17th century—History and
criticism. 3. Theater—England—History—17th century—Sources.
4. Theater—England—History—17th century—Sources. 5. Actors in
literature. I. Title.
PR658.A37M36   1991
792′.028′092242—dc20   90–35197

For Carole

Contents

CONTENTS

Preface

The initial impetus for this study began in the desire to collect and analyse play-extracts which featured professional players at work in recognizable situations. In the event this aim has had to be modified in terms of space and relevance. I have held to my determination to reprint from texts that are relatively obscure, believing there to be real virtue in associating a piece of text with its discussion. For too long a text like *Histriomastix* has been cited by critics as straight evidence of players; libel passing quite happily as fact. I have not included the texts of Shakespeare's plays, which are readily available, and elsewhere I have had to operate a rule of thumb. In some cases such as *A Mad World, My Masters,* the player scenes were too diffuse for inclusion, and I have curtailed those in *The Roman Actor* as less authentic. *The Knight of the Burning Pestle* has been excluded because it is set in a Children's Theatre, and its burlesque of citizen taste impinges only very obliquely on adult playing. I have not included aristocratic performers in private theatricals, since their authenticity too is often dubious. I have modernized the spelling wherever possible to bring it into conformity with the way Shakespeare's texts are usually presented.

Only a partial chronology of player-representation is possible because several of the key texts cannot be dated accurately. Instead I have tried to arrange the texts by way of an argument. The first group of chapters deals with itinerance, clowning, and extemporization. In part they give evidence of nostalgia for a passing age, but they also exhibit a ground-base of non-verbal, non-textual elements in all Elizabethan performance. I have included *The Mayor of Queenborough* in this group, because although it is a much later play, it exhibits many of the same characteristics.

The second group of chapters deals with a number of derogatory stage representations of players, in which evidence of playing and performance practice is often overshadowed by the contempt with which it is expressed. A brief coda to this section deals with the two principal defenders of playing. The attack upon playing is a complex matter, especially when it involves assailants who are themselves theatre practitioners and whose utterances often need to be interpreted in terms of the context in which they are voiced. It is also an important one, since the very nature of playing must have depended to a large extent on the estimation the performers and their audiences had of it. I discuss in the penultimate chapter some of the many ambiguities that underlie arguments on both sides, the controversy itself, and indeed the very act of playing which is their focus.

I have chosen to use the term 'Elizabethan Player', although a number of the texts stray into the reign of James, and one into that of his son. However as a short-hand term it seems to me preferable to 'Shakespearean', which is much over-used, as well as unfairly proprietorial, or 'Renaissance', which begs far too many questions. It is part of my argument that what the stage representations celebrate is a performance tradition, in the process of being modified, but essentially the creation of Elizabeth's reign.

I should like to thank Anne Barton, Nicholas Brooke, Michael Casey, R.A. Foakes, Andrew Gurr, Stephen Taylor, and David Wiles for reading earlier drafts and for their comments, J.R. Mulryne for his encouragement in the early stages of the project, my friend Michael Hattaway for his help and encouragement throughout, and Helena Reckitt of Routledge for her many kindnesses. My greatest debt remains to Carole, my wife, for all her support as well as her help with corrections. All the mistakes of course are my own. The book has been a long time in the coming, but lack of study-leave in the public sector does have its compensations. Whilst writing this book, I have, perforce, been involved in many years of teaching and practical experiment. I owe a debt of gratitude to the students who have worked with me on the many projects, particularly those involved in the seven-player touring version of *The Jew of Malta* and the private theatre replica production of *The Malcontent*.

E.K. Chambers' *The Elizabethan Stage* remains a marvel and a sourcebook of endless value. I would like to thank the British Library Lending Division at Boston Spa, without whose speed and resources the book could not have been written. Many of the works I have found useful are contained in the notes, but I should like to pay particular tribute to Muriel Bradbrook's *The Rise of the Common Player* and Anne

Righter's *Shakespeare and the Idea of the Play,* both of which have long
been a source of inspiration.

David Mann

Acknowledgements

I am grateful to the following institutions for permission to reproduce material in their possession: Bodleian Library, Oxford (from the title page of *Kemp's Nine Daies Wonder,* showing Will Kemp, shelfmark 4 to L 62 (12) Art); the Syndics of Cambridge University Library (from the frontispiece of the English translation of Paul Scarron's *Romans Comiques* (1676)); Henry E. Huntington Library, San Marino, California, USA (from the title-pages of William Alabaster, *Roxana* (1632), Thomas Heywood, *If You Know Not Me, Part One* (1623), Robert Armin, *The History of the Two Maids of Moreclack* (1609), Thomas Middleton and Thomas Dekker, *The Roaring Girl* (1611), Francis Beaumont and John Fletcher, *The Maid's Tragedy* (1619), Thomas Middleton and William Rowley, *The World Tossed at Tennis* (1620), Thomas Middleton, *A Game at Chess* (1624), George Ruggle, *Ignoramus* (1630), Thomas Heywood, *The Fair Maid of the West* (1631), Edward Forsett, *Pendantius* (1631), and Henry Marsh, *The Wits* (1662)); the Marquess of Bath, Longleat House, Warminster, Wiltshire (the Henry Peacham drawing of *Titus Andronicus*).

Note on the woodcuts

None of the woodcuts in this book can be regarded as unambiguous evidence of performers in actual performances. At best they can only give some indication of how contemporaries saw their players. As the frequent time-lag between performance and publication indicates, and excepting the occasional revival, many of the illustrators must never have seen the plays in performance. In some cases we cannot even be sure that the block was made for the play in hand at all. In the particular circumstances of some illustrations however, such as *A Game at Chess,* there are indications of considerable authenticity, whilst others impress with the vividness of their portrayal. The authenticity of each illustration is discussed in detail in R.A. Foakes, *Illustrations of the English Stage 1580–1642,* London, 1985.

1

Introduction
A definition of the context of study

An Excellent Actor . . . by a full and significant action of body, he
charms our attention: sit in a full Theatre, and you will think you
see so many lines drawn from the circumference of so many ears,
whiles the Actor is the Centre . . .

(John Webster)[1]

This study is concerned to examine a series of extracts from play-texts
which feature players as characters for the information they provide
about the nature of Elizabethan performance practice. In their formative stage these texts were hand-written 'scripts', copied in parts for
the actors, and intended for the two hours' traffic of the stage, and so
they generally remained throughout their active life. In normal
circumstances they were not printed, they did not become 'literature',
until they had ceased to be of value in the playhouse.

'Scripts' too in the sense of being incomplete; only one element in a
complex interaction between actors and audience, in which the desire
for that interaction preceded, and, it might be argued, overrode, any
specific text, however much it may have been revered subsequently.
Too much attention to the text, in attempting to wrest from it some
absolute, timeless, objective 'meaning', so often the purpose to which it
is now put, can distort our view of its place in the performance.
Although the scripts are virtually all we have to go on, we must learn
to look through and beyond them to the centre of the activity itself, to
which they give testimony only obliquely but which gives them their
quality and their *raison d'être*. 'The Actor', says Webster, 'is the Centre',
and this is a statement both literal and metaphoric. Positioned towards
the front of the stage and in the very middle of the auditorium, the
Elizabethan player commanded the theatre like the hub of a wheel and
was the focus of attention, whether he spoke or not. As this chapter
will go on to suggest, there are particular circumstances which led to

1

the special pre-eminence of the player on the Elizabethan stage and which justify a much greater attention to the characteristics of his performance style than they have generally received.

A play-text, however fine, can never be more than raw material, since the success of a performance depends upon the actor and audience achieving some significant shared perception of the human condition, and they do this by shaping whatever materials come to hand. This process involves therefore a fourth element in the interaction; the development of a common attitude towards the content of the script, and perhaps towards the way in which it is expressed by the playwright. A suggestion of some of the elements in this interaction is contained in the extract from *The Mayor of Queenborough,* which provides a double-role for the performer, assuming at one and the same time the role of foolish justice *and* the *persona* of the shrewd clown who plays him. In the tradition of Kemp, the performer shares with us his character's foolishness, inviting us to laugh both with and at the material; both distancing and then defining the comic world in which he lives, at once different from our world and from that of the serious plot. This process of distinguishing the actor from the material and commenting upon it is present, or potentially so, in all confrontations between performer and audience on the Elizabethan stage.

Rarely in modern criticism is the performer, as distinct from the character, recognized as a significant element in an Elizabethan play, and when he is the situation is regarded as exceptional. 'To some extent,' says Bernard Harris cautiously in his Mermaid edition, '*The Malcontent* is a play for an actor's theatre.' Martin Wine, in his edition of the same play, is more thoroughgoing: 'the frank confession of theatricalism is at the heart of the play's meaning.' It is no coincidence that such judgements are often accompanied by comparisons with modern theatre. P.J. Finkelpearl likens Marston's work to Expressionist drama, G.K. Hunter compares him to Beckett, and perhaps the most popular comparison, shared by Wine and invoked on a large scale by Michael Scott, is with Genet.[2] This use of contemporary parallels, helped by *The Malcontent's* Induction and frequent self-reference, allows us more readily to perceive how this particular play achieves its ends by theatrical means. Our failure to do this in the study of other plays, successful in their own day, is perhaps more an indication of our own limitations than of a qualitative difference in the plays concerned.

Part of the problem lies in the very process of reading a play. We are accustomed to filmed versions of Shakespeare's plays, which speak in their own, visual, language. The images in our minds as we read are often influenced by the paintings of Fuseli and Millais and others. We may still be hampered by nineteenth-century stage directions such as 'another part of the forest' which litter many editions. Modern productions of Elizabethan plays quite rightly address the expectations of their own contemporary audiences, often aiming for striking visual images, but generally performed in a post-Stanislavskian style of acting which deliberately fuses part and person. Hence the modern reader is likely to find the theatre-of-the-mind peopled not by actors, but by characters; and by literal, three-dimensional characters at that; real men and women, blackamoors and fairies in real woods or castles. In reading the plays it is difficult to take account of the dual apprehension, which the spectator is able to have, of actor and role as two separate, distinct entities; to which Hamlet's references to the clowns who speak more than is set down for them and to Lucianus's grimaces give ample, if negative, testimony. Instead many critics talk as though the central relationship were *character*–audience, rather than *actor*–audience. Even when actor/role disparity at its most extreme is thrust upon the critic, T.F. Van Laan, for instance, explains Cleopatra's reference to some quick comedian, who will 'boy' her greatness 'I' th' posture of a whore', as involving a momentary loss of what he calls *'her'* identity, which, he says, is 'utter and absolute. But only for a moment . . .'.[3]

The seamless, delicate, evanescent worlds the texts can create in the mind, as well as study-bound misunderstandings about their dependence on theatrical illusion, need to be confronted by the rigour of actual performance conditions. Illusion, certainly of the sort available in the Elizabethan theatre, operated not through tricking the audience but through their active willingness to enter into the deception. An incident at a performance of *Periander* at Oxford in 1607/8 illustrates what happened when this was not invoked. One of the student actors pretended to be a member of the audience and hissed and shouted during the prologue, 'Pox: begin your play, and leave your prating.' An observer noted that:

> The Chiefest in the hall commanded that notice should be taken
> of him, that he might afterwards be punished for his boldness, but
> as soon as it once appeared that he was an actor their disdain and
> anger turned to much pleasure and content.
>
> (*The Christmas Prince*, p. 286)[4]

The spectators were angry whilst genuinely deceived, and indeed the heckler 'had like to have been beaten for his sauciness (as it was supposed)'. It was only when they were party to the deception that the spectators' anger turned to pleasure. Furthermore, given that 'being deceived' is a voluntary process, it will be seen that breaking and then restoring the illusion, in calling forth more frequently the active early stages of audience participation, only serves to strengthen it.[5]

As many of the extracts show, the nature of the activity of playing is determined to a very large measure by the composition of the audience and its behaviour, both in the local outcome of the particular performance, and in the wider assumptions which the audience brings to the activity; it establishes the occasion and the 'rules' by which the performance operates. In the amateur, dramatic 'offerings' of dependants to their lords, depicted in Shakespeare's early plays, notwithstanding earnest sentiments of goodwill, the plays do not 'take', partly because of the ineptness of the performers, but mainly because the aristocratic auditors do not for one moment forget their own superiority.[6] At the other extreme spectators such as Sir Bounteous in *A Mad World, My Masters,* and Simon in *The Mayor of Queenborough* are so taken up by the dramatic fictions that they allow themselves to be humiliated and robbed. Only the more discriminating auditors such as Theseus and Sir Thomas More are able to follow the advice of the Chorus in *Henry V* in 'Minding true things by what their mock'ries be', perceiving both the falseness of playing and its value.

Audiences are apt to be thought of as straightforward receptors, responding directly to what they see, taking things as they are meant, but often the stage audience in an Elizabethan inner play responds inappropriately, as when Polonius bursts out at the climax of Priam's slaughter 'This is too long', and Hamlet is provoked to describe his taste, reminiscent of that of Captain Tucca, as 'He's for a jig, or a tale of bawdry'. Hamlet dismisses 'a whole theatre' as 'unskilful', 'who for the most part, are capable of nothing but inexplicable dumb-shows and noise', whilst sometimes the pleasure taken by more sophisticated members of the audience is seen to have little to do with the matter of the play, as with the Courtesan in *A Mad World, My Masters,* whose interest lies in the actors themselves, and the Empress in *The Roman Actor* who has a similar penchant and the position to satisfy it with private theatricals.[7] These observations, however contemptuously presented, testify to the importance of non-intellectual, non-literary aspects of a performance, and the love of dumb-shows and noise, or the attraction wrought by the persons of the performers, are not to be dismissed lightly. The theatre is in a large measure for itself and about itself; for its sensations, for the sound of the words, the shape of the stage configurations, the rhythms of the scenes, the process of enactment, the euphoria of collective participation. It is an art-form that speaks to us very largely through our feelings. Spectators are affected by the immediacy of the event, and by the effects of contiguity, here the primacy of the circle, multiplied by the rising galleries. Because a stage performance is of the here-and-now the audience has the sensation of witnessing something being summoned up in its midst, not unlike a religious experience or intimations from another world; uncertain and at least potentially upsetting. The extra devil that appeared at a performance of *Dr Faustus* in Exeter would have alarmed more than the performers.[8] At one and the same time spectators both fear and crave for bodily change, that surge of adrenalin which is part shocking and part stimulating; hence much of the ambivalence expressed towards the spectacle, and towards the actor too. Performers of any kind stimulate both rapport and hostility in an audience, and their skill lies to a great extent in how they juxtapose the two.[9] We can see this most clearly today in cabaret and club entertainers. Tarlton, their sixteenth-century equivalent, was by all accounts a past master at manipulating audience response; evinced in that special relief felt by every member of the audience who was not, for the moment, the victim of his witticisms. The extracts show too, in the antics for instance of Inclination in *Sir Thomas More,* and disastrously in Simon's contribution to 'The Cheater and the Clown', the survival of the medieval sense of the play as 'game', with the audience as in some sense participants, rather than merely observers.

It is very evident in the preparations for these inner plays, when the mechanics of a performance are laid out before us, how far the final product is the result of the physical processes that have led up to it, and in particular the organization and personnel of the troupe. As we grow more conscious today of the 'politics of theatre' we are beginning to discern in Elizabethan theatre a variety of aesthetic priorities conse-quent on differing production models. One of the most obvious of these is the four- or five-man itinerant troupe, so frequently illustrated in the extracts below, which reveal the effect of audiences, venues, and logistics on its dramaturgy and performance style.[10] Aristotle reports that drama began in Greece with the separation of one actor from the chorus, followed by the introduction of a second actor and then a third.[11] With this, he thought, reporting in c. 330 BC on a festival theatre which had achieved its heyday a century or so earlier, the drama had attained its mature form. One actor must have reported his own death. Two actors could engage in dialogues independent of the chorus. Three actors allowed the development of this process with a changing sequence of characters, and so on. Each change in performer resources affected the nature of the event and the relations between its parts. Four Tudor actors were presumably an answer to the conflicting priorities of how far their meagre rewards could be shared on the one hand, and the desire to sustain their sprawling, hectic, linear tales on the other. Four allowed a link man, the Vice, and encouraged the practice of each actor playing a number of parts rather than specializing in one, which had a distinctive and lasting effect on performance practice. The composition, organization, and reception of a troupe is therefore of more than incidental concern in any review of what can be learned from the evidence of the plays.

Itinerant troupes strolled the length and breadth of England in their hundreds during the century or so before the establishment of the first theatres. It is the performance practice that they evolved, with very little in the way of material resources and dependent almost entirely on their own persons and entertainment skills, which provided the basis for Elizabethan stage conventions, with remarkably little subsequent modification. Not only did itinerance continue in most years throughout the sixteenth and early seventeenth centuries, when the theatres were closed because of plague or other inhibitions, or simply, as *Histriomastix* suggests, out of term, but all productions must have been prepared with travelling in mind. Even the most well-established company was ever ready to obey a summons to perform at court, or in some nobleman's or alderman's house.[12] *Bartholomew Fair* opened one day at the new Hope Theatre amongst the bears, 'the place being as dirty as Smithfield and as stinking every whit', and was performed the next before the King at Whitehall.

Few of the plays need much more than the staging requirements detailed by Quince at his rehearsal in *A Midsummer Night's Dream*: 'here's a marvellous convenient place for our rehearsal. This green plot shall be our stage, this hawthorn brake our tiring house.' They needed somewhere to perform, and somewhere to change and enter from; and no doubt the 'houses', so often mentioned in court accounts as being specially constructed, served primarily these latter practical functions.

Recent scholarship has tended to reduce our view of the player's dependence upon even the most cherished features of the conventional image of the Elizabethan playhouse. The 'inner stage' as a miniature proscenium has long fallen into disfavour, there is little evidence for the use of flying machinery in the earlier theatres, and even the stage trap and balcony may not have been significant elements in most performances.[13] Although there has been a strong rearguard action on

PLAYERS IN FASHIONABLE DRESS

Figure 1.1 (top) Close representations of Marco Antonio de Dominis (played by William Rowley), Count Gondomar, the Spanish Ambassador (whose actual clothes were used) and Prince Charles, in Middleton's scandalous political satire, *A Game at Chess*, performed in 1624 and illustrated shortly afterwards.

Figure 1.2 (bottom) Aspatia, a girl in disguise, and Amintor, from *The Maid's Tragedy*, by Beaumont and Fletcher, performed 1611, illustrated 1619.

behalf of free-standing scenic units, which are attractive to modern critics and directors alike as practical solutions to immediate problems, their provenance is often dubious.[14] The sources or analogies offered for them mostly come from civic, religious, or courtly performances, in traditions which were repetitive and accretive, without immediate financial restriction, and designed to achieve or consolidate some kind of social cohesion, in which the provision of scenery was more often related to the status of the auditors than to dramatic considerations. Although Henslowe's 1598 property list (Appendix A) includes a few large properties, their relative scarcity should encourage caution in proposals for their use.

The dominant impression visitors leave of the Elizabethan open-air theatres was their non-representational elegance. De Witt remarks on the 'notable beauty' of the theatres he saw, and the wooden columns at The Swan which were 'painted in . . . excellent imitation of marble'.[15] Though the curtains hung on the stage may sometimes have represented locations or even moods, such as black for tragedy, it is more probable that in general they were decorative rather than representational. The stage hangings during *The Knight of the Burning Pestle* are of either the Conversion of St Paul or the Rape of Lucrece, whilst a similar curtain depicting The Prodigal Son may be the object of a joke in *A Mad World, My Masters* (II.ii).

Three inventories of costume survive amongst Philip Henslowe's papers. One of these, briefly summarized in Appendix B, indicates a number of specialist garments, mainly for low-class characters. No doubt garments were occasionally made for particular characters, but the frequency and variety of performances and the widespread concentration on upper-class characters in the plays are likely to have encouraged the regular use of a stock of costumes of the sort contained in two much bigger and more detailed inventories, one of 1598 and the other, quoted in a modernized form in Appendix B, of c. 1602. These latter inventories are very similar, and indicate the richness of the main playhouse stock, with materials of velvet, satin, silk, and cloth-of-gold, decorated with gold, silver, lace, and ermine. The frequency of black, white, and red amongst their colours is a reminder that a subsidiary pleasure of many visits to the theatre was the opportunity to see the representation of state ritual, in which these colours predominated. Many of the costumes used on the stage, we are told, were handed down from the nobility to their servants and then sold to the players.[16]

Some indication of everyday wear for people at large in sixteenth-

Figure 1.3 (left) Queen Elizabeth, from the title-page of
Heywood's *If You Know Not Me, You Know Nobody*,
performed 1605, this illustration of the same year,
based on earlier non-theatrical engravings, but
probably a fair indication of how the actor would
have been dressed.

Figure 1.4 (right) Bess Bridges, from Heywood's *Fair
Maid of the West*, written c. 1604 and illustrated in 1631,
probably from an old block, but chosen to relate the
character, as in the script, to Elizabeth.

Figure 1.5 Moll Frith, heroine of Middleton and Dekker's *The Roaring Girl*, performed 1607/8 and illustrated 1611; probably a fair indication of the appearance of the performer. Note the sharp contrast between this 'breeches' costume, in silhouette and freedom of movement, and the others on the previous page.

century Europe is given by the paintings of Breughel; loose, durable garments cut broadly on the shape of the body and serving as protection, and, in some degree, modesty. With minor variations they can be seen in illustrations of ordinary people from the twelfth century almost until our own day. Elizabethan court costumes, in marked contrast, express the principle of conspicuous consumption; vastly expensive in materials and maintenance, and grotesquely cut, with ruffs, farthingales, and peascod bellies – fashions that hindered their wearers in any serious occupation, and were redolent with the aphrodisiac of power. It is fairly evident from the preachers' detestation of this phenomenon that one of the most exciting aspects of a performance was the player strutting in this actual court finery or imitations of it. Notwithstanding the occasional and perhaps limited attempts at period authenticity, indicated by the *Titus Andronicus* drawing and references in the inventories to 'Antik sutes', the general run of playhouse costumes, pandering to the period's sartorial obses-

Figure 1.6 This drawing by Henry Peacham, c. 1595, is accompanied by selections from the text, which perhaps indicate that the figure of Aaron the Moor has been added to a tableau from I.i, in which Tamora, Queen of the Goths, sues to Titus for the life of her son. It is strongly suggestive of an actual performance, not least because it seems to indicate an attempt at authentic costuming on the sort of limited budget that would exercise a company more than it would an illustrator's imagination. The three figures on the right wear antique 'corselets', together with trunk hose in place of the strips of leather normally attached to a Roman breastplate. The costume of Titus also has an antique look, but his soldiers seem dressed somewhat at random from Elizabethan stock. The decorated garment of the huge kneeling Tamora defies classification.

Figure 1.7 A fine Devil's costume from Middleton and Rowley's *The World Tossed at Tennis,* performed and illustrated in 1620.

sions, appear to have been worn rather for display than their appropriateness to particular characters.

The discussions of acting in the plays, as in the demands made on the *Pyrgi* in *The Poetaster,* and in what we hear of acting competitions in *The Knight of the Burning Pestle* in which it is reported that Ralph 'should have played Jeronimo with a shoemaker for a wager', emphasize the semi-independent pleasures of skill for its own sake. Falstaff too introduces a competitive element into the rival representations of the King in *Henry IV Part One,* when he says, 'Judge, my masters'. Above all, *Hamlet,* that centrepiece in any discussion of the Elizabethan apprehension of playing, illustrates in the scenes with the players both a baroque, self-conscious artfulness, in which acknowledgement of the function of playing was a part, and clear evidence that this tradition

12

was no inhibition to a profound and frequently re-engaged involvement in the narrative and its embodiment of the human condition.[17]

It is likely that both stage façade and costumes had less to do with representational considerations than with providing a decorative but heightened neutrality within which the actor·had unlimited opportunity to create imaginative worlds, encouraged by the expectant circles of faces around him, but largely through his own exertions. When he failed, or when the performance was concluded, all that remained was Hamlet's 'sterile promontory', the 'bare island' of the stage from which Prospero's Epilogue begs release. The more we understand the player, the more we shall understand the plays.

2

The itinerant player and
Sir Thomas More

One characteristic of the representation of players in Elizabethan plays is the frequency with which they are shown on tour. Itinerant troupes of some sort appear in *Hamlet, Sir Thomas More, A Mad World, My Masters, The Return from Parnassus, Histriomastix, The Mayor of Queenborough, The Travels of Three English Brothers,* the anonymous *The Taming of a Shrew* and Shakespeare's *The Taming of the Shrew.* Of these *Sir Thomas More* remains in many ways the most unbiased and informative representation of the itinerant player. It offers a late sixteenth-century view of performance conditions earlier in the century, during the formative period of professional drama, and coloured no doubt by its performers' more recent experience of touring.

In his survey of the twenty-four extant Tudor texts of plays 'offered for acting', in which the number of performers and the parts they will play are generally indicated on the title-page, David Bevington shows that once the itinerant tradition had been established, four, or occasionally five, seems to have been the accepted number of players in a troupe. In two examples he noted, printers even announced plays for four players when closer inspection reveals that they would have needed more to perform them.[1] Of Augustin de Rojas Villandrando's eight categories of contemporary Spanish itinerant, it is his middle category, the *gangarilla,* that sounds most like the typical English company throughout most of the sixteenth century.[2] It consists of 'three or four men: one who can play the fool and a boy who plays the women's roles'. They charge each spectator a *quarto,* but are not too proud to accept payment in kind, 'a piece of bread, eggs, sardines, or any kind of odds and ends, which they put into a bag'. They sleep on the ground, and give performances 'in every farmyard'. Villandrando's categories range from the humble solo *bululu,* to full companies of sixteen, by 1602 genteel enough to travel by coach or litter, and no doubt gradations in some measure existed in England by the same

14

period. Although four remains a popular number in the later Tudor touring plays, six, seven or even eight begin to creep in after 1558, and by *Clyomon and Clamydes* (c. 1570), the number had risen to ten.[3]

The travelling companies that appear on-stage within the plays of this period revert however, perhaps not surprisingly, to the smaller numbers. The troupe in *Sir Thomas More,* set at the beginning of the sixteenth century, comprises the oft-quoted 'four men and a boy'. The troupe in *Histriomastix* describes itself as 'four or five', an uncertainty reflected in the *dramatis personae* which changes from scene to scene. Only three players are required in *The Mayor of Queenborough,* but they are later said not to be a proper company. Shakespeare is less specific in *Hamlet,* which has mutes and a prologue in addition to the three speaking parts. In *The Travels of Three English Brothers,* Kemp appears to be travelling alone with his boy, and the Harlequin with his wife. There may have been practical reasons for the preponderance of itinerant representations. If performer resources had to be shared between player-characters and stage audience, then perhaps the small size of a touring company would make it more credible, but the frequency of their representation suggests too a fascination with the itinerant process, especially, as in *Hamlet,* where the arrival of a group of strangers serves as a catalyst for changes amongst the members of a fixed community.

However exhilarating it may have been from time to time, touring, the players said, was dangerous and uncomfortable, and its rewards meagre. In the song in Act II of *Histriomastix* attention is drawn to the tendency of companies to split, and although Dekker suggests in *Belman of London* (1608) this was sometimes due to the ambition of the untalented, the primary reason he gives is economic. He draws a bleak picture of London players forced by plague to return to touring: companies that 'travel upon the hard hoof from village to village for cheese and butter-milk'; troupes 'that with strolling were brought near to death's door'; and 'players, by reason they shall have a hard winter, and must travel on the hoof, will lie sucking there for pence and twopences, like young pigs at a sow newly farrowed'.[4] In *Satiromastix,* he reminds Jonson of the latter's itinerant humiliations – 'thou hast forgot how thou amblest (in leather pilch) by a play-waggon, in the highway, and took'st mad Hieronimo's part, to get service among the Mimics'. Jonson in turn has Captain Tucca describe the vicissitudes of itinerant life, echoing the song in *Histriomastix:* ' "to travel with thy pumps full of gravel" . . . after a blind jade and hamper, and stalk upon boards and barrel heads to an old cracked trumpet' (*The Poetaster* III.iv.

167f.). Undoubtedly conditions on tour were less favourable than those in the capital, but Ian Lancashire has collected evidence of 334 playing troupes before 1558, which indicates the popularity of touring, at least before a comparison with regular metropolitan playing became possible, and might suggest some satirical exaggeration in these accounts.[5]

The precise origins of the early itinerant troupes are difficult to determine. The popular view that they owe some unbroken ancestry back to the Roman mime, and even further, will not bear much credence; even its most vociferous proponents admit that there was a period of several hundred years for which there is no evidence of anything like a play being performed, and it is difficult to believe that a tradition of skills could have been passed on through generations without being practised.[6] Similarities between performers of different periods are more likely to indicate a common natural mimetic propensity which is not dependent for its expression on any tradition.

The household retainer has generally been regarded as the most likely immediate antecedent of the itinerant. Recruited from other duties for the twelve-day programme of merriment at Christmas, his services were further called upon for disguisings or plays on folk themes at other seasons.[7] Eventually, so the theory goes, he and his fellows gained permission to absent themselves for the rest of the year and to stroll the countryside under the protection of their master's livery. The latter could thereby maintain his standard of entertainment at little cost to himself, and perhaps increase his reputation into the bargain. Less clearly defined were the other forms of amateur performers under the aegis of the magistrates, and generally grouped under the title 'town players'. They may have been offshoots of civic religious drama, or they may have been groups of tradesmen with purely secular ambitions, such as are parodied in *Histriomastix*. They need not necessarily have been inferior to household players. Early records often talk of small groups of 'clerks', presumably of some education, performing outside their own particular town or parish. Early evidence is confused by factors such as nomenclature, but in general it suggests the emergence by the middle of the fourteenth century of civic amateurs making short journeys in their immediate locality, but with no clear evidence of sustained itinerance until troupes, taking the name of a nobleman, start to tour from the middle or latter part of the fifteenth century.[8] By the turn of the century there is plentiful evidence of troupes on tour, in a fashion encouraged by the monarchy.

Although they maintained the fiction of liveried servants inherited

AN ITINERANT MUSICIAN

Figure 2.1 From the English translation of Paul Scarron's *Romans Comiques*, 1676.
'. . . come we must have you turn fiddler again, slave, get a bass
violin at your back, and march in a tawny coat, with one sleeve,
go Goost Fair' (*The Poetaster*)

'Better it is 'mongst fiddlers to be chief,
Than at (a) player's trencher beg relief.' (*Return from Parnassus*)

17

from an earlier generation, and most had a patron of sorts, the professional itinerants we find touring the land in the late sixteenth century were probably in social origins more akin to the despised town players. Ann Cook makes a strong case for the continued importance of patronage 'as more than a mere technicality'.[9] She points to the high correlation between a nobleman's advancement at court and the frequency with which his troupe performed there. The patron could offer real protection: stopping his players being taken as vagabonds, getting them out of prison, obtaining permission for them to play, and even subsidizing them in hard times, as in the plague payments to the King's Men during the period 1603–10. However this is not to gainsay a very real change in the economic basis of itinerance which the fiction of 'household player' served in part to conceal. The eponymous highwayman of *Ratsey's Ghost* comes upon a company of players who change the title of their troupe to whatever name they think will carry weight in that particular locality.[10] In writing to the Earl of Leicester in 1572, Burbage, Laneham, Wilson and their fellows make it clear that it is only his nominal support that they need to meet the provisions of the Act for the Punishment of Vagabonds of that year: 'not that we mean to crave any further stipend or benefit at your Lordship's hands but our liveries as we have had, and also your honour's Licence.'[11] Players of this sort are perhaps better seen as a new group emerging to meet new circumstances and new opportunities. The players themselves in their plays testify to this new economic independence. *Hamlet's* company is described as the 'tragedians of the city', there is no mention of a patron, and Hamlet's own patronage of them is as an *aficionado* from student visits to the public theatre. When the Lord in the anonymous *Shrew* play meets his household players, it is at an inn and by accident! The pretend players of *A Mad World, My Masters,* of course, invent their patron, Lord Owemuch. The egregious Captain Tucca in *The Poetaster* actually expects to get paid. He offers to pretend to act as patron in return for two shares. Perhaps most clearly a sign of the times is the burlesqued company in *Histriomastix,* in which townsmen adopt the guise of household players. They announce themselves as tradesmen – Belch, the beardmaker, Gutt the fiddlestring-maker, Incle, the pedlar – and then proceed to choose for themselves a suitably tolerant patron, 'the merry knight' Sir Oliver Owlet, whose name they can use and who remains a shadowy figure. In the less biased *Sir Thomas More* the player scene represents perhaps most clearly the accommodation that had to be made between on the one hand a large measure of independence from the patron and reliance on a popular audience (as Wit worrying about the unfavourable verdict of 'some curious citizen'), and on the other the very real need to be successful with those in power like Sir Thomas in order to survive and thrive.

The protection of the monarch was clearly different in kind from the more personal and local patronage of the household system, reflecting a shift of power under the Tudors towards centralized government. It also involved new ideas about performance excellence. Muriel Bradbrook suggests that the effect of the 1572 Act was to 'define the actor's status, restrict the number of licensed troupes, and so by a process of concentrating ability to foster the growth of professionalism', a view consonant with the later royal intervention, drawing together the best players of the time in the creation of the Queen's Men in 1583.[12]

The extracts reveal something of the problems of matching these new performance expectations with the more traditional assumptions of many of their hosts. Players arriving at a strange town would first have to gain the approval of the local civic authorities, and present their licences or other credentials. If they were not sent away, they generally sought approval through a performance before the Mayor. Mayor's plays are mentioned in *Histriomastix* and shown in *The Mayor of Queenborough*. The latter in particular is both a reminder of the humiliations which touring companies suffered at the hands of provincial magistrates and their constables, and an example of how they responded. More frequently represented in the plays, however, is the unheralded arrival of a troupe of players to offer their services to a nobleman, as they do for instance in *Hamlet*, *Sir Thomas More*, *A Mad World, My Masters*, *The Travels of Three English Brothers*, and in both versions of the *Shrew*. For most troupes no doubt such engagements were much sought after; Sir Oliver Owlet's Men in *Histriomastix*, for instance, are only too willing to abandon their performance for the Mayor when an invitation comes from Lord Mavortius, from whom they expect a larger reward. The welcome which the itinerant players' casual arrival receives, as shown by the plays, is generally warm, though we should perhaps view its authenticity with some caution. It may be not so much a reflection of what actually happened as the enactment of a politic fiction.[13] From Sir Bounteous Progress, the jovial host of *A Mad World, My Masters*, the arrival of what he takes to be genuine itinerants, provokes much excitement:

> Players? By the mass, they are welcome, they'll grace my entertainment well . . . How fitly the whoresons come upo' th' feast; troth, I was e'en wishing for 'em . . . Oh welcome,

welcome, my friends . . . Cover a table for the players. First, take heed of the lurcher, he cuts deep, he will eat up all from you. Some sherry for my lord's players there, sirrah! Why this will be a true feast, a right Mitre supper, a play and all. More lights . . .

Like another more famous incumbent of the rural bench, Justice Shallow, visitors from London set Sir Bounteous in mind of the long-gone pleasures of a misspent youth at the Inns of Court.

For all the (perhaps spurious) warmth of welcome, the extracts suggest that performing to a noble audience had its dangers and humiliations as well as its rewards. The players were obliged to perform in strange and sometimes hostile surroundings. In most cases their interlude is but a small part of a larger entertainment.[14] In *The Mayor of Queenborough* the play is planned to follow a supper for the King, something similar seems intended in *A Mad World, My Masters,* whilst in *Sir Thomas More* the play is planned more precisely to follow the main meal and precede the dessert, or 'banquet'.

Even those hosts with an enthusiastic and sympathetic attitude towards playing are conditioned, so long as it takes place in their own homes, by the older values associated with the household players. In *A Midsummer Night's Dream,* the very badness of the amateur 'Pyramus and Thisbe' asserts the status quo; it is taken by both parties as an act of homage, rather than art. As Theseus says:

> For never anything can be amiss
> When simpleness and duty tender it.

In *Sir Thomas More,* the host echoes Theseus' sentiments on the obligations of a noble auditor to assist the performance, but in the process converts a professional performance into something more like an offering: 'But if Art fail, we'll inch it out with love.'

The professional companies represented do get a better hearing at the noble houses than do the amateurs in *A Midsummer Night's Dream* and *Love's Labour's Lost,* and there is some evidence, perhaps in the behaviour of Claudius in *Hamlet,* of their potential to move their audiences. However the activity as a whole remains essentially trivial, part of a noble entertainment in which host and guest are bent on establishing and consolidating their own social roles, and in which the players can be turned on and off much as we would a wireless. No itinerant performer of an inner play is ever safe from interruption and with it the danger of loss of player concentration, loss of audience involvement, and even loss of earnings.

In 1639 Robert Willis in his *Mount Tabor* gives an account of a play which he had watched in his extreme youth, presumably sometime in the late sixteenth century, called *The Cradle of Security* (Appendix C). It shares many common features with 'The Marriage of Wit and Wisdom', the inner play in *Sir Thomas More,* and by coincidence is mentioned in its players' repertoire. Both are schematic allegories of human behaviour with clear didactic messages, but presented in an entertaining way, mixing moral instruction and lively action. They constitute examples of an important contemporary genre of drama, the Tudor moral interlude in which traditional material and traditional assumptions about theatre were being transformed to meet the needs of an emerging popular audience, which had quite different standards and expectations from that which had assisted at religious plays and courtly exhibitions. It paid now to be pleased, and not necessarily or primarily to be instructed. It grew to expect what we should call 'immediate gratification'. Its expectations had a considerable effect upon both the subject matter and its treatment in subsequent drama. The new audience would have been less tolerant of the faults of the players than in earlier traditions, but perhaps more capable of being involved in what it saw.

Both the moral interlude genre and the popular audience are treated with great contempt in *Histriomastix* and elsewhere, and it is refreshing to come upon a more positive testimony of the effect of an itinerant performance on provincial townsfolk. Although his eyes were evidently caught by bright, indicative costumes and symbolic properties, chiefly what Willis describes is the players' graphic enactment of the moral of the tale. The ladies sing the King asleep in his cradle, and when they draw back, his downfall is 'discovered'; he has been transformed into a beast. His judgement comes in the form of two old men marching round 'in a soft pace about the skirt of the stage', who strike the snout which disappears, and finally the King is carried away by wicked spirits. No doubt there was dialogue to point the moral that the King was the Wicked of the World and the old men the End of the World and so on, but what stays in Willis's mind, though he had seen it when a boy so small as to stand between his father's legs as he sat on a bench, was the visual symbolism. 'This *sight*', he says, 'took such impression in me that, when I came towards man's estate, it was as fresh in my memory as if I had seen it newly acted.' It used perhaps similar conventionalized mimes as those required in the long stage direction for the dumb show in *Hamlet,* in which the Player Queen is to express 'protestation' and 'passionate action'.

21

'The Marriage of Wit and Wisdom' in *Sir Thomas More* likewise shows how an apparently rather dry schema of the educational morality genre could be made lively and entertaining in performance. Sir Thomas, both in his anticipation, 'the theme is very good,/And may maintain a liberal argument', and later, 'A theme of some import', and in his own contribution as Good Counsel, stresses the didactic nature of the piece, in which Wit, or natural intelligence, is brought to Wisdom, or soundness of judgement (presumably through Science, knowledge), but these moral abstractions are represented on-stage in a strongly and humorously conceived encounter between a loose woman and a young gallant, egged on by an older rake, who teaches him how to make amorous advances.

The itinerant player established what control he could over the dynamics of performance by developing conventions that clearly marked the beginning of the play and adjusted the expectations of the audience. The inner plays in this selection signal their commencement in an elaborate manner. They begin with trumpets and follow this with a prologue, which helps adjust and determine the relationship between actors and audience and commonly announces the plot that is to follow. Perhaps at one stage in its development the prologue was accompanied by a dumb-show as in *A Midsummer Night's Dream,* much in the manner of the dramatic entertainments described by Lydgate in the early fifteenth century.[15] In 'The Murder of Gonzago', only the dumb-show remains, and the comments particularly of Ophelia suggest that it is not entirely comprehensible without a narrative.

Unlike its broader use in *commedia dell'arte,* the principal means for free improvisation in the interlude lay in the hands of the Vice, who served not merely as the instigator of evil and mischief within the narrative, but also as compère and often the moralist as well. In this he was the leader of the company and its most experienced performer, able to establish a direct rapport with the audience and maintain the performance through any mishaps, as well as exploiting any opportunities for spontaneous fun that might present themselves. In some plays he rarely leaves the stage and is often left alone there to occupy the audience whilst the others change. In *Sir Thomas More,* Inclination seems to be the leader of the company, and the text includes an insertion, not found in its source, in which Inclination engages in a piece of direct address:

> Back with these boys and saucy great knaves!
> What, stand you so big in your braves?

My dagger about your coxcombs shall walk,
If I may so much as hear ye chat or talk.

At an earlier stage of drama it may have been necessary for a 'whiffler'
to clear a space and to obtain the attention and silence of the assembly,
and perhaps delineate the acting area with a wooden sword. By the
fifteenth century, far from silencing an already expectant audience,
whiffling seems to have become something of a cherished convention
used to involve the audience in an active game-like relationship with
the performance, perhaps hissing and booing the tyrant who opened the
play, as in the Towneley *Resurrection,* in which Pilate threatens to hang
those members of the audience who do not clear the acting space and
shut up.[16] Always the most theatrical, the evil character could thus be
employed, half stepping out of the play, and, by casting the audience as
his followers, half drawing them into it, as a mediating, transitional
process to get the play started. The peculiarity of Inclination's speech
however is that it takes place in the middle of a scene, as though
Munday remembered and wished to repeat the technique, but had
somehow forgotten its actual purpose.

The success of English players abroad, unskilled in the native
tongues, as of Italian players in France, suggests the continuance of
non-verbal forms of entertainment throughout the sixteenth century.[17]
English players at the Danish court in 1586 including Pope and Bryan
are called 'instrumentister och springer'.[18] Simon's remark in *The Mayor
of Queenborough,* 'You are very strong in the wrists, methinks', suggests
the player accompanied his recital of their versatility with some sort of
physical display. One of the most popular set-pieces in the interlude
was the comic fight involving most of the company, in which, as the
texts 'offered for acting' show, there was a lot of noise and horseplay,
and more tumbling than violence. *Cambises* (c. 1570) has two of these
fights, one with ruffians and the other with comic countrymen, placed
equidistant in the text, one with the stage direction: 'Here let them
fight with their staves, not come near another by three or four yards.'
Common Conditions (1576) has a similar pair of scenes, one with tinkers
and the other with pirates. The second of the two fight scenes in *The
Tide Tarrieth No Man* (1576) contains the direction: 'And fighteth to
prolong the time, while Wantonness maketh her ready.' Set-pieces of
this kind were obviously popular and could be manipulated both to
please the audience and to cover awkward gaps in the action. Singing
and music are obviously important elements in all the interludes. A
study of doubling in *Cambises,* for instance, suggests that Players One

and Five were the company's musicians. In *The Tide Tarrieth No Man* by George Wapull, songs are used regularly to hammer home the moral point of a sequence, and in the 'Marriage of Wit and Wisdom' in *Sir Thomas More* some sort of dance or movement accompanies the entrance of both Wit, with his ruffling song, and Vanity, singing her 'come hither, come'. The effect of such an entrance is quite different from one straightforwardly dramatic in character, as any modern musical comedy will show; there is a break in the flow of the narrative as the character is displayed, but arguably a richer association between performer and audience thereby.

Though the resources the itinerants could carry with them would be limited in size, their plays often require quite elaborate portable properties. Means of dramatic transformations seem to have been popular, such as the snout in *The Cradle of Security*, and perhaps Inclination's bridle in 'The Marriage of Wit and Wisdom'. *Cambises* requires a whole list of gory properties; to enable one character to be flayed alive with a false skin, another to have a sword thrust up his side and a third to have his heart cut out; as well as more conventional properties such as bladders filled with vinegar. In *All for Money* (1578) by Thomas Lupton, the text requires most elaborate garments for many of the thirty-two characters played by the four actors in the company. Damnation is born with a 'terrible vizard' and a garment painted with flames of fire, and there is a 'bottle-nosed' Satan 'as deformedly dressed as may be'. Masks and loose upper garments may have been elaborate, but, by the brevity of changing-time allowed and the number of parts the actor had to play, the texts suggest on the whole that these were slipped over all-purpose basic costumes.

Perhaps the most characteristic and significant feature of itinerant practice and interlude dramaturgy alike is the use of doubling. This was not merely a convenience for enabling a small group of actors to encompass all the characters in a story but an enjoyable feature of the performance in its own right, and actively sought. Characters superfluous to the story were introduced to display the performers' versatility. In *All for Money,* for instance, the genesis of Money leading to Pleasure, Pleasure to Sin, and Sin to Damnation, is represented onstage as a series of births or spewings forth. Within a few lines, the cast of four not only plays each of the three parents and each of the three offspring, but also provides two *different* midwives for each birth. In *The Tide Tarrieth No Man,* although again there is a company of only four, the Vice is assisted by *three* lieutenants in his corruption of a series of victims. The casting implications of *Cambises* suggest that as the companies grew in size (or entered into combination) opportunities for specialization increased. There is a tyrant, a vice, a female specialist, more heavily 'loden' even than the boy in *Sir Thomas More,* together with four all-purpose actors who continue the traditions of the four-man companies, each with a wide range of generically distinguished roles. It is characteristic of the genre, as the analysis in Appendix D reveals, that the performers are perpetually in action. In *Common Conditions,* for instance, at line 1048, a cast of six somehow manages to give the impression of five characters leaving the stage and two entering.

When an actor doubles it affects his relations with each role, with the audience, with the text, and with the stage event. The performer who is continually engaged in presenting a series of characters, and perhaps carrying out the functions of stage keeper and musician as well, stands in a different relationship to the event than one who plays a single part and sits in his dressing room between stage appearances.[19] The distribution of parts in the moral interlude was organized around contrast and not specialism, often requiring the player to alternate virtuous and vicious parts. Because his parts are diverse, the player will present his characters in contrast one with another, succinctly, strongly, and more often than not, with a touch of humour. He will tend to see himself more as an entertainer and storyteller, sharing responsibility with the rest of the company for the success of the performance as a whole. Though the main roles would perhaps be cast with an eye to their suitability within the company, the exigences of playing meant that by the time the small parts were shared, the main criterion would be whether or not the actor was already on-stage. The results would be brief comic cameos displaying the actor's versatility. Mother Croote, for instance, in the four-man *All for Money*, would be very different from a real old woman, or Wantonness in *The Tide Tarrieth No Man* from a genuine fourteen-year-old strumpet. In assuming more than one part, many factors come into play that are not found outside the doubling tradition. The parts relate differently to each other, as well as to the performer. The boy in *Sir Thomas More,* for instance, as well as playing Dame Science, in presenting the two young females, Wisdom and Vanity, who pretends to be Wisdom, will be encouraged to push the moral virgin/strumpet duality of the marginalized female to either extreme.[20] The picaresque nature of the interlude genre, with very few roles that continue throughout, meant that the actors often worked in pairs, reappearing every now and then as a new pair of characters, freshly disguised and perhaps with a new dynamic between them, but still taking on some of the associations of a double-act. In *All for Money* (II.1024f.) two players appear to have alternated six cameo roles in turn. After a while the audience would find itself knowing which actor must next appear, but waiting to see in what new guise. In multiple playing the relative inappropriateness of actor to character becomes part of the pleasures of performance.

Doubling did not disappear with the establishment of regular playing in London, but continued to be frequent throughout Elizabethan and Jacobean theatre, as a glance at the *dramatis personae* of *Julius Caesar* or *Believe As You List* will show. As with *Cambises,* clowning and female parts tend to be specialist, but the broad spectrum of playing, given what little we know about the resources available, seems to have continued to stress variety and versatility. Only in the 1620s does some limited amount of type-casting emerge and then perhaps only in the Fletcher tragi-comedy school for which we have evidence, and anticipating a literalism that by the Restoration included female actresses and representational scenery.[21]

Doubling, on the other hand, was intimately bound up with a special complicity of the audience in the action of Elizabethan theatre, which was inherent in the physical space that it occupied. What had been an unavoidable necessity in the touring venues was retained as a feature of the playhouse structures themselves. The Tudor player, coming on-stage, entered into the same 'room' as that already occupied by his audience. He entered and exited the stage through doors set, for instance, in the screen of the banqueting hall, and facing much of the audience. The doors, as later in the permanent stage façade, were a key element in stage technique and a primary focus for much of the action. The Elizabethan player could not, as in a proscenium arch theatre, begin his business without establishing an accommodation with the spectators.

Exiting had its own difficulties. The clowns no doubt found their own solutions, and many exits were probably covered by attention being drawn to new entries, but the popularity of the final couplet suggests dramatists were deliberately modulating the relationship between player, audience, and narrative, and thus disengaging from whatever had been established in the scene in order to facilitate the player's exit. This in turn suggests, together with the decorated neutrality of the hall screen and later the stage façade, and probably of much of the costuming, that there were moments before leaving the stage, and perhaps after entering it, when the player was perceived as player rather than as character.

Not all players swept on with dignity. The establishment of rapport by poking the head through a curtain seems to have been widely used by stage clowns. Many entries, if not frankly comic, were potentially risible, especially where players were assuming parts obviously different in age, sex, or status from their own. The immediate effect of disguise on entry would have been very different from its continued use as the player moved forward into the three-dimensional plane of an open stage. 'Jiz' is the term coined by the Reverend Hartley to describe the distinctive outline-shape of each species of bird as it appears in motion. Each actor too has his 'jiz'; the combination of his outline, bearing, and voice. A brief moment of being deceived, face on, as the actor entered in disguise, is likely to have been succeeded by the shared amusement of recognition, whatever the dramatic context. To survive, and particularly to play tragedy, the player had to share with his audience a common acknowledgement both of the ridiculousness of impersonation and some sort of belief in its significance. Every time a player re-entered, this acknowledged conspiracy was renewed, and any change in the character's appearance, such as a change in status, or a disguise, as displayed in costume or bearing, was liable to intensify it.

Recognition of disparity however ought to be seen as a threshold rather than a barrier to subsequent imaginative involvement. In William Ringler Jr's detailed study of casting in Shakespeare's early plays, he concludes that because the Princess in *Love's Labour's Lost* was played by a man, and the fairies in *A Midsummer Night's Dream* by the mechanicals, they must all have been burlesqued.[22] However, there is no reason to suppose, as he does, that the actors were bulky or portly or gruff-speaking, and every reason to believe, though they may have made their first entrance with some archness, that subsequently the adult actors were able to sustain the spirit and atmosphere of the scenes in which they played. After all, much of the humour would be lost if the fairy world and Bottom's perception of it were not different. Disparity was an element in the total response to the plays, as a bond between audience and performer, but to be called into prominence when it was required.

Recent studies have rightly warned against the dangers of formulating a single monolithic theory of Elizabethan stage practice. If, as Scott McMillin suggests, there were substantial differences in the composition and policy of different companies, then this very probably affected their attitudes to doubling and performance style.[23] Ringler argues that Shakespeare's plays are carefully crafted so that a company of twelve men and four boys was sufficient to play all the parts, including mutes, whereas it is evident from the Lord Admiral's 'plots' for the same period that in their company gatherers were used as supernumeraries. In the plot of *Tamar Cam, Part One,* for instance, the final procession of Cannibals, Hermaphrodites, Pygmies and similar creatures requires the services, in addition to the twenty or so named actors, of a motley collection of playhouse staff including 'Gedion and Gibbs, Th. Rowley: and the red-faced fellow, Rester: Old Brown, Jeames, gils his boy & little will Barne' and 'Ned Brown'. This list has a scratch quality about it, suggesting perhaps a different approach to performance, as well as casting, from that of the Lord Chamberlain's Men.

The text of *Sir Thomas More* survives in manuscript form in six hands, thought to be a revision of an original draft by Anthony Munday, possibly in collaboration with others. Considerable uncertainty surrounds the composition and auspices of the play, but the most recent evidence points to a first performance in 1603.[24] Munday is generally regarded as the author of the player scene and some authorities have suggested Heywood as the author of Wit's stratagem at the end of this extract.

When the play opens, More is a humble City sheriff who is chosen to persuade the citizens rioting against the Lombards to lay down their arms. The immediate reward for his success is a knighthood and membership of the Privy Council, and this is shortly followed, when he pleads for clemency for the rebels, by appointment as Lord Chancellor. The latter part of the play charts the fall of More when he refuses to take the oath to the Act of Succession; his house confinement, imprisonment at the Tower, and execution. Since not surprisingly the political issues are avoided, and Henry VIII despite his behaviour remains a respected figure, attention is concentrated on the process of More's refusal rather than his motives.

In the centre part of the play, after his meteoric rise and before his much-lamented fall, there is a group of scenes representing the period of More's prosperity in which much of the action is taken up with a series of 'jests' of a chap-book humour carried out by the hero. A pompous fellow justice is deflated by having his purse cut. A clownish servant is dressed in More's clothes to test whether the 'great Erasmus can distinguish/Merit' from 'outward ceremony'. Chief amongst these scenes is our extract, which whilst serving further to demonstrate the hero's wit, humanity, modesty towards citizens, and his strong sense of justice, is otherwise a self-contained scene.

The player scene is a unique piece of evidence from the period. Unlike the other extracts reprinted here, it is neither coloured by anti-common player prejudice, as the majority are, nor does it offer an idealized picture of the players as do Heywood, Massinger, and Randolph. It is not made to serve structurally as a dénouement by the dramatist, nor as a means to some nefarious end by the characters. Indeed the very pedestrian and relatively inconsequential approach of Munday in representing the players' visit merely to flesh out an engaging picture of a warm and humane man, seems to allow its subject to emerge more clearly. Perhaps inevitably, it does call forth some incidental reflection on the relationship of Art to Life, but where in the hands of a better dramatist the scene would have been made to work harder, its patterns developed to support and extend the perspective of the play's main events, here, as evidence of contemporary itinerant practice, it appears to be uniquely pristine.

The 'Marriage of Wit and Wisdom' provides an illuminating contrast with the inner play in *Hamlet*. Shakespeare presumably contrives the playlet to echo his version of the murder of the elder Hamlet, and provides for it an especial style that enables it to be distinguished, and in part ignored, as the events amongst the stage audience, which are the central focus, unfold. Munday, on the other hand, approaches his task with a remarkable literalness. Unlike Shakespeare, who is no more precise about his itinerants' repertoire than the joke about mongrel genres, Munday takes all his titles from actual plays probably used on tour. Whereas critics disagree as to which are the 'some dozen or sixteen lines' Hamlet inserted, or even if we are to imagine they ever existed, Munday in contrast painstakingly lifts nearly all his inner-play lines from, if not the play announced, at least another of the same kind, and mentioned in their repertoire, Wever's *Lusty Juventus*. The prologue is borrowed from another educational morality, Ingelend's *The Disobedient Child*.[25] With respect to the dialogue he takes from his sources, apart from omitting the oaths, stopping the scene before it gets rude, and a couple of minor additions, Munday has done little more than change the names of his characters – Wit for Juventus, Inclination for Hypocrisy, and Vanity for Abominable Living. In substituting plagiarism for talent, Munday has perhaps unwittingly provided authenticity.

Although the players have as their patron Cardinal Wolsey, after Henry the most powerful man in the kingdom, they nevertheless subsist by casual touring.[26] The company consists of four men and a boy, and is led by the player of the Vice role. They arrive apparently by chance, and are immediately welcomed and engaged. They offer a repertoire of eight interludes, and their activity is conceived as part of a larger entertainment to which the town waits also contribute, and which has as its centre a meal that clearly takes precedence over the play. There is discussion of doubling, of extemporization and finally a short scene concerning their reward.

Since Munday's principal purpose in the scene is to illustrate his hero's humanity and extempory wit, this produces a performance context in which, relative to most other inner plays, the interlude is allowed to 'take', and the players accorded sufficient attention to enable them to display their talents and forward the narrative, at least until their own incompetence intervenes. Comments by the chief spectator, so often elsewhere an inhibition to the players and an assertion of the superior values of the audience, serve here to interpret and further develop the themes of the inner play.

The interruptions to 'The Marriage of Wit and Wisdom' and its abrupt curtailment help to keep it at a level separate from the 'real' life of the rest of the play. This is assisted by the couplet form of the borrowed interlude, and it is interesting to note that, perhaps in the excitement of the impending performance, More's own blank verse is attracted into the occasional couplet (l.50–1, l.116–17). The running problem of Luggins and his beard keeps our attention on the precarious mechanics that underlie the performance. It is not clear why the players should be so concerned about the beard; none is mentioned in the source, *Lusty Juventus*. It does not seem to qualify as an essential property, like Titivillus' head in *Mankind*, or the vizard and mace in *The Cradle of Security*, but suggests rather an over-concern with petty, realistic detail, such as is satirized in *A Midsummer Night's Dream* and used as an excuse for pilfering in *A Mad World, My Masters*. Thus a contrast is produced between the educational morality and the disinterested players who are its vehicles, taken up not with the message, but with their own immediate concerns. Wit, for instance, does not accept that the cancellation of the play is due to the King's summons, but instead ascribes it to citizen hostility, and Inclination agrees with him.

On his return, Luggins is going to have to transform himself from a breathless, threadbare secondary player to Good Counsel, a grave and sage figure of authority. Sir Thomas on the other hand is already wise and powerful, so that his extempory assumption of Luggins' part, though the performance may be halting and banal as he himself later suggests, is peculiarly fitting. It makes him for a moment the emblem of himself; the good counsellor, one who is to go to his death for his good counsel, rejected by a King with more Will than Wit (although the play is careful not to say so).

The coda to the scene, written in a different hand, contains further reflection on the relation of Art and Life, as the player of Wit uses the quality he represents to unmask a cheating manservant and obtain their proper reward. Not only does he show a natural intelligence that might make him more effective in his part (a principle the Empress asserts in *The Roman Actor*) but he chooses a dramatic fiction, searching the floor for imaginary money, in order to flush out the truth and affect real life.

Perhaps more than anything the scene pays tribute to the enduring power of the imagination and its thirst for enacted fiction, which can endure being broken and renewed, and broken again, and renewed again; a bond of involvement created by one man worrying about beards, and received by another worrying about banquets; a contract actively entered into, and inched out with love, confirming Huizinga's principle that 'The inferiority of play is continually being offset by the corresponding superiority of its seriousness'.[27]

SIR THOMAS MORE

From Act IV Scene I

Enter SIR THOMAS MORE, MR ROPER, *and* serving men *setting stools*

More: Come, my good fellows, stir, be diligent.
  Sloth is an idle fellow, leave him now;
  The time requires your expeditious service.
  Place me here stools to set the Ladies on.
  Son Roper, you have given order for the banquet?
Roper: I have, my lord, and everything is ready.

Enter his LADY

More: Oh, welcome, wife! Give you direction
  How women should be placed; you know it best.
  For my Lord Mayor, his brethren and the rest,
  Let me alone; men best can order men.   10
Lady: I warrant ye, my lord, all shall be well.
  There's one without that stays to speak with ye,
  And bade me tell ye he is a player.
More: A player, wife? One of ye bid him come in. *Exit one*
  Nay, stir there, fellows, fie, ye are too slow!
  See that your lights be in readiness;
  The banquet shall be here.[28] God's me, Madam,

31

Leave my Lady Mayoress? Both of us from the board?
And my son Roper too? What may our guests think?
Lady: My Lord, they are risen, and sitting by the fire.   20
More: Why, yet go you and keep them company;
It is not meet we should be absent both.

Exit LADY. *Enter* PLAYER

Welcome, good friend, what is your will with me?
Player: My Lord, my fellows and myself
Are come to tender ye our willing service,
So please you to command us.
More: What, for a play, you mean?
Whom do you serve?
Player: My Lord Cardinal's grace.
More: My Lord Cardinal's players? now trust me, welcome.   30
You happen hither in a lucky time
To pleasure me, and benefit yourselves.
The Mayor of London, and some Aldermen,
His Lady, and their wives, are my kind guests
This night at supper. Now, to have a play
Before the banquet will be excellent.
How think you, son Roper?
Roper: T'will do well, my Lord,
And be right pleasing pastime to your guests.
More: I prithee tell me, what plays have ye?   40
Player: Divers, my Lord: *The Cradle of Security,*
Hit Nail o'th' Head, Impatient Poverty,
The Play of Four P's, Dives and Lazarus,
Lusty Juventus, and *The Marriage of Wit and Wisdom.*[29]
More: The Marriage of Wit and Wisdom? That, my lads;
I'll none but that; the theme is very good,
And may maintain a liberal argument.
To marry Wit and Wisdom asks some cunning:
Many have wit, that may come short of wisdom.
We'll see how Mr Poet plays his part,   50
And whether wit or wisdom grace his art.
Go, make him drink, and all his fellows too.
How many are ye?
Player: Four men and a boy, sir.
More: But one boy? then I see
There's but few women in the play.

Player: Three, my Lord: Dame Science, Lady Vanity,
　　And Wisdom, she herself.
More: And one boy play them all? By'r Lady, he's loden.
　　Well, my good fellow, get ye straight together　　　　　　60
　　And make ye ready with what haste ye may.
　　(*To a servant*)
　　Provide their supper 'gainst the play be done,
　　Else shall we stay our guests here over-long.
　　Make haste, I pray ye.
Player: We will, my lord.

Exeunt servant *and* PLAYER

More: Where are the waits? Go, bid them play,
　　To spend their time awhile. How now, madam!

Enter LADY

Lady: My lord, th' are coming hither.
More: Th' are welcome. Wife, I'll tell ye one thing,
　　Our sport is somewhat mended; we shall have　　　　　　70
　　A play tonight: *The Marriage of Wit and Wisdom*,
　　And acted by my good Lord Cardinal's players.
　　How like ye that, wife?
Lady: My lord, I like it well.
　　See, they are coming.

The waits play. Enter LORD MAYOR, *so many* Aldermen *as may be, the*
LADY MAYORESS *in scarlet, with other* ladies *and Sir Thomas More's*
　　　　daughters, servants *carrying lighted torches by them.*

More: Once again, welcome, welcome, my good Lord Mayor,
　　And brethren all, for once I was your brother,
　　And so am still in heart . . .　　　　　　　　　　　　　　78

. . . .

More: . . . My good Lord Cardinal's players, I thank them for it,　　112
　　Play us a play to lengthen out your welcome –
　　My good Lord Mayor, and all my other friends –
　　They say it is *The Marriage of Wit and Wisdom*,
　　A theme of some import, how e're it prove.
　　But if Art fail, we'll inch it out with love.
　　What, are they ready?

Enter servant

Servant: My lord, one of the players craves to speak
   with you.
More: With me? Where is he?   120

Enter INCLINATION THE VICE, *ready*

Incl: Here, my lord.
More: How now? What's the matter?
Incl: We would desire your honour but to stay a little;
   one of my fellows is but run to Oagles for a long
   beard for young Wit, and he'll be here presently.
More: A long beard for young Wit? Why, man, he
   may be without beard till he come to marriage,
   for wit goes not all by the hair. When comes
   Wit in?
Incl: In the second scene, next to the Prologue,
   my lord.   130
More: Why, play on till that scene come, and by that
   time Wit's beard will be grown, or else the fellow
   returned with it. And what part playest thou?
Incl: Inclination, the Vice, my lord.
More: Gramercies, now I may take the vice if I list.
   And wherefore hast thou that bridle in thy hand?
Incl: I must be bridled anon, my lord.
More: And thou beest not saddled too, it makes no
   matter, for when Wit's inclination may gallop so fast   140
   that he will outstrip wisdom, and fall to folly.
Incl: Indeed, so he does to Lady Vanity: but we have
   no Folly in our play.
More: Then there's no wit in't, I'll be sworn: folly
   waits on wit, like the shadow on the body;[30] and
   where wit is ripest, there folly still is readiest.
   But begin, I prithee; we'll rather allow a beardless
   Wit than wit all beard to have no brain.
Incl: Nay, he has his apparel on too, my lord, and
   therefore he is the readier to enter.   150
More: Then, good Inclination, begin at a venture.

Exit INCLINATION

My good Lord Mayor, Wit lacks a beard, or else they would
begin;

I'd lend him mine, but that is too thin.
Silence, they come.

The trumpet sounds. Enter the PROLOGUE

Pro: **Now, for as much as in these latter days,**
　　Throughout the whole world in every land,
　　Vice doth increase, and virtue decays,
　　Iniquity having the upper hand;
　　We therefore intend, good gentle audience,
　　A pretty short Interlude to play at this present,　　　　160
　　Desiring your leave and quiet silence,
　　To show the same, as is meet and expedient.
　　It is called *The Marriage of Wit and Wisdom,*
　　A matter right pithy and pleasing to hear,
　　Whereof in brief we will show the whole sum;
　　But I must begone, for Wit doth appear.

EXIT PROLOGUE

Enter WIT *ruffling and* INCLINATION THE VICE

Wit [sings]: **In an arbour green, asleep where as I lay,**
　　The birds sang sweetly in the midst of the day,
　　I dreamed fast of mirth and play –
　　In youth is pleasure, in youth is pleasure.　　　　　170
　　Methought I walked still to and fro,
　　And from her company I could not go,
　　But when I waked, it was not so –
　　In youth is pleasure, in youth is pleasure.
　　Therefore my heart is surely plight,
　　Of her alone to have a sight,
　　Which is my joy and heart's delight –
　　In youth is pleasure, in youth is pleasure.

More: Mark ye, my Lord, this is Wit without a
beard. What will he be by the time he comes to the　　180
commodity of a beard?

Incl: **Oh, sir, the ground is better on which she doth go.**
　　For she will make better cheer with a little she can get
　　than many a one can with a great banquet of meat.

35

Wit: **And is her name Wisdom?**
Incl: **Aye, sir, a wife most fit**
For you, my good master, my dainty sweet Wit.
Wit: **To be in her company my heart it is set:**
Therefore I prithee to let us begone; 190
For unto Wisdom Wit hath inclination.
Incl: **Oh, sir, she will come herself even anon.**
For I told her before where we would stand,
And then she said she would beck us with her hand.
Back with these boys, and saucy great knaves!

Flourishing his dagger

What, stand ye here so big in your braves?
My dagger about your coxcombs shall walk,
If I may so much as hear ye chat or talk.
Wit: **But will she take pains to come for us hither?**
Incl: **I warrant ye; therefore you must be familiar with her** 200
When she cometh in place.
You must her embrace,
Somewhat handsomely,
Lest she think it danger,
Because you are a stranger,
To come in your company.
Wit: **I warrant thee, Inclination, I will be busy.**
Oh, how Wit longs to be in Wisdom's company!

Enter LADY VANITY singing, and beckoning with her hand

Van: **Come hither, come hither, come hither, come:**
Such cheer as I have, thou shalt have some. 210
More: This is Lady Vanity, I'll hold my life.
Beware, good Wit, you take not her to wife.
Incl: **What, unknown honesty, a word in your ear,**
You shall not be gone as yet, I swear.[31]

She offers to depart

Here's none but your friends, you need not to fray;
This young gentleman loves ye; therefore you must stay.
Wit: **I trust in me she will think no danger,**
For I love well the company of fair women:
And though to you I am a stranger,
Yet Wit may pleasure you now and then. 220

36

Van: **Who, you? Nay, you are such a holy man**
  That to touch one you dare not be bold.
  I think you would not kiss a young woman
  If one would give you twenty pound in gold.
Wit: **Yes, in good sadness, lady, that I would.**
  I could find in my heart to kiss you in your smock.
Van: **My back is broad enough to bear that mock.**
  For it hath been told me many a time
  That you would be seen in no such company as mine.
Wit: **Not Wit in the company of Lady Wisdom?**
  Oh Jove, for what do I hither come?
Incl: **Sir, she did this nothing else but to prove**
  Whether a little thing would you move
  To be angry and fret.
  What, and if one said so,
  Let such trifling matters go,
  And with a kind kiss come out of her debt.

Enter another player

(*Sotto voce*) Is Luggins come yet with the beard?
Player: No, faith, he is not come. Alas, what shall we do?

(*INCLINATION comes out of the play and speaks to SIR THOMAS*)

Incl: Forsooth, we can go no further till our fellow   240
  Luggins come, for he plays Good Counsel, and now
  he should enter to admonish Wit that this is Lady
  Vanity and not Lady Wisdom.
More: Nay, and it be no more but so, ye shall not tarry
  at a stand for that. We'll not have our play marred
  for lack of a little good counsel. Till your fellow
  come I'll give him the best counsel that I can. Pardon
  me, my Lord Mayor, I love to be merry.

(*Steps into the play as Good Counsel*)

  Oh . . . Wit, thou art now on the bow hand,
  And blindly in thine own opinion dost stand.   250
  I tell thee, this naughty lewd Inclination
  Does lead thee amiss in a very strange fashion.
  This is not Wisdom, but Lady Vanity.
  Therefore list to Good Counsel, and be ruled by me.

Incl: In truth, my lord, it is as right to Luggins' part

37

as can be. Speak, Wit.

More: Nay, we will not have our audience disappointed
if I can help it.

Wit: **Art thou Good Counsel, and wilt tell me so?**
Wouldst thou have Wit from Lady Wisdom to go?   260
Thou art some deceiver, I tell thee verily,
In saying that this is Lady Vanity.

More: **Wit, judge not things by the outward show;**
The eye oft mistakes, right well you do know.
Good Counsel assures thee, upon his honesty,
That this is not Wisdom, but Lady Vanity.

Enter LUGGINS *with the beard*

Incl: Oh, my lord, he is come; now we shall go forward.

More: Art thou come? Well, fellow I have holp to
save thine honesty a little. Now, if thou canst give   270
Wit any better counsel than I have done, spare not.
There, I leave him to thy mercy.
But by this time, I am sure our banquet's ready;
My Lord, and Ladies, we will taste that first,
And then they shall begin the play again,
Which, through the fellow's absence, and by me,
Instead of helping, hath been hindered.
Prepare against we come. Lights there, I say!
Thus fools oft times do help to mar the play.

Exeunt all, except the players

Wit: Fie, fellow Luggins, you serve us handsomely,   280
do ye not think ye?

Lug: Why, Oagle was not within, and his wife would
not let me have the beard; and by my troth I ran so
fast that I sweat again.

Incl: Do ye hear, fellows? Would not my lord
make a rare player? Oh, he would uphold a company
beyond all hope, better than Mason among the
King's Players. Did ye mark how extemporically he
fell to the matter, and spake Luggins' part almost
as it is the very book set down?   290

Wit: Peace, do ye know what ye say? My lord a
player? Let us not meddle with any such matters. Yet

38

I may be a little proud that my lord hath answered
me in my part. But come, let us go, and be ready
to begin the play again.

Lug: Aye, that's the best, for now we lack nothing.

Enter a serving man

Man: Where be these players?

All: Here, sir,

Man: My lord in post is sent for to the Court,
And all the guests do after supper part;   300
And for he will not trouble you again,
By me, for your reward, he sends eight angels,
With many thanks. But sup before you go:
It is his will you should be fairly entreated.
Follow, I pray ye.

Wit: This, Luggins, all is your negligence:
Wanting Wit's beard brought things into dislike.
For otherwise the play had been all seen
Where now some curious citizen disgraced it,
And discommending it, all is dismissed.   310

Incl: 'For God, he says true. But hear ye, sirs:
eight angels, ha! My lord would never give eight
angels – more, or less for twelve pence: either it
should be three pounds, five pounds or ten pounds;
there's twenty shillings wanting, sure.[32]

Wit: Twenty to one, 'tis so: I have a trick – my lord
comes – stand aside.

Enter MORE *with* attendants *with purse and mace*

More: In haste to Council! What's the business now,
That all so late his highness sends for me?
What seekest thou, fellow?

Wit: Nay, nothing. Your lordship sent eight angels by 320
your man, and I have lost two of them in the rushes.

More: Wit, look to that. Eight angels? I did send them
ten. Who gave it them?

Man: I, my lord. I had no more about me,
But by and by they shall receive the rest.

More: Well, Wit, 'twas wisely done; thou playest Wit
well ended,
Not to be thus deceived of thy right.

Am I a man by office truly ordained
Equally to divide true right his own,
And shall I have deceivers in my house?   330
Then what avails my bounty, when such servants
Deceive the poor receiver of what the master gives?
Go one and pull his coat over his ears.
There are too many such. Give them their right.
Wit, let thy fellows thank thee; 'twas well done.
Thou now deservest to match with Lady Wisdom.

Exit MORE with attendants

Incl: God a'mercy, Wit: sir, you had a master, Sir
Thomas More, more; but now we shall have more.
Lug: God bless him! I would there were more of his
mind; he loves our quality. And yet he's a learned   340
man, and knows what the world is.
Clown: Well, a kind man, and more loving than
many other, but I think we ha' met with the first . . .
Lug: First served he his man that had our angels, and
he may chance dine with Duke Humphrey
tomorrow, being turned away today. Come, let's go.
Clown: And many such reward would make us all ride,
and horse us with the best nags in Smithfield.

Exeunt

Glossary to *Sir Thomas More*

 41 *Divers:* several.
 66 *waits:* municipal musicians.
135 *Gramercies:* 'mercy on us!' [OED]. Exclamation of surprise.
151 *begin at a venture:* take a chance.
166 *ruffling:* swaggering.
215 *fray:* fear.
248 *on the bow hand:* you have lost your way.
269 *holp:* helped.
333 *pull his coat over his ears:* discharge him.
345 *dine with Duke Humphrey:* go hungry.

3

Evidence of players in *Hamlet*

Unlike Anthony Munday's treatment of his players, when Shakespeare's characters embark on an inner play that activity is made to
relate to and reflect on the rest of the play in a complex of associations
that often makes direct evidence of contemporary performance
practice difficult to disentangle, as for instance in the case of Ariel and
his fellow spirit-actors in *The Tempest*. There are a number of
references to them in terms of contemporary performers. Prospero
talks of Ariel's 'quality', as in *Hamlet*, the term for the profession.
Despite his magical abilities, Ariel goes off to change (I.ii. 304) like any
stage actor, and re-emerges (I. 316) dressed as a water nymph, and later
he undertakes two other boy-player roles, as the harpy and as Ceres in
the masque. Though Ferdinand sees the results as 'a most majestical
vision and/Harmoniously charming', Prospero as author and stage
manager takes a more prosaic view, of a 'trick', 'vanity of mine art'
performed by 'the rabble' and 'his meaner fellows'. Ariel too is
occasionally truculent, as well as obedient, like one bound in indentures
and chafing to be released. If Prospero is Shakespeare's own vale-
diction, and the focus shifting from the inadequacies of actors to the
problems of the playwright, it is tempting to see Ariel as a portrait of
an apprentice and a celebration of the boy player's positive capacities as
a highly skilled vehicle for the poet's intentions, interposing the
minimum of irrelevant personality, in contradistinction to the adult
player, as say Lucianus in *Hamlet* with his 'damnable faces'. Prospero
says of his performance as the harpy –

> a grace it had, devouring.
> Of my instruction hast thou nothing bated
> In what thou hadst to say.

But however much we may be persuaded by this sequence of

correspondences, none the less in the final analysis the narrative overrides any such speculation: Ariel was found by Prospero in a split pine and not in some London street.

In Bottom and his fellows in *A Midsummer Night's Dream* we are on slightly surer ground. The inner play on which they are so laboriously engaged is a play and not a vision, but though it may have been an elaborate parody of the auspices of the play itself, as an 'offering' at some Court wedding, the main *donnée* of the mechanicals' representation is that they are incompetent country amateurs in contradistinction to the accomplished performers themselves. The Lord Chamberlain's Men are burlesquing their inferiors, as the undergraduates were to do, possibly copying them, in *Narcissus*.[1] None the less there is a sense in which the play explores through parody and exaggeration the nature of playing itself. Only an author sees his creation as a whole, the players necessarily in parts; and literally so in that the written 'parts' they were given contained only their own lines. A good deal of the comedy in the discussion of how to represent Moonshine and Wall comes from the inability of the bumbling amateurs to see the purpose of this representation. Concern for detail, however, is necessary in the work of any performer. There is a sense in which the blinkered egoism so strongly displayed by Bottom is inherent in the activity itself and closely related to the energy which all acting is required to generate. Bottom's energy spills out in all directions; his constant interruptions, his desire to play all the parts, and to give impromptu tastes of them – tyrant, lover, lady, and lion – and the officious zeal with which he steps out of character to answer Theseus. He is a nuisance, and yet the necessary nuisance, for there is no doubt in the minds of his fellows that he is the finest actor of his generation, and that the play is marred and will not go forward without him. During the performance of 'Pyramus and Thisbe' when he is not on stage the piece teeters constantly on the edge of breaking down, what with Quince's stage fright and Starveling's extra-dramatic tetchiness – 'All that I have to say is to tell you that the lanthorn is the moon; I, the Man i' th' Moon; this thorn-bush, my thorn-bush, and this dog, my dog.' When it comes to it, at the moment of performance perhaps all his fellows would rather be anywhere else than in the Duke's presence chamber, but Bottom, with his self-confidence and his energy, holds the thing together, and when at its conclusion he rises from the dead with a final incongruity, he does so with all the assurance of a job well done. Not so Flute. A reluctant transvestite, he is disastrously aware of the gap between actor and part: 'Nay, faith, let not me play a woman; I have a beard coming.' Endowed with any degree of self-consciousness, to have to play another is a kind of offence against decorum and doubly so if the gap is large. In rehearsal Flute is a vivid cameo of the worst kind of actor; he does not know when to come in, and he speaks his lines in a meaningless gabble, 'cues and all'. As Demetrius concludes, Flute's woman is as bad as Bottom's man, they imitate humanity so abominably.

Perhaps the single most complex 'inner play' in Shakespeare's canon is the 'play extempore' of *Henry IV Part One* in which Falstaff takes as his subject for an improvised piece of merriment the forthcoming interview of Prince Hal with his father on the morrow. At one level the scene serves the function of contrast and parody. It exhibits the universal love of play-acting and the skill it requires, and the influence of the earlier theatre on the popular imagination. It also explores the dangers and possibilities of playing as a form of discourse. Though ostensibly a piece of fun, Falstaff continues the dialogue begun in their very first conversation, as to whether when Hal becomes king he will legitimize his low-life companions or repudiate them, and Hal uses the situation of jesting to epitomize the old man in a searing condemnation that foreshadows his final rejection in *Part Two*. The scene explores the 'given' circumstances of a performance, the *a priori* conditions that must be fulfilled by the very action of performing before others. When Hal introduces a level both private and serious before the tavern crowd, Falstaff is trapped by his own terms of reference and the public and comic nature of his amateur theatricals, so that he becomes the victim and not the master of the situation. When Hal dismisses him as 'that reverend Vice, that grey Iniquity', he leads, as so often in such discussions, into a confusion between the player and the moral status of the part he plays.

The player scenes of *Hamlet* on the other hand, as well as contributing to a running debate in Shakespeare's works about the nature of playing, appear to offer a good deal of direct information about itinerant practice. The players are travelling because of hard times in the capital caused by the popularity of the Children's Theatre, and arrive without warning. Like the other troupes featured, their numbers are small; we see three players in 'The Mousetrap', plus a prologue, and there is a reference to 'three or four mutes' who mourn and remove the body of the dead king. In his anticipation of their arrival, Hamlet lists six character-types – the king, the knight, the lover, the humorous man, the clown, and the lady – but these are perhaps more an indication of the sort of subject matter he expects, than evidence of type-casting; certainly when they arrive the players are at pains through Polonius to assert their versatility. Hamlet gives them a warm welcome, as indeed, for different reasons, does the rest of the Court. Hamlet had said that his welcome 'must show fairly outwards', but it is evident from his subsequent behaviour that he is an enthusiastic follower of the plays. He greets only two players directly, first the leading player, here a tragedian in a development away from the earlier tradition displayed in *Sir Thomas More* in which the Vice led the company, and then the boy player, now getting dangerously tall, but whose usefulness depends more, says Hamlet, on his voice not breaking. The leading player is evidently a master of his craft who can give a speech of passion from memory and with such accomplishment as to be able to produce tears on cue. He then accepts without demur to prepare a play of his host's choice for the following night and add new lines to it. As well as the opening recital of the Pyrrhus speeches, to which a good deal of attention is given, the player scenes include a discussion of acting style and a full-blown inner play.

As with all Shakespeare's performance references it is difficult to disentangle authenticity from invention. On the one hand, the Pyrrhus speeches are in an arcane, heightened, rhetorical style, distinguished from the formal but pedestrian tone of *The Murder of Gonzago,* but both suggesting the representation of a past tradition, as does the ana-chronistic dumb-show. On the other, the references to the 'late innovation' of the children indicates an immediate contemporaneity, whilst the remark about 'Hercules and his load too' invokes the very theatre in which the performance is taking place.

At the centre of *Hamlet* is the mind of its hero, through which is filtered all the material, characters, and incidents of the play. We can if we choose draw conclusions from the players' reticence, but all we actually hear from them, apart from their performances in the various inner play-material, are the First Player's brief responses, 'Aye, my lord', and 'I warrant your honour' and so on. They have none of the independent reality of the players in the final moments of their scene in *Sir Thomas More.* It is difficult therefore to discuss their part in the play independent of his perception of them.

The play offers what at first appears to be a series of excursions from the main plot, seemingly unconnected with it, such as Hamlet's conversations with the Clown and with the Norwegian Captain, but in which, as each reaches its climax, it is seen to illustrate Hamlet's predicament:

> How all occasions do inform against me,
> And spur my dull revenge!
>
> (IV.iv.31–2)

In the same way, the players, introduced by Rosencrantz and Guilden-stern for Hamlet's diversion, draw him eventually to contrast their leader's professional show of grief with what he sees to be his own reserve and inaction. They embody the dichotomy between seeming and being which is introduced in Hamlet's opening lines:

> These indeed, seem;
> For they are actions that a man might play . . .
>
> (I.iii.83–4)

Hamlet, unsettled by a supernatural visitation and acutely aware of mortality, is hungry for knowledge of things beyond the normal. 'There are more things in heaven and earth, Horatio,' he says immediately after he has seen the Ghost, 'Than are dreamt of in your philosophy.' On one level the play is a kind of spiritual quest in which the hero has a series of encounters with figures from outside the narrow claustrophobic confines of the Court, who offer opaque glimpses into other worlds. These glimpses are unstable, never reliable, but deeply felt. Sandwiched between a possibly demonic Ghost with his hints of a frightening tale that he could unfold had Hamlet the physique to withstand it, and the riddling, sepulchral promptings of the Grave-digger, stands the First Player, who, in his travelling clothes, unpainted and unprepared, at Hamlet's prompting summons up through his person in the bare presence chamber the tale and the personages of ancient myth, by turns triumphant, desperate, and heart-broken; the very stillness of the actor contrasting with the vivid imaginative world of teeming horror created.

Disturbed by the speech and the Player's tears, Hamlet dismisses all present and then in a long soliloquy beginning 'Oh, what a rogue and peasant slave am I!' he compares his own inaction in the face of real injuries unfavourably with the Player's capacity to shed real tears at a fictive story of ancient wrong. For a moment he believes that Art is showing him how he should behave in reality. He whips himself into a fury:

> it cannot be
> But I am pigeon-liver'd and lack gall
> To make oppression bitter, or ere this
> I should 'a fatted all the region kites

With this slave's offal. Bloody, bawdy villain!
Remorseless, treacherous, lecherous, kindless villain!
O, vengeance!

As he stands, one imagines, taut and assertive, he somehow catches himself as it were in a mirror, and sees himself as posturing, imitating an imitation, despicable, and ridiculous:

Why, what an ass am I! This is most brave,
That I, the son of a dear father murder'd,
Prompted to my revenge by heaven and hell,
Must, like a whore, unpack my heart with words
And fall a-cursing like a very drab,
A stallion [/scullion (F.1.)]

Whatever the last word was, or meant, the general sense is clear; he is making words, futile abuse, a substitute for action. It is only an illusion that the player tackles the same problems we face, that he experiences things as we do, for he does neither; he only delivers the lines given to him with suitable postures. The tears he sheds represent no more than an advanced control over the workings of his body. To treat life as though it were the stage leads to empty bombast and futile gestures, such as Shakespeare had recently satirized in the character of Pistol in the *Henry IV Part Two*.

A frequent playgoer, Pistol lives so vividly in the pageants he sees unfolded on the stage that he carries the play-world with him from the theatre into the street. Whereas most people keep their fantasies unspoken and make some effort to adjust to the register of public discourse, Pistol habitually behaves like a tragic hero with grand gestures, supported by half-remembered, half-understood fragments of stage dialogue. Much of the amusement comes from the contrast between Pistol's grand Byronic swagger and its tavern-brawl setting. It is Doll Tearsheet, the prostitute, who sees through him most clearly, and with most venom. She knows with the bitterness of her profession which men will stand and which will not.

Hamlet's most obvious counterpart in the play, Laertes, seems satisfied with the same sort of 'fustian': empty gestures and verbal heroics. A dashing figure at the head of a rebellion, he bursts into the palace bawling, 'O thou vile king,/Give me my father'; at a literal level surely pointless, since he knows Polonius to be dead, but a marvellously satisfying gesture. Laertes has a natural crass unselfconsciousness that allows him to leap into Ophelia's grave and demand to be covered too with earth, but when Hamlet follows him (at least in the Bad Quarto) he knows himself to be ridiculous – two people struggling in a hole and trampling down the corpse they both claim to love.

Hamlet's advice to the players in III.ii is often read as though it were counselling the development of a more 'natural' style to replace the formal mannered style attributed to the earlier generation of actors, but such an interpretation is difficult to sustain within the fable of the piece, given Hamlet's evident preference for a declamatory, orna-mented, archaic tale of slaughter, which he has already heard the First Player deliver before, and which he recalls as 'honest' and 'handsome'.

The most peculiar thing about the Advice scene however is its almost complete lack of relation to the rest of the play. Unlike the other player-scenes in Shakespeare previously discussed, it serves no dramatic function, either metaphoric or instrumental. It does not even seem to serve any practical purpose, such as to allow other players to change, since all the characters in the scenes immediately preceding it occur again at the performance of the inner play. Its only marginal claim to develop the narrative might lie in showing a headstrong young man presuming to teach experienced players their job, but the tone of the advice, which is clearly sound, militates against any such inter-pretation. One is left therefore with the strong suggestion that the Advice is an expression of authorial feeling. If that were so of course there would be less need to square *Hamlet's* taste in plays with *Shakespeare's* views on acting.

The formal/natural debate of the fifties and sixties about Elizabethan acting style largely ground to a halt with the recognition that though the result might have seemed to contemporaries to have been 'natural' or 'lifelike', the means used, as the very nature of the verse itself suggests, must have been to a very large extent 'formal'. Despite the stress in the Advice on using 'the modesty of nature' as the arbiter of acting style, its 'mirror' is a special moral mirror, 'to show virtue her own feature, scorn her own image, and the very age and body of the time his form and pressure'. It does not merely reflect back our life with the random inconsequence with which we necessarily experience it, but shapes and structures it so that the result shall be perceived more significantly than before. Just as the language 'places' the content in its moral context – as say in Claudius' opening speech in I.ii where the confidence of his sentiments is continually undercut by references to marrying his 'sometime sister' and responding to the mixture of funeral and wedding with at the same time one 'auspicious'

47

and one 'dropping', or drooping, eye – so too presumably the acting both represented the feelings and natures of the characters, and also commented upon them. Furthermore the platform of the open stage encouraged the actor not merely to represent, but to *display* his character through three hundred and sixty degrees, so that, in accord with the heightened diction, it was more immediate and more vivid than a mere reflection of ordinary life. Thus the passage stresses the importance of technique. The actor must not sacrifice emotion, but he 'must acquire and beget a temperance' that may give his expression of passion 'smoothness'. What he does must neither be 'o'erdone' nor 'come tardy off'. It does not seem to be attacking any particular style so much as bad acting *per se*, when it is insincere, disproportionate, inappropriate. As the period develops it is perhaps more a case of accumulating different registers, to meet more mannered as well as more idiomatic styles of writing, than of moving from one single style to another.

The inner play which the players perform in *Hamlet* contributes to a series of frames within frames, a 'scene of relief' in which the disposition of different groups of characters in differing relationships with the audience, and at different distances from them on the stage – messengers, observers, eavesdroppers, conspirators, and stage audiences – provide a continuum in which each observer is himself in turn a spectacle for the outer frame. Though all were alike assumed by actors, the formal nature of the inner play and the more idiomatic language of the stage observers invite the real audience to entertain the outer frames of the dramatic fiction as more 'real', life no more than a play, and itself as part of the continuum, observed by the ultimate frame, 'Heaven', as Raleigh said, 'the judicious sharp spectator' who 'sits and marks still who doth act amiss'.[2] One of the earliest and most elaborate uses of the inner play was in Kyd's *The Spanish Tragedy* (c. 1587), which had an outer frame provided by the Ghost of Don Andrea attended by the spirit of Revenge, who watched the entire play, and a further frame inside it consisting of the Spanish King and his Court brought as stage audience to an inner play at the climax of the play. In *Hamlet* the motif of watchers framing the action is repeated frequently throughout the play, as Polonius sets on Reynaldo to watch Laertes, and the King employs Rosencrantz and Guildenstern to watch Hamlet, and then places himself with Polonius to observe Ophelia 'loosed' to Hamlet. It reaches its culmination in 'The Mousetrap'; a complex web in which the observers themselves become the observed, as Hamlet and Horatio watch the King and Queen as they watch the inner play and the gradually emerging representation of their own crimes.

Like the inset views and pictures in Renaissance paintings, the inner play cannot fail to be a comment on the larger structure of which it is part.[3] Furthermore the image of frames-within-frames puts the inner play at the very centre, providing an invitation to be regarded as the ultimate focus of the drama.[4] In the case of the players' performance of *The Murder of Gonzago* there is some justification for this, as it serves both as an opportunity for a double re-enactment of the central crime, the killing of the elder Hamlet, for which revenge is sought, and as a catalyst of subsequent action, determining Claudius to plot Hamlet's death. As such it helps to deal with the central problem of revenge tragedy. Unlike, say, the love-conquers-all motif of the comedies, in which the audience's positive constructive urges go along with the wish-fulfilment of the ultimate union of the characters, revenge is a negative obsession. Kyd solves his moral problem by having his hero go mad before he exacts revenge. In the subsequent revenge plays, Marston ducks the issue of murder in *The Malcontent,* whilst the anonymous author of *The Revenger's Tragedy* in his elaborate strategies for revenge leaves us with a sense of gratuitous nastiness, leavened only by a jaunty theatricality. In *Hamlet,* Shakespeare reduces the gory mishmash of offences in his earlier attempt at revenge tragedy, *Titus Andronicus,* to the stronger focus of a single terrible crime, and improves on Kyd's stratagem of bringing the body of Horatio back at the end by keeping the murder fresh in our minds through the Ghost's rendition, and the repeated imagery of poison and ulcers, culminating in its mimed and then spoken re-enactment. The innocent players therefore are the unwitting enactors of this central image at the very heart of the play.

As the court in *The Spanish Tragedy* watches what was announced to be an entertainment for its own diversion, it emerges that the deaths of the characters, apparently simulated, turn out to have been 'real' and part of the revenge of Hieronimo. This ironic juxtaposition of art and life, with the setting and breaking of boundaries, is characteristic of the inner play. Indeed most inner plays are not really 'plays' at all if we accept Huizinga's definition of a play as 'an activity connected with no material interest, and no profit can be gained by it', for with the single exception of the interlude in *Sir Thomas More,* they are instrumental rather than expressive.[5] Rather than the inner plays being for themselves, and for the entertainment and well-being of the audience, the characters who organize them generally have an ulterior motive for which the performance is a pretext. 'In time of sports,' muses Bianca in *Women Beware Women* (V.ii. 22–3), 'death may steal in securely,/Then 'tis least thought on', whilst in *The Revenger's Tragedy* (V.i. 181–2) Supervacuo, with more than a little historical precedent, observes:

> A masque is treason's licence, that builds upon;
> 'Tis murder's best face when a vizard's on.[6]

Similarly in Middleton's comic *A Mad World, My Masters* and subplot of *The Mayor of Queenborough,* the inner plays are pretexts for theft, both make lighthearted connections between illusion and fraud, and, as in the histrionic events of *The Roman Actor* and *Sir Thomas More,* their spectators cross and re-cross the boundaries between real life and fiction. In *Hamlet,* rather than the inner play simply providing an opportunity for revenge-killing, the hero invokes the supposed capacity of mimetic representation to provoke criminals to declare their crimes, as Heywood claims to have been the case in two examples he cites in his *Apology for Actors* (1612).

It is characteristic of the inner play that it is not completed. Reality breaks in before the climax of the inner play, either through instrumental killings or cheatings, or merely through the interruption or incorporation of members of the audience. Sometimes the dramatist will have it both ways, as in *The Tempest,* and accomplish the play and still have it broken off. In 'Pyramus and Thisbe' in *A Midsummer Night's Dream* the play itself is finished and only the epilogue refused, but these are exceptions. Breaking off a play does violence to the sensibilities of those watching who have hitherto 'given' themselves to the drama, confident that it has been prepared for their amusement, that the performance is a finite whole in which they will not be called on to participate, and that what they see is only an imitation. The interruption of an inner play provides for the real audience the delicious embarrassment of watching things go wrong, and of the discomfiture of others, analogous to the pleasures of genuine extemporization, but within the safety of the narrative.

The inner play in *Hamlet,* 'The Mousetrap', breaks off as it becomes apparent that the play has some sinister extra-theatrical purpose that transgresses the accepted conventions of performance. However this does not happen immediately; the covert purpose of the event only emerges over a period of time in which Hamlet gradually encroaches on the action, and no doubt into the inner play performance area, moving from being a spectator, to a director – 'leave thy damnable faces and begin' – and then himself an enactor, a kind of hyperactive stage chorus – 'a poisons him i' th' garden for his estate . . .'. Furthermore as a result of this behaviour, his original purpose of awakening Claudius' conscience to a confession of his guilt is accompanied, and perhaps overshadowed, by a new message, that he, Hamlet, knows of the guilt. There is more than a little suggestion too that he sees himself as his father's avenger. He describes the third player on entry as: 'This is one Lucianus, *nephew* to the King.' Such a reference could only confuse the inner play's original purpose of matching the enactment to the original crime, the murder of a *brother*. This implicit threat is given further substance a moment or two later when he cues the actor of Lucianus with, 'the croaking raven doth bellow for revenge'. Lucianus is about to commit regicide not revenge, and the revenge that wells up in Hamlet's mind is surely his own on Claudius. In that Claudius immediately resolves to send Hamlet to England with instructions for his execution, the move from observer to riddling enactor was perhaps not a very wise one on Hamlet's part. But then his actions during the play-scene are a long way from the measured plotting at the end of II.ii, or the rational advice to the players on how they should perform that begins III.ii, or for that matter Hamlet's earlier commitment that the players should be heard out and the humorous man should end his part in peace. *The Murder of Gonzago* in performance is very different from what was intended by actors, audience, or princely producer.

Once the king has left the stage, Hamlet expresses his elation to Horatio in a series of semi-nonsensical verses with short skipping lines, which were delivered, one imagines, with a good deal of gesturing and comic declamation, with Hamlet perhaps capering about the stage in an exaggerated imitation of the players with whom he now claims kinship:

> *Hamlet:* Why, let the strucken deer go weep,
>   The hart ungalled play;
>   For some must watch, whilst some must sleep;
>   Thus runs the world away.
> Would not this, sir, and a forest of feathers – if the rest of my
> fortunes turn Turk with me – with two Provincial roses on
> my raz'd shoes, get me a fellowship in a cry of players, sir?

It is an access of excitement reminiscent of his first responses when the players arrived in II.ii. It is not of course the genuine light-heartedness of a free spirit, but a product of the emotional energy generated by his recent involvement in the climax of the 'Mousetrap' in which he had finally telescoped the forthcoming action into a single direct challenge to the king – 'You shall see anon how the murderer gets the love of Gonzago's wife.' There is an underlying hysteria indicated in his claim later in the sequence that he could drink hot blood, somewhat at odds with the main theme of his Advice, warning the players against an excessive representation of emotion. The testimony of both Bottom and Falstaff is that the function of true drama is to move its audience. Bottom says of his role as a lover 'that kills himself most gallant for love':

> That will ask some tears in the true performing of it.
> If I do it, let the audience look to their eyes:

Falstaff says of his coming performance:

> Well, an' the fire of grace be not quite out of thee,
> now shalt thou be moved . . .

Certainly Hamlet's own behaviour associates drama with emotion. When he wants a taste of the Player's quality he chooses a 'passionate speech', and what wells up in his mind is the epic savagery of Pyrrhus advancing on the helpless Priam. To him the stage constitutes an opportunity to express his own pent-up feelings, but with the opacity that mirrors his confusion, making Lucianus serve as cipher both for the murderer, Claudius, and for the potential revenger, himself. The inner play here serves as a psychic dimension, akin to his 'antic disposition' in the freedom of expression it offers him and the insights it allows its audience.

In a play built on patterned contrasts, of avenging princes, sons unfathered, and people going mad, the players provide several further levels to the variety of Hamlet's experience and to the dialogue he has with himself about his situation and what he ought to be doing about it. The image of Pyrrhus which the First Player summons up is like an heraldic beast, untroubled by remorse, living in a two-dimensional world in which revenge requires only the untrammelled use of his sword. For a moment, when the Player cries, Hamlet feels he is more honest, more spontaneous in expressing his feelings, and in having genuine feelings to express. Viewed in another light, the players are the unmoved, perhaps unknowing, bearers of their truths, who need to be schooled 'to speak the speech' by copying Hamlet; and then again, what they bring is trivial, false, self-indulgent, and idle 'play'; their clowns are not to be trusted. In their performance of the 'Mousetrap' the players are dignified as truth-tellers, beyond the coarse innuendo of the puppets dallying, with a quality powerful enough to stop reality in its tracks and point to the deeper meaning, the hidden guilt. And last, like their counterparts in *Sir Thomas More,* they are surprisingly prosaic; they constitute a kind of elevated normality; nameless and timeless, like the choric gardeners of *Richard II* or the minor, sturdy but unknowing figures of Greek tragedy.

Above all, the use of the players in the 'Mousetrap' suggests, theatre is a treacherous thing, difficult to control and uncertain of purpose. We see for a moment, as in the previous episode considered from *Sir Thomas More,* the underbelly of the process. It is all very well to talk of themes and messages, but a play-text is no more than a series of words said by actors, variously in character. The player of Lucianus, unaware of the larger context, concentrates on making a good job of his villainous grimaces, and Hamlet himself has more than an inkling of the uncertainties of the mimetic process as a means to any specific end. He warns Polonius to treat the players well, lest he should suffer their ill report, for they are 'the abstract and brief chronicles of the time', and later with Ophelia, Hamlet suggests the dangers of the player's truthfulness: 'Be not you asham'd to show, he'll not shame to tell you what it means.' Though we see nothing directly of this side of their personalities, Shakespeare invokes for the shabby, shady itinerant that quality Payne said made the mimus so feared in the Roman Empire, for 'with one laugh pitched to the exact pitch, the clown could destroy the kingdom, as the singer will destroy a wineglass'.[7] Elsewhere Shakespeare catches the same quality in Thersites and his 'pageant of Ajax' in *Troilus and Cressida,* in which he transfixes his victim as an object of mockery whilst retaining and asserting his independence from that representation; the sort of treatment Cleopatra fears from the 'quick comedians' and their extemporary performances, should she be taken in triumph to Rome. As the player is potentially anarchic and unreliable, so, Shakespeare suggests, is the process of performance, and the dangers and uncertainties of the audience's response to it.

4

Kemp, clowns, and improvisation

In the later years of the sixteenth century, clowning became immensely popular in the theatre, especially in the hands of Tarlton and Kemp, and clowns occur regularly in the scenes under discussion. In the first, *Pilgrimage to Parnassus*, a university play of c. 1599, Dromo begins by bemoaning the universal popularity of the clown – 'a play cannot be without a clown'. Simon in *The Mayor of Queenborough* (1619/20) testifies that the clown is still widely thought to be the best thing in a play:

> Some talk of things of state, of puling stuff;
> There's nothing in a play to a clown, if he
> Have grace to hit on't
>
> (V.i)

Sidney, in his *Apology for Poetry* (published 1595), had deplored those plays that:

> thrust in Clowns by head and shoulders, to play a part in
> majestical matters, with neither decency nor discretion.

The author of *Pilgrimage* takes a similar view, that to please their audiences playwrights had to 'drag in' a clown whether their narrative warranted it or not. To make the point crystal clear, Dromo uses a cart rope. Though presumably performed under university auspices (discussed below in Chapter 8) and self-consciously disparaging, the passage gives a concise picture of contemporary clowning.

PILGRIMAGE TO PARNASSUS

Act V

Enter DROMO, drawing a Clown in with a rope

54

Clown: What now, thrust a man into the commonwealth, whether he will or no? What the devil should I do here?

Dromo: Why, what an ass art thou? Dost thou not know a play cannot be without a clown? Clowns have been thrust into plays by head and shoulders, ever since Kemp could make a scurvy face, and therefore reason thou shouldst be drawn in with a cart rope. 5

Clown: But what must I do now?

Dromo: Why if thou can'st but draw thy mouth awry, lay thy leg over thy staff, saw a piece of cheese asunder with thy dagger, lap up drink on the earth, I warrant thee, they'll laugh mightily. Well, I'll turn thee loose to them. Either say somewhat for thyself, or hang and be *non plus*. (*Exit*) 10

Clown: This is fine i' faith: now when they have nobody to leave on the stage, they bring me up, and which is worse, tell me not what I should say. Gentles, I dare say you look for a fit of mirth. I'll therefore present unto you a proper new love letter of mine to the tune of *Put on the smock a Monday*, which in the heat of my charity I penned, and thus it begins: 15

O my lovely Nigra, pity the pain of my liver: that little gallows Cupid hath lately pricked me in the breech with his great pin, and almost killed me, thy woodcock, with his birdbolt. Thou hast a pretty furrowed forehead, a fine lecherous eye, methinks I see the bawd Venus keeping a bawdy-house in thy looks, Cupid standing like a Pander at the door of thy lips. 20

   – How like you, masters? Has any young man a desire to copy this, that he may have *forma epistolae conscribendae*? Now if I could but make a fine scurvy face, I were a king. O nature, why did'st thou give me so good a look? 25

30

(*Re-enter* Dromo, *with* Philomusus *and* Studioso)

Dromo: Give us a voider here for the fool. Sirrah, you must be gone. Here are other men that will supply the room.

Clown: Why, shall I not whistle out my whistle? Then farewell gentle auditors, and the next time you see me I'll make you better sport. (*Exeunt Dromo and Clown*) 35

55

Glossary to Pilgrimage to Parnassus

6 *scurvy*: a disease causing spots etc.; mean, ugly.
9 *awry*: crooked.
13 *be* non plus: remain in a state of perplexity.
30 forma epistolae conscribendae: a model for letter writing.
33 *voider*: a container into which waste food was swept.

Dromo in the above passage stresses the physical nature of the Kemp tradition. He counsels the Clown to grimace, adopt a comic posture with his staff, and develop grotesque business. A good clown could start an audience laughing simply by thrusting his head out through the curtain. This practice is recorded of Tarlton and of Reade, as well as Kemp, and is illustrated in *The Wits* frontispiece by an actor pretending to be Thomas Greene.[1] Simon in *The Mayor of Queenborough* gives an elaborate testimony to the humour provoked by 'peeping out' and indicates it to have been general practice (IV.ii. 134f.). This is partly no doubt a general exploitation of the peculiar appearance of the typical clown. Tarlton had a flat nose and a squint. Armin was squat and dwarf, and regularly did some sort of dog impression. Kemp had an 'ill face'. The Clown in *Pilgrimage* laments that he is too good-looking, whilst Simon counsels a good beating as the solution to a similar problem:

> 1 *Player*: This is our clown, sir.
> *Simon:* Fie, fie, your company must fall upon him and beat
> him; he's too fair, i' faith, to make the people laugh.
>
> (127f.)

We know of the clown's entry, but what of his departure? Three of the scenes associated with Kemp, from *The Return from Parnassus, The Travels of Three English Brothers,* and *Romeo and Juliet* (II.iv), each concludes with discussion as to the order of leaving the stage. The modern reader, conditioned to look for intellectual or poetic meat in the plays, is likely to skip passages of repetition, or say, here, of meaningless protocol, but some of them may reveal the imprint of long-forgotten stage business. Each of these discussions ends with Kemp having to leave first, after a show of reluctance. Clearly therefore, the Exeunt had some significance, and was probably accompanied by regular 'business', perhaps a trick of pretending that the clown was in danger of being 'goosed' by an innocent character.[2]

Some clowns no doubt had pitiful wits and little invention and deserved the castigation of the Bad Quarto of *Hamlet*, as the sort 'that keeps one suit/ of jests', and rely on catchphrases and 'blabbering with his lips'. But others, like Kemp, turned their assumed foolishness to genuinely comic account. An example of Kemp's own style may be preserved in the text of *A Knack to Know a Knave* (1592): 'Newly set forth, as it hath sundry times been played by Ed. Allen and his Company. With Kemp's applauded Merriments of the men of Gotham, in receiving the King into Gotham.' Three mad men, a Cobbler, a Miller, and a Smith, argue as to who shall deliver the welcome. The style of their dialogue illustrates a number of features common to the surviving records of Kemp's style, such as malapropisms and puns, grotesque language, 'I will . . . lay myself open to you like an oyster', and carefully 'fed' jokes, such as the Smith's 'god of our occupation' who is proved to be a cuckold, and his godhead the horn. The actual welcome is of course an anti-climax, in two silly couplets and with a petition for brewing strong-beer. On paper the jests do not immediately invite much applause. Clearly however the humour depended not so much on what was said, but rather on how it was said, on the clown's personal charisma. Often clowns played *against* their material, deliberately making it silly and, in occupying the space in front of the fiction, made fun of it.

In *Sir Thomas More* the players praise More's contribution to keeping the play afloat:

> *Inclination:* Would not my lord make a rare player? . . .
> Did ye mark how extemporically he fell to the matter, and
> spake Luggins' part almost as it is the very book
> set down?

More, on the other hand, disparages his own contribution to the performance which he says he has 'hindered': 'Thus fools oft times do help to mar the play.' In this he is perhaps reflecting a changing attitude to the aesthetics of performance; towards seeing it as an integrated whole, rather than as a loose association of parts. It is very tempting, especially in studies orientated towards Shakespeare, to describe a simple progression through the period from the independent antics of Tarlton, via Kemp, to Armin's integrated fools in *King Lear* and *Twelfth Night*, and to link them with Hamlet's outburst against the clowns who speak more than is set down for them and laugh to make others laugh. However, the more clearly Armin's portrait emerges in recent studies, the more singular he appears to have been and therefore the less suitable as evidence of some general tendency.³ A squat, dwarfish counter-tenor, he drew his characters from life, was a researcher into idiots, or 'natural' fools, and published plays and books on his findings. He seems to have established a unique collaboration with Shakespeare. If we were to look outside the Chamberlain's Men, and take, say, William Rowley instead, as a later point on the continuum; also a clown but author/collaborator of material often only loosely associated with the main plot; or Timothy Reade, still being celebrated for traditional clowning antics c. 1638, then the sequence might look quite different, and something more like traditional 'low clowning' would appear to be continuing. What does seem to decline, however, is the willingness of those playwrights who identified themselves with the intellectual and socially superior audiences to incorporate clowning into their plays. The testimony of *The Antipodes* (1636/7) and the Praeludium to *The Careless Shepherdess* (c. 1638), both perhaps by Brome, is that whilst 'The Motley Coat was banish'd with Trunk Hose' by the better poets, citizens and country visitors continue to maintain the low tastes of a former age.⁴

The university playwright of the *Pilgrimage* is of course being derogatory, but in having the clown stay longer than is strictly necessary for the criticism to be made (he takes no further part in the play) a certain ambivalence is betrayed towards clowning in the Kemp style. The clown's popularity is being deplored as his performance is being enjoyed. The same could be said of Mayor Simon, who can be seen as a representative of the unenlightened popular audience, by 1618 to be found in particular playhouses, who take delight in the clown, and have only a dim understanding of much of the rest of the play. However his own clowning performance presumably gave sustained delight to what was ostensibly a more discerning audience. These representations seem to indicate a certain lingering regret at the passing of an age, pre-eminently associated with Tarlton, Kemp's predecessor, in which the clown with his individual antics was an allowed and essential part of the social/psychological spectrum of the complete play, which thereby maintained a looser form. Jonson, who did not admit nostalgia until much later in his career, parodies what he sees as old-fashioned clowning in the Induction to *Bartholomew Fair*. His Stage Keeper is made to recall the golden age of Tarlton with a simple-minded, sentimental affection:

> Ho! an' that man had lived to have played in Bartholomew Fair, you should have seen him have come in, and have been cozen'd in

the cloth-quarter, so finely! and Adams, the rogue, have leaped
and capered upon him, and have dealt his vermin about, as though
they had cost him nothing! and then a substantial watch to have
stolen in upon them and taken them away, with mistaking words,
as the fashion is in the stage-practice.

Most of what survives of Tarlton is anecdotal and often at several
stages removed, but judging from the part of Derrick as recorded in the
memorial reconstruction of *The Famous Victories of Henry V*, he provides
an example of the non-integrated fool, at the opposite pole from his
'adopted son' Armin. Derrick operates in a separate sub-plot unrelated
to the fortunes of the play's hero, except for a solitary occasion when,
having witnessed the famous box on the ear which the Prince gives the
Lord Chief Justice, he and his stooge do a turn based upon it.
Significantly Derrick's opening dialogue concentrates on distinguishing
his clownishness. The high point of his part is an elaborate jest in which
he tricks a French soldier who has captured him. He offers to give the
soldier as ransom as many crowns as will lie on his sword. When the
dupe puts his sword on the ground Derrick snatches it, but, in that
clownish juxtaposition of shrewdness and foolishness, as he prepares
himself to decapitate the soldier, he allows the latter to run away. Thus
the play incorporates his plot as a semi-independent vehicle for the
comic *persona* which Tarlton has created and in which, judging by
Tarlton's Jests (1638), he indulges both on and off the stage. Many of the
Jests do not relate to the theatre at all and suggest that Tarlton was
primarily a banquet and tavern entertainer.

The best known of Tarlton's stage jests concern what we would now
describe as 'ad-libbing'. At one performance of *The Victories* he played
the Justice as well as the Clown, and then made fun of the doubling by
alluding humorously, as the clown, to the box on the ear he had
received as the justice. On another occasion, he turned the tables on a
persistent apple-thrower in the gallery with an extempore verse
drawing attention to the alleged moral turpitude of the man's wife.
One jest however indicates an entirely different set of performance
standards from that which obtained subsequently in the theatre:

It chanced that in the midst of a play, after long expectation for
Tarlton: being much desired of the people, at length he came
forth: where (at his entrance) one in the gallery pointed his finger
at him, saying to a friend that he had never seen him, 'That is he'.
Tarlton to make sport at the least occasion given him, and seeing
the man point with his finger, he . . . held up two fingers: the

Figure 4.1 William Kemp, dancing his way to Norwich in his morris suit, from *Kemps Nine Daies Wonder*, 1600.

Figure 4.2 Robert Armin, as the simpleton John-in-the-hospital, from his own play, *The History of Two Maids of Moreclack*, written c. 1597–9, and illustrated 1609. He is playing an old man dressed as a charity child in a blue coat.

Figure 4.3 Bubble, in an extract from John Cooke's *Greene's Tu Quoque*, written c. 1611. The illustration is from *The Wits*, 1662, a collection of 'drolls' played during the Commonwealth. Bubble, written for the clown Thomas Greene, is a foolish servant who tries to use an inheritance to turn himself into a fashionable gallant. Here, played by someone else, he wears a fool's coxcomb, and illustrates the clown's traditional curtain 'business'.

captious fellow, jealous of his wife (for he was married) and because a Player bid it, took the matter more heinously, and asked him why he made horns at him. 'No' (quoth Tarlton) 'they be fingers':

> For there is no man, Which in love to me,
> Lends me one finger, but he shall have three

– and they continue to quarrel, until the man is forced to leave in shame.

This anecdote is significant in a number of ways. First, it shows Tarlton's popularity, not as a farcical addendum to the play, but eagerly awaited as the star attraction. Second, he is not here responding to the exigences of the moment, as in the apple story, nor is he exploiting some shared humour within the narrative and its execution, as in the box on the ear. Instead, in mid-performance, he is stopping

whatever momentum the play may have had in order to indulge in comic repartee quite gratuitous to the enacted fiction. He is bringing to the performance the cachet of Jester to the Queen, different from and perhaps at odds with the function of a company player. As he exists partly outside the company, so his performance too is only inter-mittently dramatic. Furthermore, as with almost all his jests, on the stage or elsewhere, he is combative, often cruel; he stimulates hostility and a game-like competitiveness. The poor victim had merely pointed his finger, and ends up leaving the theatre in shame. He made a practice also of singing impromptu songs at the end of the performance based upon written 'themes' passed up to him from the audience. Tarlton takes his Themes as a challenge of wit; the loser to be humiliated. Generally, when he extemporizes the giver of the Theme ends up decried as 'a knave' or 'an ass'.

Though Robert Weimann is anxious for the purposes of his political thesis so to identify all 'popular' performers, he is surely right in characterizing Tarlton's style as one in which he creates his entertain-ment out of the situation he finds and develops.[5] What needs to be recognized however is that this is part of his professional technique. Wherever he appears he is greeted with a mixture of excitement *and* apprehension; his art lies in the juxtaposition of rapport and hostility. As much as he may exploit the associations of the 'community consciousness', his art remains 'for' rather than 'by' the people.

The special independent status of the clown, though a variable commodity and not usually taken to this length, remains however a prime feature in later incarnations, continuing to assert some measure of freedom and disloyalty, and a bone of contention within the general drift of dramatic practice.

Tarlton is seen as an innovator, attributed with fusing the Vice and Clown traditions and transforming the country folk jig into the theatre afterpiece.[6] He is celebrated as a national institution, equally welcome in the Queen's presence or at the City ordinary. Kemp, on the other hand, although likewise famous and celebrated, in the 1590s is continuing the tradition of independent clown into a very different theatrical era. Circumstances had changed. Many of the extra-dramatic, mediating functions of the Clown/Vice as link-man and compère at itinerant performances, which had served to meet the variable contingencies of intinerant playing when he used his invention to cover late entries and mishaps and perhaps adapt his material for particular audiences, were no longer necessary.

On the one hand, following the defeat of the Armada in 1588, one image offered by the theatre of the 1590s was that of national unity as reflected in the optimistic good-humour of *The Shoemaker's Holiday* or the chronicle plays. In this image the different social elements are seen to be in balance and the rough amalgam of the theatrical medley, as say in the plays of Greene or Peele, with the semi-independent antics of the clown, is tolerated. Lyly's prologue to *Midas* (1589) articulates this rather unsophisticated concept in which 'soldiers call for tragedies', 'courtiers for comedies', and 'countrymen for pastorals' and 'what heretofore hath been served in several dishes for a feast is now minced in a charger for a gallimaufrey'.

On the other hand, especially as the decade gathered momentum, it is also a period of rapid cultural and artistic change, in which even the recent past is despised, and new concepts of humour and of structural unity are being developed (perhaps calling into question, at least in the leading companies, the dividing line between clown and comic actor). Extemporization had produced a rougher, more variable humour less suited to the sophisticated balance achieved in Shakespeare's romantic comedies, which retains the dissonance of the clown, but carefully orchestrates it within the whole. As the seventeenth century got under way, sections of the population were separating off to form different sorts of audience at different venues, with particular tastes that could be anticipated. New assumptions were abroad about the nature of theatre, which would eventually lead to the exclusion of indecorous clowning from serious drama, and even the banishment from the stage for 150 years of Lear's fool.[7]

There appears to have been a brief period in which the positive qualities, which the spontaneous clown was seen to possess, were incorporated, as it were freshly bleeding, into the written texts, thus providing us with a fleeting glimpse of a lost tradition of extemporization – its freshness; its capacity to give the impression that the play was just for that particular audience; the intimate sense that the mirth in which they shared was their immediate *joint* creation. More than a mere adjunct to performance, extemporization in a sense exploited the quintessential characteristics of theatre: its ability to make things happen, and make them happen here and now, which premediation, total loyalty to a script, and even rehearsal, threaten to destroy, and are at best only able to simulate. An improvised performance is free to respond and adapt to its audience in a way that a scripted performance cannot. There are especial pleasures too in the danger of spontaneity; the delicious embarrassment of something about to go wrong. The Clown scene in *Pilgrimage to Parnassus* is a premeditated attempt to give

63

the impression of spontaneous clowning, with its dangers and embarrassments. The Clown is thrust against his will onto the stage, with nothing prepared, and is merely given a catalogue of gross antics to perform, said to be the clown's stock-in-trade, and told to improvise. He must sink or swim:

> Dromo: . . . Either say somewhat for thyself, or hang and
> be *non plus*. (*Exit*).

Once the Clown gets out his crumpled piece of paper with the love-letter on, the audience are able to relax a little; they know he now has material for jesting; they will not have to witness him lost for words, or any further uneasy silences. Shirley echoes a similar effect in the concluding lines of *The Cardinal* (1641) when the clown, Pollard, is 'thrust upon the stage, and falls'; presumably impelled by the author's boot. At first he seeks revenge by asking the audience not to clap, and only finally relents. Martin Holmes suggests that Kemp spoke the Epilogue to *Henry IV Part Two*, offering to dance to please the audience:[8]

> If you look for a good speech now, you undo me; for
> what I have to say is of mine own making; and what, indeed,
> I should say will, I doubt, prove mine own marring

It too suggests, artfully, a performer unprepared, uneasy, modest, as the magic of the fiction dissipates around him.

The extent to which Kemp improvised, and the precise nature of the activity involved, remain uncertain. Much depends on what is meant by the current Elizabethan term 'extemporization'; as today with the word 'improvisation', it can be used to describe a number of different activities. There are at least five involved in the group of extracts under discussion. First it can be used of the activities preceding and subsequent to the play-proper. Although Posthast in *Histriomastix* uses the term 'extempore' a good deal, he does so of prologues and songs on themes which conclude the entertainment rather than of plays themselves. Jigs, similarly outside the main text, were likewise an opportunity for improvisation. Even before Kemp left the Chamberlain's Men and danced his way to Norwich, he was celebrated for his jigs, which concluded the performances in the theatres. So popular was Kemp that the early entries of the *Stationer's Register* suggest a general belief that a jig would succeed only if his name were attached.[9] The jigs, his dancing journeys, and the ballads indicate that Kemp, like Tarlton, had a firm basis as a professional entertainer outside the theatre, which can be expected to have marked the distinctiveness of his contributions to it.

Richard Brome makes a useful distinction between two types of extemporization within the main play in the scene in *The Antipodes* where the patron/director, Letoy, with Hamlet's advice very much in mind, is giving instructions to a company of private players. First of all he castigates the practice, illustrated by Tarlton above, of stopping the dramatic action for independent mirth:

> *Letoy*:   when you are
>   To speak to your co-actors in the scene
>   You hold interlocutions with the audience.
> *Byplay*: That is a way, my lord, has been allowed
>   On elder stages to move mirth and laughter.
> *Letoy*: Yes, in the days of Tarlton and Kemp,
>   Before the stage was purged from barbarism,
>   And brought to the perfection it now shines with.
>
>   (II.ii. 43f.)

Whether Brome ever saw Kemp perform is uncertain. He began his theatrical career as Jonson's 'man', apparently in a domestic capacity, before he took to playwrighting. He is first mentioned in 1614 in *Bartholomew Fair*. In any event, Brome makes a clear distinction between this sort of loose clowning, which he condemns, and what he calls performing 'extempore':

> *Letoy*: Well, sir, my actors
>   Are all in readiness, and, I think, all perfect
>   But one, that never will be perfect in a thing
>   He studies; yet he makes such shifts extempore,
>   (Knowing the purpose what he is to speak to)
>   That he moves mirth in me 'bove all the rest.
>   For I am none of those poetic furies,
>   That threats the actor's life in a whole play
>   That adds a syllable or takes away.
>   If he can fribble through, and move delight
>   In others, I am pleased.
>
>   (II.i.14f.)

Brome is here advocating a less severe aesthetic than that Shakespeare put into the mouth of his prince/director. The Clown cannot remember every detail of his written lines, but, knowing the general drift, 'the purpose what he is to speak to', makes up substitutes on the spot.

Furthermore, he makes a habit of doing so, and that, says Letoy, is itself a source of pleasure and amusement. One distinctive feature of this form of extemporization is that apparently the Clown is the only person in this company to use it, and has some kind of licence for it, but Brome implies that the result must aid, and not significantly damage, the total performance. Part of the fun of this technique, what he calls 'fribbling', is in resisting the danger of the dramatic flow being impeded. In *The Mayor of Queenborough* the same word is used in a less favourable view of the practice of bluffing through with a rough approximation of the lines. Bad Quartos give plentiful evidence of the same sort of thing. Interestingly Letoy gives the same reason for Byeplay's 'shifts extempore' as the character Kemp does in *The Travels* when he agrees to perform with Harlequin, because he is 'somewhat hard of study'.

What Brome commends is different again from what we may describe as a fourth type of extemporization, that of the *commedia dell'arte*, in which spontaneous dialogue was used to implement a given scenario, aided by set pieces or 'lazzi', and performed by a more-or-less fixed set of characters or 'masks'. This tradition is widely known in England at the time, but though characters and situations are frequently borrowed, their technique of performance itself is generally regarded as a foreign practice.[10] The single exception appears to be Kemp's participation with Harlequin in *The Travels of Three English Brothers*. He seems quite willing to improvise in the Italian style and his comments with respect to unfamiliar performance conventions are restricted entirely to the subject of actresses. However, it is not clear how closely Day's conception approximates to genuine *commedia* usage. It does not seem to involve a scenario, nor is the problem of performing in a foreign language touched on. Kemp talks of 'extemporal *merriment*', and from the way he sets about it, full of sexual *double-entendre*, the intended play shows every sign of turning into something very like a jig, where the plot, more obviously than in a play, is no more than a vehicle for the central activity of bawdy improvisation. Having escaped the Lord Chamberlain's Men and their new aesthetic standards, no doubt Kemp would not be averse to extending post-play extemporizing into the play itself. 'Extemporal merriment' too, with its overtones of an earlier festive amateur tradition, would serve to describe the improvisation involved in Falstaff's tavern game in *Henry IV Part One*.

What emerges then from Brome's discussion, and within the main play as distinct from its periphery, is the (perhaps general) acceptance of a style which he calls 'extempore', which involves a freer treatment of the script than normal, but which is to be distinguished from either Tarlton's 'interlocutions' or *commedia dell'arte* proper. As such it is consonant with the greater opportunities for more personal, more charismatic delivery allowed by the less poetical, less elaborate language which was given to clowns.

Kemp's contribution to *Romeo and Juliet* may be a borderline case between embroidering a script, and being given a free hand to invent at will. D. Fenton gives a number of examples of scripts which call for actors to make up their own lines, as in Greene's *Tu Quoque*: 'Here they two talk and rail what they list; and then Will Rash speaks to Staines.'[11] This type of extemporization involves more than the non-dramatic interlocutions of the Tarleton type, or modern ad-libbing. Spaces are left in the script to be filled in by the clowns. We know Shakespeare wrote the part of Peter with Kemp in mind.[12] The assignment of servant parts generally in the play is not very clear, but even if Kemp appeared in all the servant scenes, he would not have had many lines. In Act II scene iv, Peter appears as the Nurse's escort. Apart from saying 'Anon' at the beginning and end of the scene, he is given only one speech of any substance:

> *Nurse*: And thou must stand by too, and suffer every
> knave to use me at his pleasure?
> *Peter*: I saw no man use you at his pleasure; if I had, my
> weapon should quickly have been out, I warrant you.
> I dare draw as soon as another man, if I see occasion in
> a good quarrel, and the law on my side.
>
> (II.iv.149f.)

Brief though it is, the speech offers the clear lines of a bawdy and cowardly character, and a relationship with the Nurse which is potent for comic development. However it is difficult to believe that Will Kemp, sharer and chief clown, merely spoke these lines and did nothing else throughout the rest of this scene, especially given the testimony of Brome that in the days of Tarlton and Kemp:

> The fools and jesters spent their wits, because
> The poets were wise enough to save their own
> For profitabler uses.
>
> (*The Antipodes*, II.ii.51f.)

Perhaps, therefore, at this stage in his career, Shakespeare was sometimes content to get Kemp on and off, and to suggest comic possibilities for extemporary development? Obviously this can be no more than speculation. There is a double irony in attempting to put together written evidence of an unwritten tradition of clowning which is both highly physical and often dependent on the immediate humorous possibilities of a particular moment. At best one can sometimes only point to holes where it might have been.

One further aspect of Elizabethan improvisation remains to be touched on. All the types of unwritten dialogue so far discussed have been in some measure spontaneous. The general assumption is that clowns respond to the particular circumstances of the moment, even though they may have a repertoire of stock gags they can work in or fall back upon. However there is some evidence, not merely in reported editions of the play but also in certain authorized texts passed to the printer by the book-keeper, which suggests that the clown's elaboration of the original text through extemporization was repeated in further performances, and subsequently written down. Peter Davison, in a comparison of the 1604 and 1616 editions of *Dr Faustus,* gives a fascinating reconstruction of what the clowns made of Marlowe's original script.[13] The printer's foreword to *Tamburlaine* surely indicates that he had a record of those 'fond and frivolous gestures' which he then chose to omit. The title-page of *A Knack to Know a Knave* claims to include Kemp's merriments (although critics are not entirely agreed that it does). If Davison is right, and not only did the clowns modify the script through improvisation, sharpening the humour by incorporating what 'works' in performance, but their modifications were subsequently recorded and became part of the working script, then this may reflect further on the nature and status of this activity during the period.

The Travels of Three English Brothers was a topical play, the product of a collaboration between Day, Rowley, and Wilkins, and performed in 1606/7 at The Curtain, and possibly at The Red Bull. It exaggerated the adventures of the three Sherley brothers, which were still continuing when the play was performed.

In 1600, Kemp, having broken with the Lord Chamberlain's Men, danced his morris to Norwich and subsequently wrote a pamphlet, *Kemp's Nine Days Wonder,* in which he announced his intention of dancing across the Alps to Italy. The journey was undertaken and he met Sir Anthony Sherley in Rome in 1601. It is possible, if perhaps unlikely, that Kemp played himself in this scene. His subsequent career is obscure. He was back from his Continental trip and playing with

Worcester's Men by the winter of 1602/3, and The Curtain seems to have been a favourite stamping ground of his. 'Kempe, a man' was buried at St Saviour's in 1603, a bad year for the plague, but the entry seems ungenerous for the greatest clown of his time and Kemp was a common enough name. Therefore it is possible that he could have still been alive in 1606/7. He was certainly dead by 1608.[14] In any event the style attributed to him could be reproduced in print by a variety of people, as here by the combination of Day, Rowley, and Wilkins. However, since Day had worked with Kemp, and although he sets the meeting in Venice, and not Rome, and three years after the event, the scene does have some sort of loose claim to be an historical record.

The play is romantic and naively pro-English and pro-Christian. Anthony becomes an envoy of the Persians in their attempts to persuade European kings to join them against the Turk. His younger brother, Robert, remains behind as hostage and then rises to become a general. Both for a time fall victim to jealous Persians. Thomas, the elder brother, is betrayed and falls into the hands of the Turks, which leads to a scene of graphic torture. At the end of the play, the elder brothers are released from prison, and their enemies unmasked, whilst Robert, now cleared of treason, marries the Sophy's niece.

The Kemp episode is more or less self-contained. We do not meet him again, as only two lines of the prologue to the play with Harlequin are spoken before an evil Jew has Sir Anthony arrested for debt:

> *Prologue*: Our act is short, your liking is our gains;
>   So we offend not, we are paid our pains.
> *Jew*: No more of this, we'll have a Jewish Jig.
>   To your business . . .

As an inner-play it must hold some sort of record for brevity.

Harlequin, or as the text calls him 'Harlaken', is taken here as the generic name for a *commedia* actor, rather than as the character-type, or 'mask', since his speciality turns out to be Pantalone. *An Almond for a Parrat* (1590), attributed to Nashe and dedicated 'To that most Comical and conceited Cavalier Monsieur du Kempe, Jest-monger and Vice-gerent General to the Ghost of Dick Tarlton', tells of a meeting with Francatrip 'Harlicken' at Bergamo (the home of the 'mask' of that name), to whom, according to this testimony, Kemp's fame had spread.

Warmly welcomed by Sir Anthony, Kemp deliberately misconstrues all that is said to him from the very beginning of the exchange, so that his answers are unexpected and droll. He directs everything towards that most copious of subjects for *double-entendre*, sexual activity, the traditional province of the fool from his origins in fertility rites. Asked an innocent question about new plays, he puns on the sexual meaning of 'play', and says that most gentlemen prefer copulation to drama. Pressed further, he alludes to *England's Joy*, which sounds like a play, but was instead a hoax; a fact presumably known by the audience but not by the expatriate Sir Anthony.[15] Hence Kemp establishes a shared intimacy with the audience from which the other characters are excluded, so that they become the objects of mockery.

It is from this basis – of intimacy on the one hand, and a sharpened awareness of double meanings on the other – that he goes on to make fun of foreign actors in the person of Harlequin, giving particular attention to the latter's wife. This enables him to increase his rapport with the audience by stimulating chauvinism (whilst giving some indication of the impropriety with which actresses were associated by the English).[16] Even whilst arranging the performance, Kemp is able to play a witty servant to Harlequin's innocent Pantaloon, interpreting as bawdy everything he says; 'do tricks in public', ''tis only her practice', 'keep my wife', a 'common thing' (pudendum), and 'take up' (her skirts). He can do so because he is not as firmly located in the fiction of the scene as are the other characters. Part of him is, as it were, lounging at the edge of the stage, poking fun, purposelessly, at all that passes by.

FROM *THE TRAVELS OF THREE ENGLISH BROTHERS*

(*Sir Anthony Sherley is in Venice, organizing a banquet*)

Enter a servant

Serv: Sir, here's an Englishman desires access to you.
Sir Ant: An Englishman? What's his name?
Serv: He calls himself Kemp.

Enter KEMP

Sir Ant: Kemp! bid him come in. Welcome, honest Will.
    And how doth all thy fellows in England?   5
Kemp: Why, like good fellows, when they have no money
    live upon credit.
Sir Ant: And what good new Plays have you?
Kemp: Many idle toys, but the old play that Adam and Eve
    acted in bare action under the fig tree draws most of   10

the Gentlemen.

Sir Ant: Jesting Will.

Kemp: In good earnest it doth, sir.

Sir Ant: I partly credit thee, but what Play of note
have you?   15

Kemp: Many of name, some of note, especially one; the
name was called *England's Joy*. Marry he was no Poet
that wrote it! he drew more Conies in a purse-net than
ever were taken at any draught about London.

Enter servant *with* HARLEQUIN *and his* WIFE

Serv: Sir, here's an Italian Harlequin come to offer a   20
play to your Lordship.

Sir Ant: We willingly accept it. Hark, Kemp;
Because I like thy gesture and thy mirth.
Let me request thee play a part with them.

Kemp: I am somewhat hard of study, and like your honour;   25
but if they will invent any extemporal merriment, I'll put
out the small sack of wit I ha' left in venture with them.

Sir Ant: They shall not deny't: Signior Harlequin he is
content: I pray thee question him – (*Whisper*)

Kemp: Now, Signior, how many are you in company?   30

Harl: None but my wife and self, sir.

Kemp: Your wife! Why, hark you, will your wife do
tricks in public?

Harl: My wife can play.

Kemp: The honest woman, I make no question; but how if   35
we cast a whore's part or a courtesan?

Harl: Oh my wife is excellent at that; she's practised
it ever since I married her; 'tis her only practice.

Kemp: But, by your leave, and she were my wife, I had
rather keep her out of practice a great deal.

Sir Ant: Yet, since 'tis the custom of the country,   40
Prithee make one; conclude upon the project:
We neither look for Scholarship nor Art
But harmless mirth, for that's thy usual part. (*Exit*)

Kemp: You shall find me no turn-coat. But the project;   45
come, and then to casting of the parts.

Harl: Marry, sir, first we will have an old Pantaloon.

Kemp: Some jealous Coxcomb.

Harl: Right, and that part will I play.

Kemp: The jealous Coxcomb?

Harl: I ha' played that part ever since –   50

Kemp: Your wife played the Courtesan.

Harl: True, and a great while afore; then I must have a
    peasant to my man, and he must keep my wife.

Kemp: Your man, and a peasant, keep your wife? I have
    known a Gentleman keep a peasant's wife, but 'tis not   55
    usual for a peasant to keep his master's wife.

Harl: Oh 'tis common in our country.

Kemp: And I'll maintain the custom of the country.

(Offers to kiss his wife)

Harl: What do you mean, sir?

Kemp: Why, to rehearse my part on your wife's lips: 60
    we are fellows and amongst friends and fellows, you
    know, all things are common.

Harl: But she shall be no common thing, if I can keep
    her several. – Then, sir, we must have an
    Inamorato that must make me Cornuto.   65

Kemp: Oh for love sake let me play that part.

Harl: No, ye must play my man's part, and keep my wife.

Kemp: Right; and who so fit to make a man a Cuckold as
    he that keeps his wife.

Harl: You shall not play that part.   70

Kemp: What say you to my boy?

Harl: Aye, he may play it and you will.

Kemp: But he cannot make you jealous enough.

Harl: Tush, I warrant you, I can be jealous for nothing.   75

Kemp: You should not be a true Italian else.

Harl: Then we must have a Magnifico that must take up
    the matter betwixt me and my wife.

Kemp: Anything of yours, but I'll take up nothing of
    your wife's.

Harl: I wish not you should: but come, now am I your Master.

Kemp: Right, and I your servant.   81

Harl: Lead the way then.

Kemp: No, I ha' more manners than so: in our Country
    'tis the custom of the Master to go in before his wife,
    and the man to follow the master.   85

Harl: In –

Kemp: To his Mistress.

Harl: Ye are in the right –
Kemp: Way to Cuckold's-haven: Saint Luke be your speed.

(*Exeunt*)

Glossary to *The Travels of Three English Brothers*

9f. Most gentlemen like fornication best.
18f. *Conies*: lit. rabbits; here 'dupes'.
19 *draught*: trawl.
25 *hard of study*: cannot learn lines.
32 *tricks*: sexual activities.
39 *practice*: as above.
47 *Coxcomb*: fool, from his headware; here 'jealous fool' i.e. cuckold.
64 *Several*: separate.
   Inamorato: a lover.
65 *Cornuto*: a cuckold.
89 *Cuckold's haven*: a harbourage on the Thames.

5

Clown as justice
The Mayor of Queenborough

The Mayor of Queenborough is one of a number of plays attributed to
Thomas Middleton, sometimes in association with William Rowley,
which contain inner plays or masques in domestic settings that provide
a pretext by which groups of characters effect some kind of non-
dramatic purpose; robbery in *A Mad World, My Masters* (c. 1606) and,
incidentally, in the present play, reformation in *The Spanish Gypsy*
(c. 1623), exposure in *Your Five Gallants* (c. 1605), and revenge in
Women Beware Women (1621); whilst in *No Wit, No Help Like a Woman's*
(c. 1613) the performers intend revenge but achieve no more than a
display of toothless envy. In the last three of these plays the performers
are amateurs taking part in domestic masques, and therefore not to our
immediate purpose, whilst *The Spanish Gypsy* is a tasteless farrago of
musical comedy gypsies who all turn out to be nobles in disguise, and
whose pretensions to be itinerants are very thinly conceived. The
itinerant players in *A Mad World, My Masters* have rather more
substance, though they too turn out to be imposters. Only in *The Mayor
of Queenborough* are the players, though dishonest rogues, none the less
genuine professionals.

Middleton cannot be said to be deeply stirred by the appropriateness
of the player paradigm, or the possibilities of the stage to teach.
Although his stage auditors may be relieved of some of their worldly
possessions by means of the stratagems that pass for plays, and though
reality may be confused with fiction so as temporarily to disturb or
excite them, they remain unchanged by their experiences. What his
plays celebrate is the carnival quality of occasional dramatics, their
potential for anarchy, and the access of energy infused by the
itinerants.

There is no direct evidence that Middleton himself was a player, but
by the age of twenty-one he was reported as having left Oxford, and to
be 'remaining in London accompanying the players', which suggests a

close and presumably sympathetic association. His presentation in the two plays of players as rogues is less a genuine indictment of the profession than a symptom of the fascination in which the Elizabethan middle-class intelligentsia held the London underworld, at least as a source of racy imaginative literature. Many of the 'coney-catching' pamphlets were written by dramatists and are linked to the stage by the general associations made between criminality and inventive deceit.

Our play is now more commonly called *Hengist, King of Kent*. In early references, however, it appears as *The Mayor of Queenborough*, a testimony to the initial popularity of its comic subplot, the final scene of which forms the extract under consideration. Modern critics have largely accepted the findings of R.C. Bald's 1938 edition that the play was composed in c. 1619/20, and that it is entirely the work of Middleton.[1] When the text surfaced in 1641 it was in the possession of the King's Men and the first printed edition in 1661 described it as having been performed at Blackfriars. Various suggestions have been put forward as to its original auspices.

The main plot concerns the arrival of the Saxons in England. The hero-villain Vortiger, after failing to depose the saintly Constantius by trickery, murders him and takes his throne. He quells an uprising by using the services of the Saxons, Hengist and Horsus. Given only as much land as can be covered by a hide, Hengist has it cut into narrow strips and so encloses enough space for a castle. To consolidate his position, he sends for his daughter, Roxena, to entice King Vortiger, who succumbs and, under the tutelage of Roxena's secret lover, Horsus, puts away his Queen, Castiza. After various episodes the evil characters all die on the burning castle walls and order is restored.

Simon, the comic hero of the subplot, is the tanner who cut the hide into strips, and under Hengist's patronage he prospers. Hengist becomes King of Kent, and Simon becomes Mayor of Queenborough. There is an obvious sense in which Simon can be seen to be parodying the main plot. He too has his rebellion in the form of Oliver, the fustian weaver and puritan, and much of what he says as Mayor is in a tone of burlesque tyranny. He is grandly assertive and threatens violent punishments, but everything is scaled down in size until it becomes ridiculous. Oliver's punishment is watching a play, the triumphant bonfires will be of peas-straw, and only one of the bells will ring. When Simon throws off his gown to take part in the play, the satin forepart of his doublet, in a period obsessed with sartorial distinctions, is seen to have a canvas back. The nature of his burlesque of tyranny is encapsulated in his final threat to Oliver, 'I will have/His eyes pulled out *for a fortnight.*' Only in his clown-world could such a punishment be temporary.

Commentators agree on the parallels offered by the subplot, but only those who see the whole play as travesty can accept that this justifies its length and its obvious anachronisms. In general however most critics are content on the one hand to recognize its structural irrelevance, whilst at the same time acknowledging the quality of its humour. In performance it works well as a brief self-contained play – perhaps the most satisfyingly complete in the selection – showing the rise and fall of a comic tyrant, which is genuinely funny. It intertwines effectively the two elements of the visit of the players and the humiliation and triumph of Oliver, the puritan, both to satisyfying resolutions. The brief entry of Hengist at the end of the extract, his summons to battle and Simon's inappropriate response, illustrates the gulf between the two plots.

The players who appear in *The Mayor of Queenborough*, although they are 'professed cheaters' and 'only take the name of country comedians to abuse simple people . . .' (l. 357), are more genuine than those in *A Mad World, My Masters,* Middleton's other essay in itinerant deceit. Follywit and his companions had no play, but these players have 'a printed play or two, which they bought at Canterbury for sixpence', and from what we can see before Simon spoils it, are prepared to act it out quite effectively. Like bad players everywhere, they have not learnt all their lines, and 'fribble out the rest'. Rather than being pure imposters, they represent the tail-end of the player-spectrum, below what is acceptable, and precisely the sort of opportunist scoundrels against whom the Act for the Punishment of Vagabonds of 1572 was intended.

They arrive, like all the other itinerants in this collection, un-announced, but conveniently to be incorporated into a larger entertain-ment which is already in hand. They offer their first performance, as was the custom, to the Mayor, who decides to monitor it in advance of a performance before the King of Kent in order to ensure that it is good enough and not 'dangerous'. As with the other touring groups represented here they offer a repertoire of plays, seven in number, from which their host may choose. Like Hamlet's visitors they claim versatility 'from the hug to the smile, from the smile to laugh, from the laugh to the handkerchief', but the selection they offer seems to concentrate on cheating.

In his creation of Simon, Middleton draws upon a long tradition of clownish figures in authority, echoing, perhaps with some nostalgia, the earlier comic creations of Kemp, who seems to have specialized in characters, either as servants or officials, who inhabited a comic world of their own, ineffectual and yet insulated from disaster by their own special self-confidence and humour. Shakespeare wrote the part of Dogberry for him in *Much Ado About Nothing* (1598) shortly before Kemp left the Chamberlain's Men. It has many features in common with the justice's speech given to him in *The Second Part of the Return from Parnassus*. Both are foolish men holding offices of power; pompous, overweening, and inordinately ponderous.

It is not surprising that the justice and the constable should be objects of fun. It is on their whims and prejudices that the fortunes of the strolling player so much depended, and the frequency with which they are represented in the plays is a reminder of how the players took their revenge. Jonson in *Bartholomew Fair* (whilst himself focusing much of the play around a comic justice) made fun of the comic watch as a theatrical convention with references to the watch stealing upon Adams and Tarlton and taking them away with 'mistaking words'.

In *A Mad World, My Masters,* working new variants on the old theme, Middleton offers a comic justice and his new constable. The 'real' constable, having arrested the pretend players, brings them to Sir Bounteous, the justice, sitting at a performance, and enters with mistaking words:

> May it please your worship, sir, here are a company of *auspicious* fellows . . .

whereupon Sir Bounteous takes him for a player, and directs him towards what he believes to be his fellow upon the stage:

> To me? Puh, turn to th' justice, you whoreson hobby horse!

Turning to his companions in the audience, he observes:

> This is some new player now; they put all their fools to the constable's part still.

This prompts Follywit and his companions to gag the constable and incorporate him into their stratagem.

When Middleton creates Simon, the eponymous Mayor of Queenborough, he works another variation on the justice-as-fool by having his clownish tanner promoted to Mayor. It is perhaps this play Gossip Tattle has in mind in Jonson's *The Staple of News* (1626), when she says:

> the fool . . . is the very justice o' peace of the play and can

commit whom he will, and what he will, error, absurdity, as the
toy take him, and no man say black is his eye, but laugh at him.

Except for the arbitrary and unusual circumstances of his elevation,
Simon would have remained one of the traditionally oppressed.
Through his untypical, spontaneous antics in the seat of power, he
questions and satirizes the behaviour of its normal incumbents, those
who, up and down the land, still betray their own shortcomings in the
very act of asserting the dignity of their office.

Simon's behaviour is deliciously inappropriate. He considers himself
so important he must employ a deputy to shake people's hands, and yet
he sees nothing incongruous in pissing out the fire at bedtime. His
domestic hints on making a pan-pudding out of beating cushions on
which millers have sat is an imaginative satire on citizen frugality.

Middleton has created in Simon an unjustly neglected comic figure,
who carries on many of the traditional features of the Elizabethan
Clown. The text in a sense offers the elements of two scripts; one the
character of Simon in the play, and, in the other, cues for the performer
of that part in his relationship with the stage event and its audience. He
engages the audience in a running commentary of jokes which are less
an expression of his character in the fable than a semi-extra-dramatic
relationship established between spectator and player; as in Simon's
comments on the retreating footman (l. 35-6).

Although Simon habitually calls his aldermen 'neighbours', the term
seems to encompass the audience too:

> For you must imagine now, neighbours, this is
> The time when Kent stands out of Christendom,
> For he that's king here now was never christened.

The comic choric tone he employs, and his insistence that the events of
the main plot take place at a different historical time than that of
himself and the audience, seem to be suggesting the independent reality
of the clown. That his loyalty to the amusement of the audience is
always greater than that to the fable is well illustrated in his reply to
the Felt Monger (l. 347f.), who has pointed out that it is Simon's own
fault the meal was thrown in his face because he told the player to do
his worst:

Simon: His worst? That's true, but the rascal hath done his best.

His comic resilience allows us to enjoy the word-play without being
over-much worried about his physical discomfort. In this sort of

clown–audience rapprochement all the other characters/actors serve as stooges, objects of amusement, deficient in this comic/ironic dimension which the Clown shares with his audience, for, although it is the convention of the Clown to be both shrewd and blundering, there is a sense in which the mind that enjoys the jokes in this play is sharper than the surface character we are offered.

Simon is made to represent the half-understanding common auditory when he says:

> *Simon*: . . . I have known a great man poisoned in a play –
> *Glover*: What, have you, master mayor?
> *Simon*: But to what purpose many times, I know not.
> *Glover*: Methinks they should not destroy one another so.
> *Simon*: Oh, no, no! he that's poisoned is always made
>   privy to it; that's one good order they have among them.
>
> (l. 150f.)

Presumably he is referring to the convention of using the inner play to murder a member of the stage audience. The Glover however takes it that it is the actor, not the character, who is being killed, and Simon's answer only furthers a confusion which is to become the reason and the means for his own direct entry into the play. Unlike Sir Thomas More, whose behaviour in attempting to shore up the entertainment is entirely logical, Simon is involved in a clown-logic which continually undercuts everyday expectations and assumptions, in a world not so much of topsy-turveydom or simple inversion, but of confusion.

Although Simon sees himself as something of a *cognoscente*, insisting that the clown must 'have the grace to hit on 't', and even offers the glimmerings of an aesthetic of clowning: the 'clown sets off the king', once the play begins, in his determination to take his own reality into the play, he seems (if only for our amusement) to be unable to distinguish reality from illusion. His insistence that a clown should be serious and not 'clownish' itself creates much of the humour of affronted dignity. It also echoes Nashe's story of the country justice who would not let the audience laugh at Tarlton because he wore the Queen's livery. Furthermore, it relates to that tradition by which the clown brings our foolishness into question. The proposition 'the fool is he who thinks he is not a fool' implies, in the anarchic clown-logic, either that the wise man is he who says he *is* a fool, or that we are all fools. Set against the latter view however is Simon's assertion that 'every man is not born to it'. Along with the all-encompassing folly

that Simon's imitation of a magistrate implies is that enduring sense of
the separateness of the Clown identified by William Willeford:

> And even when the fool loudly and convincingly proclaims that
> we are fools, too, what the fool is partly remains the fool's secret,
> though he may pretend to disclose it.[2]

THE MAYOR OF QUEENBOROUGH

Act V Scene I

Enter SIMON, GLOVER, FELT MONGER, *and other of his brethren,*
AMINADAB, *and* servants

Simon: It is not that rebel, Oliver, that traitor to my year,
  'prehended yet?
Amin: Not yet, so please your worship.
Simon: Not yet, sayest thou? How durst thou say, 'not yet', and
  see me present? Thou malapert, thou art good for nothing but   5
  to write and read! Is his loom seized upon?
Amin: Yes, if it like your worship, and sixteen yards of fustian.
Simon: Good, let a yard be saved to mend me between the legs,
  the rest cut in pieces and given to the poor. 'Tis heretic fustian,
  and should be burnt indeed; but being worn threadbare, the   10
  shame will be as great: how think you neighbours?
Glover: Greater, methinks, the longer it is wore:
  Where being once burnt, it can be burnt no more.
Simon: True, wise and most senseless – How now, sirrah?

Enter a footman

  What's he approaching here in dusty pumps?   15
Amin: A footman, sir, to the great King of Kent.
Simon: The King of Kent? Shake him by the hand for me.
  Thou 'rt welcome, footman: lo, my deputy shakes thee!
  Come when my year is out, I'll do 't myself.
  If 'twere a dog came from the King of Kent,   20
  I keep those officers would shake him, I trow.
  And what's the news with thee, thou well-stewed footman?
Foot: The King, my master –
Simon: Ha!
Foot: With a few Saxons,   25

Intends this night to make merry with you.
Simon: Merry with me? I should be sorrow else, fellow,
    And take it in ill part; so tell Kent's king.
    Why was I chosen, but that great men should make
    Merry with me? There is a jest indeed!   30
    Tell him I look for't; and me much he wrongs,
    If he forget Sim that cut out his thongs.
Foot: I'll run with your worship's answer.
Simon: Do, I prithee.   (*Exit* footman)
    That fellow will be roasted against supper;   35
    He's half enough already; his brows baste him.
    The King of Kent! the King of Christendom
    Shall not be better welcome;
    For you must imagine now, neighbours, this is
    The time when Kent stands out of Christendom,   40
    For he that's king here now was never christened.
    This for your more instruction I thought fit,
    That when you're dead you may teach your children wit. –
    Clerk!
Amin: At your worship's elbow.   45
Simon: I must turn
    You from the hall to the kitchen tonight.
    Give order that twelve pigs be roasted yellow,
    Nine geese, and some three larks for piddling meat,
    And twenty woodcocks: I'll bid all my neighbours.   50
    Give charge the mutton come in all blood raw,
    That's infidel's meat; the King of Kent's a Pagan,
    And must be served so. And let those officers
    That seldom or never go to church bring it in,
    'Twill be better taken. Run, run. (*Exit Aminadab*)   55
    Come hither now.
    Take all my cushions down and thwack them soundly,
    After my feast of millers; for their buttocks
    Have left a peck of flour in them: beat them carefully
    Over a bolting-hutch, there will be enough   60
    For a pan-pudding, as your dame will handle it.
    Then put fresh water into both bough-pots,
    And burn a little juniper in the hall-chimney.

(*Exeunt* servants)

Like a beast as I was, I pissed out the fire last night
and never dreamt of the king's coming.   65

Re-enter AMINADAB

How now, returned so quickly?
Amin: Please your worship, here are a certain company
  of players –
Simon: Ha, players!
Amin: Country comedians, interluders, sir, desire your worship's   70
  favour and leave to enact in the town-hall.
Simon: In the town-hall? 'Tis ten to one I never grant them that.
  Call them before my worship. (*Exit Aminadab*) – If my house
  will not serve their turn, I would fain see the proudest he lend
  them a barn.   75

Re-enter AMINADAB *with* players

Now, sirs, are you comedians?
2 Player: We are, sir; comedians, tragedians, tragi-comedians,
  comic-tragedians, pastorists, humourists, clownists, satirists:
  we have them, sir, from the hug to the smile, from the smile
  to the laugh, from the laugh to the handkerchief.   80
Simon: You are very strong in the wrists, methinks. And must
  all these good parts be cast away upon pedlars and maltmen,
  ha?
1 Player: For want of better company, if it please your worship.
Simon: What think you of me, my masters? Hum; have you   85
  audacity enough to play before so high a person as myself?
  Will not my countenance daunt you? For if you play before
  me, I shall often look on you; I give you that warning
  beforehand. Take it not ill, my masters, I shall laugh at you,
  and truly when I am least offended with you: it is my humour,   90
  but be not you abashed.
1 Player: Sir, we have played before a lord ere now, though we
  be country actors.
Simon: A lord? ha, ha!
  Thou'lt find it a harder thing to please a mayor.   95
1 Player: We have a play wherein we use a horse.
Simon: Fellows, you use no horse-play in my house;
  My rooms are rubbed: keep it for hackney-men.
1 Player: We'll not offer it to your worship.

Simon: Give me a play without a beast, I charge you.   100
2 Player: That's hard; without a cuckold or a drunkard?
Simon: Oh, those beasts are often the best men in a parish, and
    must not be kept out. But which is your merriest play? That
    I would hearken after.
2 Player: Your worship shall hear their names, and take your   105
    choice.
Simon: And that's plain dealing. Come begin, sir.
2 Player: *The Whirligig, The Whibble, The Carwidgeon*.[3]
Simon: Hey-day! What names are these?
2 Player: New plays of late. *The Wildgoose Chase*.   110
Simon: I understand thee now.
2 Player: *Gull Upon Gull*.
Simon: Why, this is somewhat yet.
1 Player: *Woodcock of our side*.
Simon: Get thee further off then.   115
2 Player: *The Cheater and the Clown*.
Simon: Is that come up again?
    That was a play when I was 'prentice first.
2 Player: Aye, but the cheater has learned more tricks
    of late,   120
    And gulls the clown with new additions.
Simon: Then is your clown a coxcomb; which is he?
1 Player: This is our clown, sir.
Simon: Fie, fie, your company must fall upon him and beat him:
    he's too fair, i'faith, to make the people laugh.   125
1 Player: Not as he may be dressed, sir.
Simon: Faith, dress him how you will, I'll give him that gift, he
    will never look half scurvily enough. Oh, the clowns that I
    have seen in my time! The very peeping out of one of them
    would have made a young heir laugh, though his father lay   130
    a-dying; a man undone in law the day before (the saddest
    case that can be) might for his twopence have burst himself
    with laughing and ended all his miseries. Here was a merry
    world, my masters!
    Some talk of things of state, of puling stuff;   135
    There's nothing in a play to a clown, if he
    Have grace to hit on't; that's the thing indeed:
    The king shows well, but he sets off the king.
    But not the King of Kent, I mean not so;

The king is one, I mean, I do not know. 140
2 *Player*: Your worship speaks with safety, like a rich man;
  And for your finding fault, our hopes are greater,
  Neither with him the clown, nor me the cheater.
Simon: Away, then; shift, clown, to thy motley crupper.

Exeunt Players

We'll see them first, the king shall after supper. 145
Glover: I commend your worship's wisdom in that, master
  mayor.
Simon: Nay 'tis a point of justice, if it be well examined, not to
  offer the king worse than I'll see myself. For a play may be
  dangerous: I have known a great man poisoned in a play – 150
Glover: What, have you, master mayor?
Simon: But for what purpose I know not.
Felt monger: Methinks they should not destroy one another so.
Simon: Oh, no, no! he that's poisoned is always made privy to
  it; that's one good order they have among them. – (*A shout* 155
  within) What joyful throat is that? Aminabad, what is the
  meaning of this cry?
Amin: The rebel is taken.
Simon: Oliver the puritan?
Amin: Oliver, puritan, and fustian-weaver, altogether. 160
Simon: Fates, I thank you for this victorious day!
  Bonfires of peas-straw burn, let the bells ring!
Glover: There's two in mending, and you know they cannot.
Simon: 'Las, the tenor's broken! Ring out the treble!

Enter OLIVER, *brought in by* officers

I'm over-cloyed with joy. – Welcome, thou rebel! 165
Oliver: I scorn thy welcome, I.
Simon: Art thou yet so stout?
  Wilt thou not stoop for grace? Then get thee out.
Oliver: I was not born to stoop, but to my loom:
  That seized upon, my stooping days are done. 170
  In plain terms, if thou hast anything to say to me, send me
  away quickly, this is no biding-place: I understand there are
  players in thy house; despatch me, I charge thee, in the name
  of all the brethren.
Simon: Nay, now, proud rebel, I will make thee stay: 175

And to thy greater torment, see a play.

Oliver O devil! I conjure thee by Amsterdam!

Simon: Our word is past;

    Justice may wink a while, but see at last.

    (*Trumpet sounds*) The play begins. (*Oliver attempts to escape*)   180

    Hold, stop him, stop him!

Oliver: Oh that profane trumpet! Oh, oh!

Simon: Set him down there, I charge you, officers.

Oliver: I'll hide my ears and stop my eyes.

Simon: Down with his golls, I charge you.   185

Oliver: O tyranny, tyranny! Revenge it, tribulation!

    For rebels there are many deaths; but sure the only way

    To execute a puritan, is seeing of a play.

    Oh, I shall swound!

Simon: Which if thou dost, to spite thee,   190

    A player's boy shall bring thee aqua-vitae.

        Enter FIRST PLAYER *as* FIRST CHEATER

Oliver: Oh, I'll not swound at all for't, though I die.

Simon: Peace, here's a rascal! List and edify.

1 *Player*: I say still he's an ass that cannot live by his wits.

Simon: What a bold rascal's this! He calls us all asses at first   195

    dash: sure none of us live by our wits, unless it be Oliver

    the puritan.

Oliver: I scorn as much to live by my wits as the proudest of

    you all.

Simon: Why, then you're an ass for company; so hold your   200

    prating.

        Enter SECOND PLAYER *as* SECOND CHEATER

1 *Player*: Fellow in arms, welcome! The news, the news?

Simon: Fellow in arms, quoth he? He may well call his fellow

    in arms; I'm sure they're both out at the elbows.

2 *Player*: Be lively, my heart, be lively; the booty is at   205

**   hand. He's but a fool of a yeoman's eldest son; he's**

**   balanced on both sides, bully; he's going to buy**

**   household stuff with one pocket, and to pay rent with**

**   the other.**

1 *Player*: And if this be his last day, my chuck, he shall   210

**   forfeit his lease, quoth the one pocket, and eat his meat**

in wooden platters, quoth the other.

Simon: Faith, then he's not so wise as he ought to be, to let
such tatterdemallions get the upper hand of him.

1 Player: **He comes.** 215

Enter THIRD PLAYER AS CLOWN

2 Player: **Aye, but smally to our comfort, with both his
hands in his pockets. How is it possible to pick a lock,
when the key is on the inside of the door?**

Simon: O neighbours, here's the part now that carries away the
play! If the clown miscarry, farewell my hopes for ever; the 220
play's spoiled.

3 Player: **They say there is a foolish kind of thing called a
cheater abroad, that will gull any yeoman's son of his
purse, and laugh in his face like an Irishman. I would
fain meet with some of these creatures: I am in as good 225
state to be gulled now as ever I was in my life, for I
have two purses at this time about me and I would fain
be acquainted with that rascal that would take one of
them now.**

Simon: Faith, thou mayest be acquainted with two or three, 230
that will do their good wills, I warrant thee.

1 Player: **That way's too plain, too easy, I'm afraid.**

2 Player: **Come, sir, your most familiar cheats take best,
They show like natural things and least suspected.
Give me a round shilling quickly.** 235

1 Player: **It will fetch but one of his hands neither, if it
take.**

2 Player: **Thou art too covetous: let's have one out first,
prithee; there's time enough to fetch out the other after.**
(*Starts his cheat*) **Thou liest, 'tis lawful current money.** 240
(*They draw their weapons*)

1 Player: **I say 'tis copper in some countries.**

3 Player: **Here is a fray towards; but I will hold my hands,
let who will part them.**

2 Player: **Copper? I defy thee, and now I shall disprove
thee. Look you, here's an honest yeoman's son of the 245
country, a man of judgement.** (*Doffs his hat*)

3 Player: **Pray you be covered, sir; I have eggs in my cap,** and cannot put it off.

2 Player: **Will you be tried by him?**

1 Player: **I am content, sir.** 250

Simon: They look rather as if they would be tried next sessions.

1 Player: **Pray give your judgement of this piece of coin, sir.**

3 Player: **Nay, if it be coin you strive about, let me see it; I love money.** (*Takes one hand out of his pocket to hold the coin*) 255

1 Player: **Look on it well, sir.** (*They pick his pocket*)

2 Player: **Let him do his worst, sir.**

3 Player: **You'd both need wear cut clothes, you're so choleric.**

2 Player: **Nay rub it, and spare not, sir.** 260

3 Player: **Now by this silver, gentlemen, it is good money; would I had a hundred of them!**

2 Player: **We hope well, sir. – The other pocket and we are made men.** (*Exeunt* FIRST *and* SECOND PLAYERS)

Simon: O neighbours, I begin to be sick of this fool to see him 265
thus cozened! I would make his case my own.

3 Players: **Still would I meet with these things called cheaters.**

Simon: A whoreson coxcomb; they have met with thee.
I can no longer endure him with patience. 270

3 Player: **Oh my rent! My whole year's rent!**

Simon: A murrain on you! This makes us landlords stay so long
for our money.

3 Player: **The cheaters have been here.**

Simon: A scurvy hobby-horse, that could not leave his money 275
with me, having such a charge about him! A pox on thee for
an ass! Thou play a clown! I will commit thee for offering
it. – Officers, away with him!

Glover: What means your worship? Why, you'll spoil the play,
sir. 280

Simon: Before the King of Kent shall be thus served,
I'll play the clown myself. – Away with him!

Officers seize THIRD PLAYER

3 Player: With me? If it please your worship, 'twas my part.

Simon: But 'twas a foolish part as ever thou playedst in thy

life: I'll make thee smoke for it; I'll teach thee to understand 285
to play a clown; thou salt know every man is not born to it.
– Away with him quickly! He'll have the other pocket
picked else; I heard them say it with my own ears.

Re-enter SECOND PLAYER *as* SECOND CHEATER
See, he comes in another disguise to cheat thee again.

Exit THIRD PLAYER *with officers*

2 Player: Pish, whither goes he now?

Simon: Come on, sir, let us see what your knaveship can do at 290
me now: you must not think you have a clown in hand. The
fool I have committed too, for playing the part. (*Throws off
his gown, discovering his doublet with a satin forepart, and a canvas
back*)

2 Player: What's here to do?

Glover: Fie, good sir, come away: will your worship 'base
yourself to play a clown? 295

2 Player: I beseech your worship let us have our own clown; I
know not how to go forward else.

Simon: Knave, play out thy part with me, or I'll lay thee by
the heels all the days of thy life. – Why, how now, my
masters, who is it that laughed at me? Cannot a man of 300
worship play the clown a little for his pleasure, but he
must be laughed at? Do you know who I am?
Is the king's deputy of no better account among you?
Was I chosen to be laughed at? – Where's my clerk?

Amin: Here, if it please your worship. 305

Simon: Take a note of all those that laugh at me, that when I
have done, I may commit them. Let me see who dare do it
now. – And now to you once again, Sir Cheater: look you,
here are my purse strings; I do defy thee.

2 Player: Good sir, tempt me not; my part is so written, that I 310
could cheat your worship if you were my father.

Simon: I should have much joy to have such a rascal to my son.

2 Player: Therefore I beseech your worship pardon me; the part
has more knavery in it than when your worship saw it at
first: I assure you you'll be deceived in it, sir; the new 315
additions will take any man's purse in Kent or Christendom.

Simon: If thou canst take my purse, I'll give it thee freely: And
do thy worst, I charge thee, as thou'll answer it.

2 Player: I shall offend your worship.

Simon: Knave, do it quickly.   320

2 Player: Say you so? Then there's for you, and here is for me.
   (*Throws meal in his face, takes his purse, and exit*)

Simon: Oh bless me! Neighbours, I am in a fog,
   A cheater's fog; I can see nobody.

Glover: Run, follow him, officers.

Simon: Away! Let him go; he will have all your purses,   325
   if he come back. A pox on your new additions! They spoil
   all the plays that ever they come in: the old way had no
   such roguery in it. Call you this a merry comedy, when a
   man's eyes are put out in't? Brother Honeysuckle – (*Exit
   Aminadab*)

Felt Monger: What says your sweet worship?   330

Simon: I make you deputy to rule the town till I can see again,
   which will be within these nine days at farthest. Nothing
   grieves me now, but that I hear Oliver the rebel laugh at
   me. A pox on your puritan face! This will make you in love
   with plays as long as you live; we shall not keep you   335
   from them now.

Oliver: In sincerity, I was never better pleased at an exercise.
   Ha, ha, ha!

Simon: Neighbours, what colour was the dust the rascal threw
   in my face?   340

Glover: 'Twas meal, if it please your worship.

Simon: Meal! I am glad of it; I'll hang the miller for selling it.

Glover: Nay, ten to one the cheater never bought it; he stole it
   certainly.

Simon: Why, then I'll hang the cheater for stealing it, and the   345
   miller for being out of the way when he did it.

Felt Monger: Aye, but your worship was in the fault yourself;
   you bid him do his worst.

Simon: His worst? That's true, but the rascal hath done his
   best; for I know not how a villain could put out a man's   350
   eyes better, and leave them in his head, as he has done mine.

Re-enter AMINADAB

Amin: Where is my master's worship?

Simon: How now, Aminadab? I hear thee, though I see thee
    not.

Amin: You are sure cozened, sir; they are all professed 355
    cheaters: they have stolen two silver spoons, and the clown
    took his heels with all celerity. They only take the name of
    country-comedians to abuse simple people with a printed
    play or two, which they bought at Canterbury for sixpence;
    and what is worst, they speak but what they list of it, and 360
    fribble out the rest.

Simon: Here's an abuse to the commonwealth, if a man could
    see to look into it.
    But mark the cunning of these cheating slaves,
    First they make Justice blind, then play the knaves. 365

Hengist (without): Where's master mayor?

Glover: Od's precious, brother! The King of Kent is newly
    alighted.

Simon: The King of Kent!
    Where is he? That I should live to this day, 370
    And yet not live to see to bid him welcome!

Enter HENGIST *attended*

Heng: Where is Simonides, our friendly host?

Simon: Ah, blind as one that has been foxed a seven-night!

Heng: Why, how now, man?

Simon: Faith, practising a clown's part for your grace, I have 375
    practised both my eyes out.

Heng: What need you practise that?

Simon: A man is never too old to learn; your grace will say so,
    when you hear the jest of it: the truth is, my lord, I meant
    to have been merry, and now it is my luck to weep water 380
    and oatmeal; I shall see again at supper, I make no doubt of
    it.

Heng: This is strange to me, sirs.

Enter a GENTLEMAN

Gent: Arm, arm, my lord!

Heng: What's that? 385

Gent: With swiftest speed,

If ever you'll behold the queen, your daughter,
Alive again.
Heng: Roxena?
Gent: They are besieged: 390
Aurelius Ambrose, and his brother Uther,
With numbers infinite of British forces,
Beset their castle, and they cannot 'scape
Without your speedy succour.
Heng: For her safety 395
I'll forget food and rest; away!
Simon: I hope your worship will hear the jest before you go.
Heng: The jest! Torment me not.
Simon: I'll follow you to Wales with a dog and a bell, but I
will tell it you. 400
Heng: Unseasonable folly! (*Exit with attendants*)
Simon: 'Tis a sign of war when great men disagree.
Look to the rebel well, till I can see;
And when my sight's recovered, I will have
His eyes pulled out for a fortnight. 405
Oliver: My eyes? Hang thee!
A deadly sin or two shall pluck them out first;
That is my resolution. Ha, ha, ha! (*Exeunt*)

Glossary to *The Mayor of Queenborough*

7 *fustian*: a coarse cloth made of cotton and flax.
49 *piddling meat*: for picking at; a side-dish.
60 *bolting hutch*: a container for sifting bran.
62 *bough pots*: vessels for holding ornamental branches etc.
95/6 *mayor*: pun on 'mare'.
98 *rubbed*: cleaned.
135 *puling*: whining, feeble.
144 *crupper*: lit. strap passing under horse's tail; here with *Motley*,
variegated, parti-coloured: fool's costume.
185 *golls*: hands.
189 *swound*: faint.
214 *tatterdemallions*: ragamuffins.
258 *cut*: slashed.
259 *choleric*: angry.
272 *murrain*: pestilence.

361 *fribble*: see pp. 65–6.
373 *foxed*: drunk.

6

Attacks on the common player

One of the peculiarities of the evidence provided by contemporary stage representations of the professional player is the frequency with which they attack and condemn him. In the adults' own plays, such as *Hamlet, Sir Thomas More,* the Induction to *The Malcontent,* and the two *Shrew* plays, they represent themselves as might be expected as unassuming workaday professionals.[1] It is not until *The Roman Actor* in 1626 that we get an idealized self-portrait. Five of the representations of players in this selection, on the other hand, are frankly derogatory, and range from witty satire to straightforward abuse. One of their characteristics, not surprisingly, is that they appear to have been performed by other than adult professionals. Ben Jonson's *The Poetaster* was performed in 1601 at Blackfriars by the Children of the Chapel. The *Pilgrimage to Parnassus* (c. 1599) and *The Second Part of the Return from Parnassus* (c. 1603) were two of three plays performed by members of St John's College, Cambridge. The auspices, authorship, and date of *Histriomastix* are unknown, but P.J. Finkelpearl has made a strong case for its performance by members of the Inns of Court.[2] A fifth play, Robert Tailor's *The Hog Hath Lost his Pearl,* was performed at Whitefriars in 1613 by London apprentices and its social attitudes can be seen as a throwback to the earlier group.

It is difficult for the modern reader to understand why the performers of these plays should see themselves as so superior to what they represent in performance, and why they are so critical, so unyieldingly condemnatory. *The Poetaster*, for instance, presents a picture of smelly, parasitical, greedy, dishonest fleshmongers, whilst *Histriomastix,* much the most extensive treatment of players, seems designed as a catalogue of all their venial shortcomings, without a single extenuating feature.

In subsequent chapters it will be suggested that these hostile representations of the common player, often quoting directly from those who would condemn all dramatic mimesis, take much of their tone from their institutional contexts. The penultimate chapter will consider how far they were serious in their condemnation, and what they meant by using the play-form to present it.

Although it is on the specific objections to the profession of player that many Elizabethan attacks turn, including those in the plays under review, the ground-base of hostility, as expressed for instance by Rainolds against Gager's university theatricals, concerns the very act of mimesis. Characteristically it is expressed in moral and theological terms; as being wrong, against God's teachings, and betraying and debasing his creation. However beneath what now may seem an obsessive concern for theological niceties that no longer have much validity, there are deep-rooted objections to impersonation that our own age would term 'psychological', relating to the threat it makes on personal integrity and psychic wholeness, which some of the plays in the selection themselves explore, and which remain relevant to any discussion of the acting process.

Play-acting was associated by its critics with change and weakness, with the destruction of recognized boundaries and categories. Because each performance was immediate, and at least potentially spontaneous, is was a continuous threat to orthodoxy and authority. In particular it was identified with the ascendancy of the emotions, which were seen as man's point of weakness, and against which there must be perpetual vigilance. Man's reason is a besieged city, ever in danger of being sacked. The mind has to be held by force to the course of virtue. Players, said Gosson, 'set . . . abroach strange consorts of melody, to tickle the ear; costly apparel, to flatter the sight; effeminate gesture, to ravish the sense; and wanton speech, to wet desire to inordinate lust' (*School of Abuse,* 1579). The result of the assault on the senses was to 'draw the bridle from that part of the mind, that should be ever be curbed, from running our head: which is manifest treason to our souls, and delivereth them captive to the devil' (*Plays Confuted in Five Actions,* 1582).

The stage, it was claimed in numerous pamphlets issued from the late 1570s onwards, incited spectators to all manner of evils:[3]

If you will learn how to be false and deceive your husbands, or husbands their wives, how to play the harlots, to obtain one's love, how to ravish, how to beguile, how to betray, to flatter, lie, swear, forswear, how to allure to whoredom, how to murder, how to poison, how to disobey and rebel against princes, to

consume treasures prodigally, to move to lusts, to ransack and
spoil cities and towns, to be idle, to blaspheme, to sing filthy
songs of love, to speak filthily, to be proud, how to mock, scoff,
deride any nation . . . shall not you learn, then, at such interludes
how to practice them?

(John Northbrooke, *A Treatice wherein Dicing etc,* 1577)[4]

Women were considered particularly vulnerable to being corrupted by
such spectacles. Anglo-phile Eutheo reports:

Some citizens' wives, upon whom the Lord for example to others
hath laid his hands, have even on their deathbeds with tears
confessed that they have received at those spectacles such filthy
infections, as have turned their minds from chaste cogitations,
and made them of honest women light housewives.

(Anglo-phile Eutheo: *A Second and third blast of retrait from plays and
theatres,* 1580)

Transvestitism figures prominently in the preachers' attacks, partly
because it was a perceived impropriety, and partly because it was
subject to a direct prohibition in *Deuteronomy* xxii.5: 'The woman shall
not wear that which pertaineth unto a man, neither shall a man put on a
women's garment: for all that do so are abomination unto the Lord thy
God.'

Lacking any more specific Divine commandments concerning theatricals, the opponents of the theatre had perforce to extend the use of
this passage to condemn all assumption of the garments and behaviour
of others. So Gosson uses it as a base from which to attack the very
principle of mimesis:

In Stage Plays for a boy to put on the attire, the gesture, the
passions of a woman; for a mean person to take upon him the title
of a Prince with counterfeit port, and train, is by outward signs
to show themselves otherwise than they are, and so within the
compass of a lie . . .

(Stephen Gosson, *Plays Confuted in Five Actions etc.,* 1582)

The formulation 'within the compass of a lie' discounts the element of
pretence in play-acting in favour of an all-consuming concentration on
the actor becoming the part he plays, and being guilty of the crimes he
represents; and so betraying his own personality to his eternal
perdition. Players, according to William Prynne in *Histrio-mastix, The
Player's Scourge* (1633) 'unman, unchristian, uncreate themselves'.

The Devil was widely considered to be the best actor, precisely because he lacked the personal integrity that inhibits or modifies impersonation. Therefore the more effective the player, the more he was likely to be regarded as kin to the Devil. Furthermore, the Devil operated through deceit, which was both the means of performance and an important element in the subject matter and plot motifs of plays. The Theatre, like the Devil, its opponents said, makes deception attractive. This is especially so in the Machiavel character convention, which became enormously popular in the theatre of the 1590s. It embodied a gleeful hypocrisy in which, under the guise of virtue, beauty, love, and friendship, it systematically destroyed all those in whom these qualities were found. It was itself the inheritor of a long tradition of energetic, charismatic vice-figures, played by the leading actors of the early itinerant troupes, in which as A. Weirum points out, 'the organic association of play acting with disguised evil . . . was part of the theological inheritance from the Middle Ages'. It was a permanent reminder to the player of the danger in which he stood:[5] 'beware, therefore, you masking Players, you painted sepulchres, you double dealing ambidexters, be warned betimes . . . lest God destroy you in his wrath' (Philip Stubbes, *Anatomy of Abuses,* 1583).

So far this discussion has avoided using the word 'puritan' of the opponents of the stage. As Margot Heinemann has shown, not all puritans were anti-theatre, nor all opponents of theatre puritans.[6] However in accepting this view we risk ignoring a substantial body of contemporary Elizabethan and Jacobean usage, particularly in the plays themselves. Furthermore, whereas the objections dealt with above have a long tradition going back to the early Church, there is a substantial group of objections to playing which more obviously cohere around a political stance that in many ways anticipates the values of the opposition party in the Civil War, and led amongst other things to the closure of the theatres in 1642.[7]

In part they were economic. A number of writers have suggested that early attacks from 1577 were concerned mainly with the deleterious effects of playing upon trade and manufacture, in drawing especially the younger artisans and factors from their gainful employment, rather than upon its alleged moral dangers.[8] The preachers likewise objected primarily to the competition of players on the Sabbath, drawing their congregations away, and receiving as gifts money that ought to have gone in alms. William Ringler has pointed out that the sudden flush of tracts and sermons from 1576/7 was a direct consequence of the erection of the first purpose-built theatres, The

Theatre and The Curtain, in Finsbury Fields in the same years – 'the sumptuous Theatre houses', as Northbrooke calls them, 'a continual monument of London's prodigality and folly'.[9]

It is perhaps a paradox of revolution that many of those who themselves seek social change, however extreme, ground their aspirations on images drawn from the past: here that of plays as amateur pastimes and mirth in hall. Opponents of the theatre objected in particular to the combination of professional players and the Court as a new, wasteful, and dangerous phenomenon. They decried the development under this royal protection of a new profession of player. 'So howsoever he pretends to have a royal Master or Mistress', Cocke could jeer at *A Common Player*, 'his wages and dependence prove him to be the servant of the people.' 'Yea, the acting of Stage-plays can never be made a lawful profession, because Plays themselves are but recreations, which must not be turned into professions' (William Prynne, *Histrio-mastix,* 1633).

They insisted upon an ultra-conservative view that money should only change hands for some tangible commodity. The anonymous author of *A Refutation of the Apology for Actors* fuses the two meanings of 'play' in order to deny that acting was work – 'but to avoid work, like brave and noble beggars, they stand to take money of everyone that comes to see them loiter and play'.[10] Therefore, says Anglo-phile Eutheo, they 'juggle in good earnest the money out of other men's purses into their own hands'. Prynne, for all his general prolixity, sums up the opposition case very neatly: 'Stage-plays in their best acception are but vanities or idle creations, which have no price, no worth or value in them: they cannot therefore be vendible because they are not valuable.'

Hence playing was little more than theft: 'they cosen and mock us with vain words, and we pay them good money,' complains the anonymous 'I.G.'. The spectator, says Hall, leaves the theatre regretting that he has allowed the prurient expectations of his lecherous imagination to mislead him into parting with hard cash:

> Now when they part and leave the naked stage,
> 'Gins the bare hearer in a guilty rage
> To curse and ban and blame his likerous eye
> That thus hath lavished his late half-penny:
>
> (John Hall, *Virgidemiarum,* 1597)

Not all critics were content to play safe and confine their attack to the weaker element in the Court-player association. Anglo-phile

Eutheo criticized the covetousness of noblemen in being too mean to maintain their players and therefore encouraging them to travel, 'offering their service, which is a kind of beggary', whilst Rankins went further: 'The Prince must be pleased, therefore the subject be diseased. For this is poison to some, which is medicinable to other, and of particular good, by abuse may spring a general evil' (William Rankins, *A Mirror for Monsters,* 1587). Despite his elaborate disclaimers, the drift of his meaning is fairly clear: princes poisoned their kingdoms in pursuit of their own pleasure.

A more popular tack however was to try to break the association, by showing the players to be subversive or even treasonous. The opponents drew attention to satire on the King: 'Furthermore, there is no passion wherewith the king, the sovereign majesty of the Realm was possessed, but is amplified, and openly sported with, and made a May-Game to all the beholders' (Henry Crosse, *Virtue's Common-Wealth: the High-way to Honour,* 1603).[11]

However despite these local indignities, the tolerance of playing by the monarchy continued as it had under Elizabeth, with the Stuart kings often taking a more personal interest in its details and regulation. Under Elizabeth, Gosson could inveigh in 1582 that:

> in a commonwealth, if private men be suffered to foresake their calling because they desire to walk gentleman-like in satin and velvet, with a buckler at their heels, proportion is so broken, unity dissolved, harmony confounded, that the whole body must be dismembered and the prince or the head of it cannot choose but sicken.

Yet the nobility continued to allow their cast-off, once-worn garments to percolate down to the players, and despite these warnings of imminent peril, even commented approvingly on their use. So Rowland Whyte in a letter to Sir Robert Sydney, 1599:

> Two days ago, the overthrow of *Turnholt* was acted upon a stage, and all your names used that were at it; especially Sir Francis Vere, and he that played that part got a beard resembling his, and a watchet satin doublet, with hose trimmed with silver lace . . .

It is an oddity of the controversy that many of the very same arguments against players used by writers in total opposition to the stage were mustered by playwrights themselves, in pamphlets, or when writing with an eye to other auspices, such as the universities, the Inns of Court, the Children's companies or the London apprentices. It is the object of much of the remainder of this study to try to examine what they meant by this often violent reiteration.

Evidence of playwright hostility falls broadly into two bands. In the early 1590s a group of writers, notably Greene and Nashe, wrote a series of pamphlets in which they bemoaned the humiliating necessity of university graduates to write for the stage and the exploitation they thereby suffered at the hands of the grasping and upstart players. What particularly provoked their ire was the growing tendency amongst the players of dispensing with the scholar poets' services in favour of their own home-grown player-poets; upstart crows, beautified, said Greene of Shakespeare, with the poets' own feathers. Act Three of *Histriomastix* directly dramatizes this conflict, and the extract from *The Hog Hath Lost his Pearl* shows the contempt with which the scholar-poet held his servitude, here reduced to penning a Jig, the very lowest form of dramatic writing. The three *Parnassus* plays, written at Cambridge at the turn of the century, perhaps with the time-lag of provincial imitation, adopt the same tone of outraged contempt as their university predecessors of ten years earlier.

By 1600, however, the metropolitan climate had changed. Greene, Marlowe, and Kyd all died in the early 1590s. The Children's Theatre, which had rivalled the popularity of the adults at Court, was in eclipse by 1590, and did not re-emerge until c. 1599/1600. Shakespeare almost alone amongst the major poets continued writing through the decade, which saw at its close a new generation of writers emerge. Jonson was eight years Shakespeare's junior, Marston eleven years. When these writers returned to the attack, their target was an adult theatre which had enjoyed considerable success, and though they could no longer employ quite the same dog-in-the-manger tone towards the player-poets as their predecessors, they were no less virulent, and had at their disposal, in the form of the newly re-opened Children's Theatres at St Paul's and Blackfriars, a weapon that could be honed to a fine edge.

Part of the hostility of the playwrights could be said to be inherent in the activity itself. The tasks of writing a play and performing it, especially as they were conceived at the beginning of the seventeenth century, require very different skills and conditions, and this must often have led to conflicts of interest. In the adult companies the players held the purse-strings and called the tune. The poet was given an advance, 'in earnest', after showing a resumé of the plot, or a first act, and this allowed the players to supervise the subsequent composition. Notwithstanding the obligation to have a prompt copy licensed by the Master of the Revels, once completed the players appear to have been able to make further changes to the text, using their own experience of what 'works' on-stage to cut and adapt. There is plenty of evidence to suggest that from the writer's point of view texts fared even worse when revived on tour; extemporized and garbled, as some of those surviving texts based on memorial reconstruction show.

The new Children's Theatre of 1600 on the other hand offered the writer a new status. The Children were trained to do as they were told, with a whip if necessary.[12] Not only did the poets have more opportunity to join the managements of the Children's companies and share their financial rewards, but they had much greater artistic freedom to develop new forms, and, with a receptive, relatively select audience, to introduce new content.[13] The re-opening of the indoor theatres brought a new sense of competitiveness into the London scene, stimulating a, very probably exaggerated, class-consciousness in both performers and audience, and an access of parody and imitation; in short a new vogue in theatre. It was one that could be used by those writers disenchanted with the adult companies, to settle old scores, as Jonson is said to have done after a quarrel with the Chamberlain's Men over the failure of *Every Man Out of His Humour* in 1599.

7

The Poetaster, the 'War of the Theatres', and the Children

Jonson's representation of the player Histrio in *The Poetaster,* and his subsequent discussion of contemporary playing, which includes a vivid description of an unnamed adult company and an acute parody of the adult repertory put into the mouths of children, constitutes one of the most interesting, as well as formidable, pieces of evidence to be considered in this study. Jonson wrote the play for the Children of the Chapel in 1601, as a contribution to the so-called 'War of the Theatres', narrowly beating his rivals' *Satiromastix* in speed of production. In it he defends himself in the character of Horace, the Latin satirist, from various attacks on him, and in turn satirizes Marston in the character of Crispinus and, to a much lesser extent, Dekker as Demetrius. In Dekker's *Satiromastix* all three characters appear again, but with Horace/Jonson this time as the butt of the satire, and the others represented in a more favourable light.

The 'War of the Theatres' is a term which can be used in the wider sense to subsume aspects of inherent or general antagonisms in the theatre that came to the surface around 1600, but it is perhaps best more narrowly applied to an hypothesis which attempts to set the acknowledged antagonisms in *The Poetaster* and *Satiromastix* in the context of a larger group of plays with Jonson at its centre. As such it incorporates elements of both playwrights versus players and children versus adults, but in the fiction of the 'War' – as indicated in Dekker's term 'the *Poetomachia*' – both groups of performers are also seen as mere footsoldiers in the battle of mighty opposites, the poets themselves.

The exact dimensions of this quarrel are never likely to be known. Several scholars at the end of the nineteenth century, notably Small and Penniman, attempted to tease from the plays of Jonson and Marston supposed portraits of each other and of their contemporaries, but the process is an unsatisfactory one.[1] Read today, the plays rarely seem as preoccupied with the quarrel as these critics were. In assessing the value of each play as evidence of contemporary stage practice or attitudes to playing, it is difficult to determine how far the individual dramatist is concerned to pillory particular opponents, and how far his interest is rather in traditional forms of invective and in loyalty to his own imaginative fiction.

Roscoe Small summarized the generally accepted basis of evidence for the quarrel.[2] There were four main items. In William Drummond's notes on his conversations with Ben Jonson in 1619, he recalls that Jonson 'had many quarrels with Marston, beat him, and took his pistol from him, wrote his Poetaster on him; the beginning of them were, that Marston represented him on the stage'. Jonson wrote an *Apologetical Dialogue* for the publication of *The Poetaster* in 1602, in which he answers the charges made against him in *Satiromastix*. He claims that his play was a reluctant defence, because for 'three years/They did provoke me with their petulant styles/On every stage'. In the same year, Dekker wrote an address, *To the World*, for his publication of *Satiromastix*, in which he referred to 'that terrible *Poetomachia*, lately commenced between Horace the second, and a band of lean-witted Poetasters'. Great interest has been taken in his reference to 'a *band*' of Poetasters, and its implication for the involvement of other poets as well as Marston, who seems to be clearly implicated in the play's composition. The fourth piece of evidence, the reliability of which is questioned below, is a speech given to Will Kemp in *The Second Part of the Return From Parnassus*:

Oh, that Ben Jonson is a pestilent fellow, he brought up
Horace giving the Poets a pill, but our fellow Shakespeare
hath given him a purge that made him bewray his credit.

Around these four pieces of evidence, Small constructed an elaborate theory whereby the quarrel began with Munday giving some offence in lost plays for the Admiral's Men in 1598, to which Jonson replied in the original versions of *The Case is Altered* and *Every Man In His Humour*. Meanwhile in *Histriomastix*, here ascribed to Marston, the latter was thought to have curried favour by attacking Munday and the adults, and by giving a flattering portrait of Jonson as Chrisoganus, which misfired. Jonson replied in *Every Man Out of His Humour* by ridiculing Marston's vocabulary. The quarrel then became more heated, with more obvious and more venomous portraits of each other, through Marston's *Jack Drum's Entertainment*, Jonson's *Cynthia's Revels*, and Marston's *What You Will*, culminating in Jonson's *The Poetaster* and

Dekker's *Satiromastix,* and finally, Small said, Shakespeare's contribution to the War in *Troilus and Cressida* (although this final attribution has gained even less general acceptance than most of the rest). The anonymous Cambridge writer of *The Second Part of the Return from Parnassus,* according to Leishman, weighed in on the side of Jonson, as further means of supporting Hall in his satirical tussle with Marston.[3]

Whether the 'War' was quite as extensive as the above account suggests remains in question. The subsequent chapters of this study stress the importance of the institutional context of the plays, in some measure gainsaying the stress on the personal antagonisms favoured by earlier critics. However there is no doubt that in the minds of the principal participants some sort of quarrel took place. It was fought out in the public arena of the theatres, and it involved the professional players, who are represented unfavourably in three of the plays associated with it.

The relationship between the two chief plays in the quarrel, *The Poetaster* and *Satiromastix,* remains a puzzle. The orthodox theory, as expressed for instance by O.J. Campbell, is that Jonson found out that Dekker and the others were preparing to put him on-stage in *Satiromastix,* and wrote and had his play put into performance by the Children of the Chapel before the other was ready.[4] However, as almost everything satirical in Dekker's play refers to, or is modelled on, *The Poetaster* – the final scene for instance has a similar arraignment and the same central characters – it is difficult to see what preparation against Jonson could have preceded the completion of *The Poetaster.* Although it is hard to believe that Dekker's other plots in the play have the substance, or even the potential, to fill a complete play by themselves, they are none the less quite unrelated to the Horace plot, as though, as Small argues, Dekker had a half-finished tragedy with a comic subplot to which he appended 'as best he could' the scenes against Jonson.[5] Perhaps the most telling factor is the relatively casual treatment of the chief author of *Satiromastix* in *The Poetaster.* If Jonson's real purpose had been to answer, or even anticipate, Dekker's work, he would hardly have given so much attention to Marston and so little to Dekker. The suspicion therefore remains that *The Poetaster* is really more of a provocation than a genuine defence.

Immediately before the extract under review, Horace/Jonson is introduced for the first time being pestered by the now frankly ridiculous Crispinus/Marston, who boasts of being a scholar, a new-turned poet, a satirist, a gentleman and stoic, as well as an architect, dancer, and singer. Horace becomes desperate to escape from him but is unable to do so until the arrival of Minos, an apothecary, with two *lictors* or sergeants to arrest Crispinus for an unpaid debt of sweetmeats. However help for Crispinus is at hand in the form of Captain Tucca, a braggard captain, attended by his two *pyrgi* or pages. Tucca flourishes his sword and demands the gentleman's release. Instead he is disarmed by a *lictor*. Tucca then fawns on the *lictors*, and cajoles Minos to have Crispinus released and his sword returned. At this point Histrio enters and the extract begins.

At first, taking Histrio by his fine clothes and manner to be a person of consequence, Tucca treats him with deference, but then returns to his arrogant bullying when he realizes he has been deceived by a mere player. He threatens to force Histrio to return to his former life as a penniless itinerant, or even a musician, the very lowest form of life. When Histrio is sufficiently apologetic, Tucca unbends and suggests a supper at the player's expense. He introduces Crispinus, now his protégé, as a new writer who will make Histrio's company prosperous, and forces the player to give Crispinus an advance, which the hapless Minos is induced to supplement. Tucca's purpose in all this, apart from a general love of interfering and manipulating, is to 'skelder'; that is to obtain a percentage of all money that changes hands.

In a passage which obviously bore closely on contemporary events, Tucca goes on to enquire of the repertory of Histrio's playhouse, taking exception to innovatory styles of satire, burlesque, and 'humours' (such as Jonson was himself introducing). Histrio assures him that his house is innocent of these, and that they are to be found at the theatres on the other side of the Tiber(/Thames).

Tucca then has his pages audition for Histrio. The *pyrgi* go through their paces in a variety of styles, but in the end, the extempore performance is for its own sake; Tucca refuses to hire the *pyrgi* out, because, he says, they would be turned into male prostitutes, a charge he repeats later, suggesting the players acted generally as procurers of flesh. Instead he returns to the subject of the players' dinner which he is demanding of Histrio, and gives trenchant thumbnail portraits of four more of the latter's company. Demetrius (Dekker) is then noticed and there follows a discussion of *Satiromastix*, then said to be in preparation. They admit they know nothing to Horace/Jonson's disrepute, but they will make things up, because they have been eclipsed by the children and need the money. The scene ends with the return of one of the pages on the shoulders of Minos, impersonating 'the Moor'. Tucca offers to be the patron of Histrio's company in return for money. He inveighs against Horace, which is the cue for the latter's reappearance and their hasty departure.

The general assumption has been that Histrio's troupe is the Lord Chamberlain's Company, who were subsequently to perform *Satiromastix*, and that they were being contrasted with the current performers of the play themselves, the Blackfriar's Children, on the opposite side of the Tiber/Thames. If so, 'seven shares and half', to whom Tucca sends greetings, is presumably one of the Burbages. On the other hand there is some evidence to relate the satire to the other major London troupe, the Lord Admiral's Men. Dekker was mainly a writer for them, and their new theatre, The Fortune, seems to be mentioned directly (l. 11) and probably referred to obliquely as 'your Triumphs' in contradistinction to 'your Globes' (l. 86). Many of the targets parodied by the *pyrgi* can be traced to the Admiral's repertoire. As part of what was to become identified as the low-brow northern circuit, together with The Curtain and the unrefurbished Red Bull, the Admiral's Men at The Fortune attracted audiences from the northern suburbs, and could therefore satisfy the either-side-of-the-Tiber antithesis by being contrasted with the Chamberlain's Men in Southwark, with their newer theatrical fare including the *Every Man* plays written by Jonson himself.

The evidence could also be read to suggest that the rival adult troupes are being lumped together in the attack. This would seem to be supported by the generic name 'Histrio', which Jonson chooses for his player, and Envy's general inquiry in the Induction:

> Are there no players here?
> . . . they could wrest,
> Pervert and poison all they hear or see,
> With senseless glosses and allusions . . .

In these circumstances the players could be excused for thinking they were all indicated. However in his *Apologetical Dialogue* Jonson claimed that he had not been attacking the profession at large, but that he only meant to tax 'some' and that the rest were foolish to take offence. Certainly the descriptions of the players are highly specific and there seems to be a case for suggesting they were modelled on individuals: 'your eating player' the 'lean Polyphagus', obviously a great fat man; Aenobarbus, 'the out-of-tune fiddler'; Aesop, 'your politician', presumably their business manager, who 'smells ranker than some sixteen dunghills', and who appears briefly later as an informer; 'Frisker, my zany', perhaps some sort of scribe or plagiarist of Jonson; and 'your fat fool', 'my Mango', a procurer. The fat fool is to be invited as part of the entertainment at the feast Tucca is demanding, but he must not use his 'over-familiar playing face' to beg presents or to get out of hand. The implication is that the fool is much the same in the tavern as on the stage, and the general drift of Tucca's comments suggests each player bases his performance closely on his own personal and physical characteristics – though this is possibly less a statement of fact than, taking up the puritan charge, part of the calumny (perhaps because of these players' alleged paucity of talent?). If, as seems likely, these portraits are those of individuals, nevertheless they are also collectively informed by a sardonic vision, which Jonson possesses or assumes, of the Common Player as glutinous, smelly, extrovert, and dishonest.

At the heart of his attack, however, there is an ambivalence towards his targets, evident in the full-throatedness of the parts he writes, and in his various more direct insertions of his own vitality into the plays through self-dramatization. Although in *The Poetaster* Jonson refers repeatedly to the adult players in terms which stress the low class of their audience and the coarse nature of their style; as in 'twopenny tearmouth', 'stinkard', and 'penny-biter'; and although this play is an important contribution to establishing that sense of superiority in both matters (discussed below) which the Children's Theatre claimed, and on which its brief popularity may have depended, nevertheless Jonson could not completely divorce himself from his own antecedents. Dekker in *Satiromastix* reminds him of his humble beginnings as an itinerant player in a provincial company:

> thou has forgot how thou amblest (in leather pilch) by a play-waggon, in the highway, and took'st mad Hieronimo's part, to get service among the mimics . . .

> (IV.i.130f.)

His opponents would not let him forget that he had made his début in the now despised *Spanish Tragedy*. There is mention of it elsewhere, coupled with the return of charges of humiliating poverty, such as Jonson had made against Dekker:

> and when thou ran'st mad for the death of Horatio: thou borrowed'st a gown of Roscius the Stager (that honest Nicodemus) and sent'st it home lousy, did'st not?

> (I.ii. 355)

Jonson is well qualified then to describe the vicissitudes of itinerant life. It is implied also in *Satiromastix* that Jonson owes his fellows, the players, a kindness in his more recent distress in prison in 1598 after a scuffle in which he killed a fellow player and was near execution for it (IV.iii. 202f.). Nor is the attack on the adults in *The Poetaster* the mark of a final rift with them. Within two years he was back writing for The Globe with *Sejanus* (1603). Thus any real disengagement from his erstwhile companions is more rhetorical than actual.

Evident in much of Jonson's work, and at tension with the idealist, there is the 'humorous' man; carnal, egocentric, with boundless energy and combativeness. In the creation and deployment of Captain Tucca – behind the obscure Captain Hannam, beyond the tradition of *il bragadaccio* and *miles gloriosus*, beneath even the continuation of Jonson's own seam of braggard captains such as Bobadill and Shift – lies a close association with its author.[6] This is true, notwithstanding either Jonson's own clear identification of the better part of himself with Horace, and its acceptance by the opposition in *Satiromastix*, nor Tucca's discomfiture at the end of the play. To begin with Tucca is the mouthpiece of Jonson's attack on the players. Second, he possesses many of the qualities that Jonson himself seems to have possessed, or of which he approved in his actions. As well as being similarly indigent, Tucca is arrogant and confident of his own superiority in his dealings with almost everyone, and not only does he have a magnificent turn of phrase and a rich store of derogatory epithets, but he uses language to manipulate others, and therefore, like the Poet, as his principal means of livelihood. He has an energy and a resourcefulness which it is difficult to resist.

Penniman and Campbell in their earlier studies were under the misapprehension that Tucca himself was a player and the *pyrgi* his apprentices.[7] This error is not altogether inexcusable, since Tucca has many similarities with the very people he is attacking, and this is part Jonson's joke, and part a layer of ambiguity that suggests mixed feelings towards the quarry, acknowledging perhaps his own participation in their common endeavour. Robert Greene in *A Quip for an Upstart Courtier* gives a description of an 'Applesquire' which sounds remarkably as one might imagine Tucca:

a huge ruff about his neck wrapped in his great head like a wicker cage, a little Hat with a brim like the wings of a doublet, wherein he wore the Jewel of Glass, as broad as a chancery seal: after him followed two boys in cloaks like butterflies: carrying the one of them his cutting sword of choler, the other his dancing rapier of delight . . . . At length coming near, I might discern *a Player* . . .

Jonson, of course, identified more fully with Horace, as the spokesman of his more deeply-held convictions about the place of poetry in society, but Tucca is more than a *jeu d'esprit*. There is a good deal of Jonson's carnal identity about him, which could be expressed perhaps more confidently through a traditional character-convention, though here performed by a child, which can be enjoyed, laughed at, and finally punished; not unlike the grotesque, egocentric hero that Molière modifies from the *commedia dell'arte* and adapts for himself in, say, *School for Wives*, or the *persona* of the conservative countryman that Aristophanes creates (and perhaps plays?) in *The Acharnians*.

There is however an even more direct level at which Jonson represented himself on stage, which forms part of the context for his satire in *The Poetaster* and his subsequent aggrieved and violent response to *Satiromastix* in the *Dialogue*. In the final scene of *Satiromastix*, in close imitation of *The Poetaster*, Horace/Jonson, together with his creature Asinus, are brought before the King for trial. They have assumed the costumes of satyrs, as Horace desires to be a 'Timonist'. The King installs Crispinus/Marston as his deputy, as the more honourable Caesar had done Virgil in the first play. Horace/Jonson is then crowned with stinging nettles and under this rather unsubtle discomfort is made to swear an oath to abjure his customary behaviour (Appendix E).

The oath consists of eight articles which between them create a vivid and quite engaging picture of Jonson's egocentric foibles. The whole passage seems to have the authentic ring of Jonson – ebullient, socially aspiring, insecure, and extravagantly self-centred. It is the little touches that ring most true, such as his behaviour in drawing attention to himself in the gallery whilst watching his own play, or leaping onto the stage at the end to ingratiate himself with the more influential playgoers and set the whole house talking about him. There is a wealth of humorous observation in the fifth article which contrasts the way in which Jonson wheedles his friends to attend his opening performances with lots of self-depreciation, and then preens himself subsequently, converting the good opinions thus solicited into homage and adulation. The final picture at the tavern pokes gentle fun at his excitable inventiveness, under the stimulus of drink, good company, and the desire to sing for his supper and thus avoid paying his share of the bill. It has much of the flavour of Tucca's anticipation of the players' feast in *The Poetaster*, and is a reminder of a whole tradition of anecdotes linking Jonson and tavern life, from Beaumont on the Mermaid Tavern, through Shakespeare's supposed fatal drinking bout with him, and Drummond's observation that drink was one of his elements, to his presiding over the Apollo Club at the Devil Tavern. The charges are highly particularized, with vivid detail: in the theatre, in the tavern, and at the bookbinder's; as from the viewpoint perhaps of an actor, a drinking companion, or a fellow poet; and they bear out the testimonies of his Scottish host William Drummond, and his friend James Howell.

The satirical portrait of Jonson in *Satiromastix* does not however exist in isolation. In many respects it is following the parameters of a complex entertainment-convention *already laid down by Jonson himself*. The articles of the oath, for instance, charge Jonson with being conceited, meddlesome in his own productions, and a parasitical *bon viveur* in the tavern. Yet in his own dramatic writings Jonson had already touched on the self-same shortcomings. In the Epilogue to *Cynthia's Revels*, given to a boy to speak, although Jonson admits that for him to proudly approve his own play 'might tax the maker of Self-love', he does so anyway:

> I'll only speak what I have heard him say,
> 'By –, 'tis good, and if you like't, you may.'

When he attempts in the Prologue to *The Poetaster* to deal with adverse comments on this passage, it is to hedge and justify himself, rather than deny it. The Induction to *Cynthia's Revels* contains a thumbnail portrait of an interfering author:

> we are not so officiously befriended by him, as to have his presence in the tiring house, to prompt us aloud, stamp at the book holder, swear for our properties, curse the poor tireman, rail the music out of tune, and sweat for every venial trespass we commit, as some author would . . .

Although this is coupled with a disclaimer that this is how *other* authors behave, none the less in its fullness, and in consideration of later more frank self-portraits, for instance in *Bartholomew Fair* and *The Staple of News*, it is probably a piece of ingenuous self-advertisement.

Finally in *Every Man Out of His Humour* (1599) Jonson anticipates *Satiromastix*'s satirical account of his tavern behaviour in Buffone's description of Asper, and even gives a cue for attacks upon his appearance:

> This is that our Poet calls 'Castalian liquor', when he comes
> abroad (now and then) once in a fortnight, and makes a good
> meal among Players, where he has *Caninum appetitum* . . . and
> looks villainously when he had done, like a one-headed
> CERBERUS . . .

It is evident therefore that rather than simply acknowledging that he
has become a public figure and being 'willing to play on this as part of
his art', as Alexander Leggatt suggests, it is more the case that Jonson
was setting out to draw attention to himself.[8] Given all this, it may
come as something of a surprise that Jonson should appear so upset by
the attacks on him in *Satiromastix* as to describe them as 'all excrement'.

One reason perhaps is the very public nature of the rebuke, as Sir
John Davies says in *Witte's Pilgrimage*, 'before Knights and Lords'.
Furthermore the title-page of *Satiromastix* indicates that Dekker's play
had the unusual distinction of being performed both by the Chamberlain's Men and the Paul's Boys. Add the complicity of the Admiral's
Men, if that is what Tucca means by Histrio having 'fortune' on his
side, then it is beginning to look as though all his peers have joined
together against him – as he says, 'their whole tribe'. And not only his
enemies; in his *Dialogue*, Jonson, talking of the players, regrets that
'Some better natures' were involved, and given the relatively good-
natured tone of the eight articles, perhaps their invention, it was
probably their defection that hurt him most.

There are frequent references in *The Poetaster* to Marston's red hair
and his little legs, as well as to his genteel origins which seem
particularly to have upset Jonson. The lines with which Crispinus is
confronted in the final scene are taken from Marston's plays, and
Tucca's description of the style of Crispinus is very like that of the
recently completed *Antonio* plays:

> high, lofty, in a new stalking strain, bigger than half the rhymers
> i' the town again; he was born to fill thy mouth, Minotaurus, he
> was, he will teach thee to tear and rant.

It seems likely then that the boy who played Crispinus was got up to
look like Marston and attempted a close imitation of him, and it is to be
expected that when the time came the performers of *Satiromastix*
replied in kind, and Jonson's personal peculiarities were imitated as an
object of mirth both at The Globe and at St Paul's.

There is of course a world of difference between self-dramatization
and the satirical representation by others. Jonson makes it clear he is

very aware of his own enormities, but the two sides of the self-portrait Jonson provides do not seem equally genuine; there is a seam of poems fairly obviously intended to provide a more coolly composed, idealized fiction in order to offset the more genuine and spontaneous mani-festations of his carnal egocentric personality. At the heart of Jonson's persistent self-presentation in his work is a desire to be seen to rise above all detraction, and to be loved and respected for it. To do so, like all solo performers, Jonson must maintain that delicate equilibrium of attraction and repulsion, significance and foolishness. It is an equil-ibrium that is upset by the imitation of others, whether it be to flatter, as perhaps in *Histriomastix*, or decry, as in *Satiromastix*. Only if he can control the context can Jonson justify his arrogance by his honesty, and leaven his self-mockery by the generous humour with which it is presented.[9]

The Children of the Chapel Royal, the company which performed *The Poetaster*, were singing in 'disguisings' by 1501, performing plays under Richard Edwards in the 1560s, and established in a playhouse at Blackfriars in 1576. The early history of their rivals, the choirboys at St Paul's Cathedral, appears very similar. They were performing plays by the 1520s, and though several masters contributed to their development it was Sebastian Westcott, master for thirty-five years (1547–82), who established Paul's as the most popular performers at Court during the first half of Elizabeth's reign.[10] By 1575 he had a regular playhouse close to, or even inside, the cathedral. Both companies seem to have been subject to inhibitions on playing in the 1580s, and both resumed playing around the turn of the century. After a brief blaze of glory St Paul's playhouse was shut down in 1607, whilst the Chapel company lingered on until 1613, losing its connection with the Chapel proper in 1606 and handing Blackfriars back to the adults in 1608.

Pioneering studies of the Children have perhaps been too inclined to generalize, about the satirical and unwholesome nature of their material for instance, or their all-purpose parodic acting style, or uniformly aristocratic audience. It is perhaps more in keeping with what we know, not only of the rapidly changing theatrical and social conditions around them, but of the changing composition of the children's companies themselves, that we should expect all these things to be more variable in their applicability too.

Commentators have rightly pointed to the significance of the fifteen or so years' gap that separates the two periods of the Children's popularity on the London stage. Although their revival was more obviously a commercial venture, it was perhaps anticipated in their earlier phase of activity more than has been supposed. At St Paul's, the contiguity of chancel and theatre, as close as a matter of yards if as Reavley Gair suggests the theatre was located in the Chapter House precincts, enabled the boys to continue to serve in the choir whilst performing plays perhaps once or twice weekly.[11] The Blackfriars venture, on the other hand, from its inception involved separate locations for playing and for the children's ecclesiastical duties. Although there is disagreement as to whether this implies two separate groups of boys, it is a signal feature of the situation that both Farrant in 1576 and Nathaniel Giles in 1600 started up a Blackfriars' company at a time when each was able to combine the posts of masters of both the Windsor and the London chapels, and able perhaps to use the joint resources of twenty-two boys to maintain whatever choral establishment was required, together with a separate acting company.[12] This would explain why, on Farrant's death in 1580 and the end of the plurality, it was necessary to augment the Blackfriars' company with Paul's. If so, it suggests some measure of continuity of practice between the two periods.

Further evidence of early commercialism at the rival playhouse is suggested by the details of Westcott's will in 1582, which indicates the presence on his property of seven ex-choristers whose ages have been estimated as ranging from 16 to 30 years.[13] This is not clear proof that they were members of a theatrical company, since the cathedral made general provision for the maintenance of ex-choristers, which included accommodation in Sermon Lane, but it is suggestive, especially set against the evidence elsewhere of the tendency for the average age to rise in youthful troupes the longer they played.

In 1606 the commission of the Master of the Chapel Royal, Giles, appears to forbid him to use his choristers for playing:

> for that it is not fit or decent that such as should sing the praises of God almighty should be trained up or employed in such lascivious and profane exercises.

This curtailed the power of impressment and presumably encouraged the maintenance of the existing troupe, and the continuance of ex-choristers in it, so that the average age steadily rose during the decade, through adolescence to early manhood.[14] The issue of age is an important one since it relates closely to that of performance style. Middleton's group of comedies written a few years later for Paul's, c. 1604–6, seem written for the developing skills of an adolescent company and to capitalize on their natural vivacity. The form and plots are highly contrived, the characters often grotesques and the incidents farcical. The overall impression the plays give is one of immense vitality, and, whatever the moral dubiousness of the events in absolute terms, of good humour, wish-fulfilment, and a celebration of comic invulnerability. From 1609, when the King's Men took over Blackfriars and removed an important part of their operation indoors, whatever distinctions in theatre venue and ambience that remained between the men and the growing boys would have been further modified.

In the context of this graph of changing age-groups and performance styles, there is an especial significance in the strong case made by Reavley Gair for regarding the re-opening of Paul's around 1599 as a fresh start with a new company of young boys, who are introduced, in their own persons and for the first time, in the Induction to Marston's *Antonio and Mellida*. Thereafter in the body of the play attention is drawn to the new techniques being adopted.[15]

The evidence, both in the play-texts written for them, and in the details of their recruitment, suggest their rivals at the Chapel Royal, also recommenced their dramatic operations with a new and very young company. Henry Clifton in 1600, complaining to the Star Chamber at the impressment into the Chapel Royal of his son (on his way home from school), indicates that it was part of a larger operation in which eight boys were taken up, amongst them Nathan Field and Salathiel Pavy. This sounds more like the re-establishment of a playing company than the routine replenishment of a small choir. Furthermore Clifton alleged that the Blackfriars syndicate were abusing their powers by choosing boys who could not sing. *Cynthia's Revels* written the following year by Jonson for the Blackfriar's company has an Induction which, in a similar manner to *Antonio and Mellida*, introduces the young players in their own persons in a highly artistic piece of contrived naturalism. In distinguishing them from the parts they play in the stylized, mannered piece that follows, it draws attention to the peculiarity of the process and to their diminutive size; they are described as 'tits', 'wrens', 'emmets', and 'pismires'. *The Poetaster*, written for the same company later in 1601, can be expected to share some of the same quality of self-conscious innovation. It is likely that some of the piquancy of the children's representation of the adult player's repertory by the *pyrgi*, Tucca's diminutive pages, lies in the novelty and juniority of the revived company, making its own mark in performance style in contradistinction to the adults, as their playwright attempted to do in subject matter.

Like Lyly's ill-fated attempts to perpetuate the courtly, dream-like contemplation of Love-in-Idleness of the 1580s, all was subject to change, and the freshness of the Children was soon to lose its bloom. When James re-licensed the Chapel Children on his accession in 1603, they became the Children of the Queen's Revels, with no reference to their ecclesiastical function. Very probably it was the exploitation of the Children for satire, particularly of the King himself, which led subsequently to a curb on fresh recruits and therefore their loss of youthful distinctiveness.

Both companies in the first year or two of the century, when they were young and precocious, may well have tried to develop an exclusive aristocratic/intellectual clientele by creating an ambience of superiority, and one equally pleasing to Jonson's purpose in scoring off his enemies, and to their scrambling investors. Marston's jibe in the Induction to *Jack Drum's Entertainment*, that attendance at the public theatre involved being 'choked/With the stench of Garlic', and 'pasted/To the barmy Jacket of a Beer-brewer', may be less a statement of fact than a deliberate exaggeration to encourage an air of exclusiveness at the private theatre, with what *Antonio and Mellida* describes as its 'select and most respected auditors'.[16]

Whatever the attitude of those who came to the private theatres around 1600, and whatever their social origins, the particular ethos of performance, which may have lasted only for a matter of months rather than years, appears to have been strongly influenced by three features which are well attested in contemporary commentary. First, the boys were musical; they played instruments as well as sang; the performance began with music, it punctuated the acts, and Marston at least had an eye to its effect as an augmentation of, or counterpoint to, the stage action.[17] On the whole though, it would be wrong to equate their use of music with, say, post-romantic film scores. Early seventeenth-century music plumps almost entirely for one of only two moods, either a lilting gaiety, now almost beyond recall, or a haunting sadness. Most of the music performed in the private theatres therefore, apart from its obvious ceremonial and supernatural applications, must have been incidental; decorative rather than dynamic. Whilst it was performed the action of the play was muted or supplanted by other pleasures of a different order which music gives. Music bulked so large in the Children's Theatre that, according to the Induction to *The Malcontent*, their texts were correspondingly shorter.

Second, something of the same sense of the importance to the event of the incidental and decorative is echoed in the frequent reference to the beauty and gracefulness of the performers. The children in *The Knight of the Burning Pestle*, burlesquing citizen behaviour in the private theatre, are frequently made to refer to their own charm:

> *Wife*: Sirrah, didst thou ever see a prettier child? How it
> behaves itself, I warrant ye, and speaks, and looks, and
> perts up the head?
>
> (I.i. 94–5)

Jonson has his mock gallant in the Induction to *Cynthia's Revels* complain that the boys are not pretty enough. Dekker, in what is surely the private theatre dimension of his composite, all-embracing satire of the theatre in the *Gull's Hornbook* (1609), advises his Gull that: 'By sitting on the stage, you may (with small cost) purchase the dear acquaintance of the boys . . .'. Cokes in *Bartholomew Fair*, anticipating that the puppets will be a children's company, indicates the potential of the young performers for exploitation:

> I would fain see them, I would be glad to drink with the young
> company; which is the tiring house? . . . Have you none of your
> pretty impudent boys now, to bring stools, fill tobacco, fetch ale,
> and beg money, as they have at other houses?
>
> (V.iii. 60–3)

The period is too far away to be able to come to any final judgements about the prevalence of homosexuality in this phenomenon. The opponents of the stage were always ready to find it, with a hatred that suggests some measure of their own conscious vulnerability. On the other hand, an aesthetic response to physical beauty could be said to complement the grace of the movements and the harmony of the sounds, and relate to a much larger cultural phenomenon stretching back to the Middle Ages in which innocence and purity were expressed through androgynous representations of angels and the Virgin Mary. When the puppet Dionysus finally shames the puritan Busy in *Bartholomew Fair*, he shows that he has no sexual organs at all beneath his tunic, and something of the same lack of sexual consciousness seems to inform the casual way in which characters change dress and identity in children's plays, such as the Amazon disguise in *Antonio and Mellida* and the promised sex-change at the conclusion of *Gallathea*.

Finally, it can be argued that sitting on the stage was essentially, if not exclusively, a private theatre phenomenon.[18] In an age when rank or wealth could procure most things, and rules though plentiful lacked the machinery of enforcement, even at Court where over crowding was common and the Chamberlain had to clear a space by laying about him with his staff of office, if someone was sufficiently powerful then no doubt he sat where he chose in *either* theatre. On the other hand, sitting on the stage, as comments show, interfered with the performance. The Tireman says to the supposed city gallants in Webster's Induction to the adult version of *The Malcontent* (1604), 'Sir, the gentlemen will be angry if you sit here', and Sly replies, 'Why? we may sit upon the stage at the private house'. Sly goes on to satirize the obtrusive self-display of the private theatre gallant, and, in refusing to leave the stage, because he is 'one that hath seen this play often, and can give them intelligence for their action', is presumably threatening to interrupt the play in order to instruct the performers. It is one thing to patronize the impudent youths, in their musical, decorative, satirical entertainment, but quite another to infringe upon the acting space of an adult company, whose itinerant tradition has come to place a high value on control over the circumstances of performance. Furthermore, the effect on sightlines of sitting on the stage is likely to have been quite different in the public theatre. Stools might form a casual extension of the side box seating in an indoor theatre, but they would block the view, especially of those in the yard, at a public theatre.

In short, therefore, the private theatres at the turn of the century, perhaps quite briefly, offered the spectators a different relationship to the performers than that which obtained in the adult outdoor playhouses, partly because the activity itself was different; a more distanced, self-conscious, contemplation of human behaviour, spiced by beauty, artifice, music, and a kind of innocent vivacity.

It is unfortunate that so much attention has been given to the term 'parody', licensed as R.A. Foakes points out by Jonson himself, with its associations of triviality and repetition.[19] The quality of the Children as performers was not by its nature satiric; it was neutral. Goethe talks of an actor studying the idiosyncrasies of women: 'he has learned to know them, and reproduces them as artist; he plays not himself, but a third, and, in truth, a foreign nature.'[20] The Children offered a similar sort of distanced representation of the adult world. We come to understand a particular sort of person, says Goethe, 'so much the better because someone has observed and meditated on their ways, and not the process itself, but the result of the process is presented to us'. In the dialogues that Jonson gives to Asotus and Amorphous in *Cynthia's Revels*, he catches that experience in which truths come to us by so circuitous a route as to appear both objective and as though freshly minted, the familiar made strange. In Act II there is a lesson on how to make faces, with a catalogue from merchant to courtier, and in Act III another on how to woo a lady with sentiments learned by rote but delivered with an air of spontaneity.

Parody is the *application* of the Children's special quality in a particular social and theatrical context, which provided a nexus for the children's mimetic vivacity on the one hand, and the combative, satirical penchant of the writers who gathered round them on the other. There is every reason to suppose they could draw tears as well as laughter. They inherited a long tradition of pathetic heroines, and there are many individual testimonies to the power of the child actor to move, from Pavy's old man, to the apprentice Desdemona at Oxford in 1610, who 'implored the pity of the spectators by her very face.'[21] The hero of Chapman's *Bussy D'Ambois*, for instance, may be too callow and overweening for modern tastes, but the play is not a straightforward parody, is clearly meant to be in sympathy with Bussy's humanist assertion of manliness, and is in danger of collapse unless taken with some, perhaps arch, seriousness. However it was as vehicles for satire that the children were chiefly celebrated, and if the testimony in *Hamlet* is to be relied on, the 'little eyases, that cry out on the top of the question, and are most tyrannically clapped for 't', were feared as well as enjoyed.

The *pyrgi* passage in *The Poetaster* may give some indication of the quality of that satire when aimed directly at their rivals. It consists of a whole gallery of popular character conventions and sensational 'dramatic' effects: 'the doleful strain', 'the amorous vein', 'the horrible fierce soldier', 'the ghost', 'the lady', and finally, after going offstage to get ready, 'the Moor'; all no doubt sharply distinguished and strongly presented. All the performers in the play are boys, but the *pyrgi* are able to present their own status and characteristics, and to strike more directly at the opposition; presenting a picture of the 'rumbling player' in miniature, and contrasting it with their own sophisticated and sharper talent. Their display suggests that much of the pleasure is 'theatrical', both pejoratively in what the common people enjoy, and more appreciatively in their own satire upon it. Assuming so many roles at such speed draws attention to the performers' versatility and élan, qualities so evidently demanded for instance in the performance of the Third Child/Anaides the Impudent in *Cynthia's Revels*. The dual awareness of role and player, and the attention drawn to the disparities and felicities of their conjunction, fed a self-consciousness that percolated into mainstream theatre, as seen most obviously in the King's Men's enthusiastic appropriation of *The Malcontent*.

The Poetaster is an uneven play, due in part to Jonson's mixed motives at the time of writing. On the one hand, Jonson desired to justify his own position by linking his personal aspirations and indignities to the wider Augustan tradition, all of which he found it easier to assert than show. In particular the first half of the fifth act, in which the claims of Horace/Jonson to be the 'eyes' of Caesar's 'pilot' are tendered, and Virgil's artistic supremacy established, is extremely undramatic, offering mutual compliments in place of conflict or debate.[22] Even when the conspirators rush on to impeach Horace for what they allege is his treasonous emblem, there is an air of shadow-boxing, since Caesar does not for one moment accept the charge. On the other hand, Jonson also desired to forestall and humiliate his current enemies through ridiculing their individual behaviour.

Perhaps because of this mixture of motives, the play has a weak structure. It begins by being focused on Ovid, whose plot is terminated in his banishment in Act Four; whilst Horace is not introduced until Act Three, nor Caesar until Act Four, and Virgil not until the final act. There is some inconsistency between the three sequences in which Crispinus is involved. The courting of Chloe, the pestering of Horace, and the final punishment do not cohere into a single whole. The character seems much more ridiculous in the second for instance than in the first, and the final judgement is *literary* and does not sort well with the earlier satire on Marston's appearance and behaviour; there is very little connection between how his work is described and what we see of it.

In Jonson's early plays there is a tendency simply to link together a series of static, satirical, prose 'characters', in the tradition of Theophrastus, for which the stage is by no means an ideal medium. In one sense, the history of Jonson's development as a dramatist is one of finding more appropriate 'dramatic' contexts for these 'characters', so that by *Volpone* (1606) for instance, they are becoming less incidentally satiric and more integrated into genuine drama. In *The Alchemist* (1610) he is able to whisk his vividly realized figures on and off with great dexterity, as in the opening *in medias res* quarrel where the 'characters' take the form of pauses for breath in the physicalized argument, and the whole thing is held together by the central image of the house of illusions. In his mature plays, Jonson is able to find a single physically represented metaphor which incorporates most of the action. In *The Poetaster*, however, he is only able to anticipate the technique in the last scene, in the administration of the emetic which causes Crispinus to vomit up all his unwholesome vocabulary. For the rest, the play is a mixture of self-justification and self-aggrandizement, invective, and city comedy.

It thus exploits, if largely in a negative way, the capacities of its child performers. The Children's theatre-ambiance – their musical talent, their grace and precocity, together with the practice by members of the audience of sitting on-stage – may have encouraged an atmosphere more conducive to a recital or to an intimate satirical review, rather than the stimulation of strong emotion or the evocation of vivid imaginary worlds. Such a performance ambiance could perhaps accommodate a looser association of parts, more vocal music, and less concern for the dynamics of the sort of story-line that would have been demanded in the public theatres. It may have promised a better hearing for *The Poetaster* and its sister play *Cynthia's Revels*, for Jonson's prolix 'characters', court allegories, and strong expressions of opinion.

THE POETASTER

Act III Scene I

(HISTRIO passes by)

Captain Tucca: . . . What's he that stalks by there? Boy,
    Pyrgus, you were best let him pass, sirrah; dog, ferret, let
    him pass, do.[23]
2 Pyrgus: 'Tis a player, sir.
Tucca: A player? Call him, call the lousy slave hither.   5
    What will he sail by, and not once strike or vail to a Man-
    of-War, ha? Do you hear? You – player, rogue, stalker –
    come back here. *(Histrio returns)* No respect to men of
    worship, you slave? What, you are proud, you rascal,
    are you proud? Ha? You grow rich, do you, and purchase,   10
    you two-penny tear-mouth? You have fortune, and the
    good year on your side, you stinkard? You have,
    you have?
Histrio: Nay, sweet Captain, be confined to some reason. I
    protest I saw you not, sir.   15
Tucca: You did not? Where was your sight, Oedipus? You
    walk with hare's eyes, do you? I'll ha' 'hem glazed, rogue.
    And you say the word, they shall be glazed for you. Come,
    we must have you turn fiddler again, slave, get a bass violin
    at your back, and march in a tawny coat with one sleeve to   20

Goose Fair, and then you'll know us. You'll see us then, you will, gulch, you will? Then, (*Mimicking Histrio*) – 'Will 't please your worship to have any music, Captain?'

Histrio: Nay, good Captain.

Tucca: What? do you laugh, Owlglass? Death, you   25
perstemptuous varlet, I am none of your fellows: I have commanded a hundred and fifty such rogues, I.

1 Pyrgus (*aside*): Ay, and most of that hundred and fifty have been leaders of a legion.

Histrio: If I have exhibited wrong, I'll tender satisfaction,   30
Captain.

Tucca (*unbending*): Sayest thou so, honest vermin? Give me thy hand, thou shalt make us a supper one of these nights.

Histrio: When you please, by Jove, Captain, most willingly.

Tucca: Dost thou swear? Tomorrow then; say and hold, slave.   35
There are some of you players honest gent'man-like scoundrels, and suspected to ha' some wit, as well as your poets; both at drinking, and breaking of jests: and are companions for gallants. A man may skelder ye now and then of half a dozen shillings or so. Dost thou not know that   40
Pantolabus there? (*Pointing to Crispinus*)

Histrio: No, I assure you, Captain.

Tucca: Go, and be acquainted with him, then. He is a gent'man, parcel-poet, you slave. His father was a man of worship, I tell thee. Go, he pens high, lofty, in a new stalking strain;   45
bigger than half the rhymers i' the town again. He was born to fill thy mouth, Minotaurus, he was. He will teach thee to tear, and rant, rascal. To him, cherish his muse, go. Thou hast forty, forty shillings I mean, stinkard. Give him in earnest, do; he shall write for thee, slave. If he pens   50
for thee once, thou shalt not need 'to travel, with thy pumps full of gravel', any more, after a blind jade and a hamper and stalk upon boards, and barrel heads, to an old cracked trumpet –

Histrio: Troth, I think I ha' not so much about me, Captain.   55

Tucca: It's no matter. Give him what thou hast, Stiff toe. I'll give my word for the rest: though it lack a shilling, or two, it skills not. Go, thou art an honest shifter. I'll ha' the statute repealed for thee.

    Minos, I must tell thee, Minos, thou has dejected yon   60
gent'man's spirit exceedingly. (*Pointing to Crispinus*) Dost

observe, dost note, little Minos?

Minos: Yes, sir.

Tucca: Go to, then, raise; recover, do. Suffer him not to
droop in prospect of a player, a rogue, a stager. Put   65
twenty into his hand, twenty sesterces I mean, and let
nobody see. Go, do it. The work shall commend itself.
Be Minos. I'll pay.

Minos: Yes forsooth, Captain. (*During the following exchange
Minos gives the money surreptitiously to Crispinus.*)   70

2 Pyrgus (*aside to the other page*): Do we not serve a notable
shark?

Tucca (*to Histrio*): And what new matters have you now afoot,
sirrah? ha? I would fain come with my cockatrice one day
and see a play, if I knew when there was a good bawdy   75
one, but they say you ha' nothing but humours, revels, and
satires, that gird and fart at the time, you slave.

Histrio: No, I assure you, Captain, not we. They are on the
other side of the Tiber. We have as much ribaldry in our
plays, as can be, as you would wish, Captain. All the   80
sinners i 'th' suburbs come and applaud our action daily.

Tucca: I hear you'll bring me o' the stage there; you'll play me,
they say. I shall be presented by a sort of copper-laced
scoundrels of you. Life of Pluto, and you stage me, stinkard,
your mansions shall sweat for't, your tabernacles, varlets,   85
your Globes, and your triumphs.

Histrio: Not we, by Phoebus, Captain. Do not do us imputation
without desert.

Tucca: I wu' not, my good two-penny rascal. Reach me thy
neuf. Dost hear? What wilt thou give me a week, for my   90
brace of beagles here, (*Gestures to Pyrgi*), my little point-
trussers? You shall ha' them act among ye. (*To one of them*)
Sirrah, you pronounce. Thou shalt hear him speak in King
Darius' doleful strain.

1 Pyrgus (*in a voice of stage lamentation*):   95
O doleful days! O direful deadly dump!
O wicked world and worldly wickedness!
How can I hold my first from crying thump,
In rue of this right rascal wretchedness!

Tucca: In an amorous vein now, sirrah. Peace.   100

1 Pyrgus (*playing a rejected lover*)
Oh, she is wilder, and more hard withall,[24]

121

Than beast, or bird, or tree, or stony wall.
Yet might she love me to uprear her state:
Ay, but perhaps she hopes some nobler mate.   105
Yet might she love me to content her sire:
Ay, but her reason masters her desire.
Yet might she love me as her beauty's thrall:
Ay, but I fear she cannot love at all.

Tucca: Now the horrible fierce soldier, you, sirrah. (*to the*   110
other page)

2 Pyrgus: **What, will I brave thee? Ay, and beard thee too.**[25]
A Roman spirit scorns to bear a brain
So full of base pusillanimity.

Histrio: Excellent.[26]   115

Tucca: Nay thou shalt see that will ravish thee anon. Prick up
thine ears, stinkard. The Ghost, boys.

1 Pyrgus (*as the Ghost*): **Vindicta.**

2 Pyrgus (*in terror*): **Timoria.**

1 Pyrgus: **Vindicta.**   120

2 Pyrgus: **Timoria.**

1 Pyrgus: **Veni.**

2 Pyrgus: **Veni.**

Tucca: Now, thunder, sirrah, you, the rumbling player.

2 Pyrgus: Aye, but somebody must cry (**'Murder'**) then, in a   125
small voice.

Tucca: Your fellow-sharer there shall do't. Cry, sirrah, cry.

1 Pyrgus: **Murder, murder!**[27]

2 Pyrgus: **Who calls out 'murder'? Lady, was it you?**

Histrio: O, admirable good, I protest.   130

Tucca: Sirrah, boy, brace your drum a little straighter, and do
the t'other fellow there, he in the- what sha' call him? –
and yet, stay too.

2 Pyrgus: **Nay, and thou dalliest, then I am thy foe,**
And fear shall force what friendship cannot win;   135
Thy death shall bury what they life conceals,
Villain, thou diest, for more respecting her –

1 Pyrgus: **O, stay my Lord.**

2 Pyrgus: **– than me.**
Yet speak the truth, and I will guerdon thee: 140
But if thou dally once again, thou diest.[28]

Tucca: Enough of this, boy.

2 Pyrgus (*continues to rant as they talk*):

Why then lament therefore: damn'd be thy guts
Unto King Pluto's hell, and princely Erebus;   145
For sparrows must have food.[29]

Histrio: 'Pray, sweet Captain, let one of them do a little of a
   lady.

Tucca: Oh, he will make thee eternally enamoured of him
   there. Do, sirrah, do. 'Twill allay your fellow's fury a little.   150

(As the other Pyrgus continues to strut)

1 Pyrgus (as a love-lorn Lady):
Master, mock on: the scorn thou givest me,
Pray Jove, some lady may return on thee.

2 Pyrgus (not responding in character): Now, you shall see me do   155
   the Moor. Master, lend me your scarf a little.

Tucca: Here, 'tis at thy service, boy.

2 Pyrgus: You, Master Minos, hark, hither a little. *(They exeunt)*

Tucca: How dost like him? Art not rapt? Art not tickled now?
   Dost not applaud, rascal? Dost not applaud?   160

Histrio: Yes. What will you ask for 'hem a week, Captain?

Tucca: No, you mangonizing slave, I will not part from 'em.
   You'll sell 'em for enghles, you. Let's ha' good cheer
   tomorrow night at supper, stalker, and then we'll talk.
   Good capon, and plover, do you hear, sirrah?   165
      And do not bring your eating player with you there; I
   cannot away with him. He will eat a leg of mutton while I
   am in my porridge, the lean Polyphagus. His belly is like
   Barathrum, he looks like a midwife in man's apparel, the
   slave. Nor the villainous-out-of-tune fiddler Aenobarbus,   170
   bring not him. What has thou there? Six-and-thirty, ha?

Histrio: No, here's all I have, (Captain) some five-and-twenty.
   Pray, Sir, will you present and accommodate it unto the
   gentleman.
      For mine own part I am a mere stranger to his   175
   humour. Besides, I have some business invites me hence,
   with Master Asinius Lupus, the tribune.

Tucca: Well, go thy ways, pursue thy projects. Let me alone
   with this design. My Poetaster shall make thee a play, and
   thou shalt be a man of good parts in it.   180
      But stay, let me see. Do not bring your Aesop, your
   politician; unless you can ram up his mouth with cloves.
   The slave smells ranker than some sixteen dunghills, and is
   seventeen times more rotten.

Marry, you may bring Frisker, my zany. He's a good   185
skipping swaggerer; and your fat fool there, my Mango,
bring him too: but let him not beg rapiers, nor scarves, in
his over-familiar playing face, nor roar out his barren bold
jests, with a tormenting laughter, between drunk and dry.
Do you hear, stiff toe? Give him warning, admonition,   190
to forsake his saucy glavering grace and his goggle eye. It
does not become him, sirrah. Tell him so.
    I have stood up and defended you, ay, to gent'men, when
you have been said to prey upon puisnes, and honest
citizens, for socks, or buskins, or when they ha' called you   195
usurers or brokers, or said you were able to help to a piece
of flesh – I have sworn I did not think so. Nor that you
were the common retreats for punks decayed i' their
practice. I cannot believe it of you –
Histrio: Thank you, Captain. Jupiter, and the rest of the gods   200
    confine your modern delights, without disgust.
Tucca: Stay, thou shalt see the Moor, ere thou go'st. (*Enter
    DEMETRIUS*) What's he with the half-arms there, that salutes
    us out of his cloak, like a motion? ha?
Histrio: O, sir, his doublet's a little decayed. He is   205
    otherwise a very simple honest fellow, sir, one Demetrius,
    a dresser of plays about the town here. We have hired him
    to abuse Horace, and bring him in a play, with all his
    gallants: as Tibullus, Maecenas, Cornelius Gallus, and the
    rest.   210
Tucca: And, why so, stinkard?
Histrio: Oh, it will get us a huge deal of money (Captain) and
    we have need on't; for this winter ha's made us all poorer,
    than so many starved snakes. Nobody comes at us, not a
    gentleman, nor a –   215
Tucca: But you know nothing by him, do you, to make a play of?
Histrio: Faith, not much, Captain, but our Author will devise,
    that that shall serve in some sort.
Tucca: Why, my Parnassus here, shall help him, if thou wilt.
    Can thy author do it impudently enough?   220
Histrio: Oh, I warrant you, Captain, and spitefully enough too.
    He has one of the most overflowing rank wits in Rome. He
    will slander any man that breathes, if he disgust him.
Tucca: I'll know the poor, egregious, nitty rascal, and he have
    these commendable qualities, I'll cherish him – stay, here   225

comes the Tartar –

(*2 PYRGUS enters on MINOS' shoulders and stalks about the stage,
wearing TUCCA's scarf as a turban, and pretending to be a huge
MOOR*)

– I'll make a gathering for him, ay, a purse, and put the poor   230
    slave in fresh rags. Tell him so, to comfort him.
(*Prompting the Pyrgus to start*) – Well said, boy.

2 *Pyrgus*: **Where art thou, boy? Where is Callipolis?**
    Fight earthquakes in the entrails of the earth,
    And eastern whirlwinds in the hellish shades;   235
    Some foul contagion of th' infected heavens
    Blast all the trees; and in their cursed tops
    The dismal night-raven, and tragic owl
    Breed, and become forerunners of my fall.[30]

Tucca: Well, now fare thee well, my honest penny-biter.   240
    Commend me to seven-shares and a half, and remember
    tomorrow. – If you lack a service, you shall play in my
    name, rascals, but you shall buy your own cloth, and I'll ha'
    two shares for my countenance. Let thy author stay with
    me.   245
Demetrius: Yes, sir. (*Exit Histrio*)
Tucca: 'Twas well done, little Minos. Thou didst stalk well.
    Forgive me that I said thou stunk'st, Minos: 'twas the
    savour of a poet I met sweating in the street hangs yet in
    my nostrils.   250
Crispinus: Who? Horace?
Tucca: Aye, he. Dost thou know him?
Crispinus: Oh, he forsook me most barbarously, I protest.
Tucca: Hang him, fusty satyr, he smells all goat; he carries a
    ram, under his arm-holes, the slave. I am the worse when I   255
    see him. (*Aside*) Did not Minos impart?
Crispinus: Yes, here are twenty drachmas he did convey.
Tucca: Well said. Keep 'em, we'll share anon. (*Aloud*) Come,
    little Minos.
Crispinus: Faith, Captain, I'll be bold to show you a mistress of   260
    mine, a jeweller's wife, a gallant, as we go along.
Tucca: There spoke my genius. Minos, some of thy eringoes,
    little Minos, send. Come hither, Parnassus, (*to Crispinus*) I

must ha' thee familiar with my little locust here.
(*Gesturing to Minos*) 'Tis a good vermin, they say. See, here's   265
Horace and old Trebatius, the great lawyer, in his com-
pany. Let's avoid him now. He is too well seconded.
(*Exeunt*)

Glossary to *The Poetaster*

 6 *Vail to a man-of-war*: merchant ships were supposed to dip their
    colours or topsails to warships.
17 *hare's eyes*: open but asleep.
    and = if (used repeatedly in this extract).
22 *gulch*: glutton or drunkard.
26 *perstemptuous*: presumptuous.
27 The number of a company (H&S).
29 *a legion* of lice (a common joke).
39 *skelder*: begging by disbanded or wounded soldiers (H&S).
41 *Pantolabus*: grab-all, nickname for a buffoon in Horace (H&S).
44 *parcel-poet*: part-poet.
47 *Minotaurus*: the half-bull, half-man of Cretan mythology.
50 *in earnest*: as an advance.
52 *jade*: sorry horse.
58 *it skills not*: it doesn't matter.
59 *statute*: against Vagabonds.
66 *sesterces*: Roman coins. Like *drachmas* later.
68 *Be Minos*: act up to your name, be just (H&S).
74 *cockatrice*: harlot, mistress. Lit: a mythical creature.
81 *suburbs*: synonymous with brothels etc.
85 *mansions*: stage houses.
89 *I wu'*: I will.
90 *neuf*: fist.
91/2 *point-trussers*: pages, who helped fasten the laces tying doublet to
    hose.
93 *pronounce*: declaim.
98 *first*: fist(?).
106 *sire*: father.
108 *thrall*: prisoner/slave.
118 *Vindicta*: revenge.
119 *Timoria*: dread.
122 *veni*: I come.
131 *Brace your drum*: stand up straight.

140 *guerdon*: reward.

156 *The Moor*: perhaps the Muly Mahamet in the Battle of Alcazar.

162 *mangonizing*: dealing in flesh.

163 *enghles*: male prostitutes.

167 *away*: 'I cannot get rid of' (Parfitt).

168 *Polyphagus*: 'eating to excess' (H&S).

169 *Barathrum*: abyss, devouring gulf (H&S).

170 *Aenobarbus*: red beard.

173 *accommodate*: 'bring to accept' (Parfitt).

191 *glavering*: fawning.

194 *puisnes*: innocents.

195 *Socks or buskins*: footwear of classical actor.

196 *help to a piece of flesh*: procure.

198 *punks*: prostitutes.

203 *half-arms*: pun on weapons and poverty.

204 *motion*: puppet, or puppet-play.

216 *by*: of.

243 *buy your own cloth* for liveries.

244 *countenance*: patronage.

261 *A gallant*: used of the fashionably dressed of either sex.

262 *Eringoes*: candied root of sea holly, used as an aphrodisiac.

8

University drama and
The Return from Parnassus

The latter part of the sixteenth century saw the development of a new kind of university graduate. There had been an increasing tendency amongst the upper classes to send their sons to university, creating a new ambience in which future men of letters of lower social origins could gain tastes and aspirations above their means:[1] 'My gentry', as a character puts it in Marlowe's *Edward II*, 'I fetched from Oxford'. At the same time changing social and economic patterns denied such men the traditional careers through the accustomed channels of patronage and preferment.[2] The Reformation had closed off many ecclesiastical destinations, and inflation reduced the value of incomes dependent on rents, which together with the gradual concentration of the nobility in London, in part a Tudor policy, led to a diminution of provincial households.

The consequent graduate unemployment is reflected most sharply in the three *Parnassus* plays written at St John's College, Cambridge, between 1598 and 1603 for performance by its members, which constitute an almost unbroken lament for the fate of the poor scholar, in a world which scorns learning and virtue, and is niggardly in its rewards even when he prostitutes his talents in writing for the stage, or performing on it. *Pilgrimage to Parnassus* follows the progress of two undergraduates, Philomusus and Studioso, through the perils and distractions of obtaining their degrees. The two parts of *Return from Parnassus* chart their subsequent disenchantment as they learn by bitter experience of the low esteem in which genuine learning is held and are reduced to exploring various branches of popular writing, such as ballads, pamphlets, and satires, and sink finally to the level of auditioning as hired men for the Lord Chamberlain's company. In doing so, they provide a unique face-to-face confrontation between the common player and his institutional rival.

At the beginning of the *Second Part of the Return from Parnassus,* there is a detailed if rather supercilious review of contemporary literature. No-one gets off scot-free, although, as for instance in the discussion of Marston where criticism is mingled with admiration, certain pre-dilections do emerge. The plays reveal a lively interest in London literary life and the popular theatre not entirely compatible with their wholesale dismissal. Why then should the university playwrights, and those who enthusiastically performed and received these plays, express such strong and disparaging views about a London theatre, which they evidently both enjoyed and imitated? Part of the reason for this seems to have been the very special circumstances under which the plays were written and performed. To a modern reader it may seem that the straightforward prose of the two players is more sympathetic than the convoluted and hysterical verse of the scholars, full of snobbery and self-pity, but even allowing for some measure of self-mockery, it must be recognized that they express the feelings and values of their community, and one determined to assert its superiority at a time when the separate identity of the two traditions seems in danger of being lost.

For many educated Elizabethans, the two universities formed the middle layer of a three-tier system, starting in the grammar schools and culminating in a period of residence at one of the Inns of Court. Drama became increasingly popular in all three types of institutions, due partly to the general humanist assumptions about its place in education, consonant with other revisions in the curriculum, and further encouraged at the universities by the development of the college system. The late fifteenth century saw a quickening of interest in Roman drama across Europe. From 1486 a number of commentaries appeared on Vitruvius, bent on reconstructing classical theatre and leading eventually to the building of the Teatro Olimpico at Vicenza. Editions of Terence, some of them illustrated, were published in the 1490s at Lyons, Strasbourg, London, and Venice, and at Paris in 1505. At about the same time there were attempts to revive classical stage practice in performances of plays by Terence and Seneca, notably under Pomponius Laetus in Rome, and then to imitate them with a home-grown Italian product, the *Commedia Erudita.*

During Elizabeth's reign the use of plays as an accepted educational strategy appears to have become widespread.[3] By the 1540s Ralph Radcliffe was attempting ambitious dramatic activities at his school in Hitchin. In 1550 the Statutes of Edward VI for the Free Grammar School at Bury St Edmunds provide for the 'chaster plays of Plautus and Terence' being taught to the third form. The annual Westminster School Latin play dates from 1561. Under Thomas Ashton in the 1570s Drama became a weekly activity at Shrewsbury School. The ban on the use of the Merchant Taylors' Hall by Mulcaster's boys in 1574 is one of the first pieces of evidence of public performances by children.

There were a number of attractions to the humanist educators of the sixteenth century in performances of Terence. The Latin language was at the centre of Elizabethan education to an extent which it is difficult to comprehend today. For the educated it was a second language, and an entry to historical, classical, and international thought and culture in general, and to ecclesiastical preferment, medicine, and law in particular. Francis Bacon, for instance, wrote his serious work in Latin and only his more trivial in English. Pupils at school were required to imitate classical authors in their own compositions, and also to speak fluently in Latin. Great stress was placed on rhetoric and oral argument.The plays of Terence in particular served these purposes admirably. He had long been admired for his style and his sentiments; only his storylines occasionally gave offence, and this was remedied by a 'Christian Terence' movement of imitations on more edifying themes, particularly that of the Prodigal Son. As time went on perhaps it was the temptations of a broader audience which led to the occasional introduction into the schools of plays in the vernacular.

The performance of a play was considered an effective vehicle for encouraging a kind of graceful boldness which the Elizabethans found attractive and called 'audaciousness', or, as by the Merchant Taylors when they did not like it, 'impudent familiarity'. Later, in 1660, Hoole recommends that schoolboys should perform comedies as:

> an excellent means to prepare them to pronounce orations with a grace, and I have found it an especial remedy to expel that subrustic bashfulness and unresistible timorousness which some children are naturally possessed withal . . .
>
> (W. Hoole, *New Discovery of the Old Art of Teaching Petty School,* 1660)

As with the schools, the performance of plays at the universities, along with the ceremonies for the Lords of Misrule, were written into the college statutes, as at St John's College, Cambridge in 1545. There is evidence of plays on religious themes at the universities from the late fifteenth century, and these are joined from c. 1540 by plays of theological controversy by Grimald, Christopherson and others.[4] Greek play manuscripts were circulating in Oxford from c. 1456 and reached the syllabus by 1517. Classical tragedy, mainly the works of Seneca, with occasional Latin adaptations of the Greek tragedies, was being revived at the universities by 1551. Seneca's influence spread through much of the academic, as well as the popular drama, of the 1580s and 1590s, at its best assimilated with native traditions, as in Richard Legges's trilogy *Richard Tertius* at St John's College, Cambridge in 1579/ 80. In the 1580s William Gager at Oxford based a series of plays on classical models, with varying degrees of faithfulness and success, but with considerable originality and invention

However the most enduring influence on university drama was that of the Roman Comedy. Terence was on the Cambridge syllabus by 1502 and on that of Oxford by c. 1505, and his plays were being performed by 1510/11, those of Plautus by 1522–3, and by 1536 the movement was gaining momentum and the Latin plays were joined by revivals of Aristophanes. During the 1560s records of Roman Comedy are particularly frequent, mainly at Trinity College. By 1583 these had given way in popularity to Latin versions of their Italian imitations, the *Commedia Erudita*, which in turn provoked native adaptations and imitations at the universities by 1578/9 (anticipated at the Inns of Court by Gascoigne's *Supposes*, 1566).

Although there appears to have been a steady trickle of performances in English of academic humanist drama at the universities, one peculiarity of the general corpus of university drama was that except for occasional Greek, it was predominantly performed in Latin. This was so to such an extent that when asked to prepare an English comedy for the Queen at Christmas the university authorities at Cambridge in 1592, could claim (perhaps as an excuse for their reluctance) that their actors had so little practice in that language, that they were unwilling to perform in English.

Neither the use of Latin, nor the humanist justification for the educational uses of drama, satisfied those at the universities who held to the fundamental objections to mimesis itself. Opponents of the university play refused to distinguish its actors from those of the professional theatre. Both, said Rainolds, incurred the Roman *infamia*, which barred actors from various civil rights and warranted excommunication.[5] Nichols quotes an account of one Dr Preston, a tutor, who was called on to coach his student for a female part in *Ignoramus*, 1615/16: 'the Doctor declined, not conceiving, he said, that his friends intended Mr Morgan *for a player*.'[6] Supporters of the university stage, however, seem to have been in the majority, and on this occasion included Mr Morgan's guardians. When a sub-tutor, Samuel Fairclough, refused to play a similar part in the same play and cited *Deuteronomy* in his defence, the Vice-Chancellor 'endeavoured to laugh him out of his reason'.

The defenders of the university stage, as of school plays, were anxious to make a clear distinction between the educational benefit of occasional performances, described by the Earl of Leicester, Chancellor of Oxford University, in 1584 as 'commendable and great furtherances of Learning', and the infamy of playing for money and on a regular basis. So absolute was the distinction considered to be between the two activities that university dramatists like Legge and Preston signed petitions demanding the banning of the itinerants. Gager, himself a prolific dramatist, and Rainolds' chief adversary, makes a clear distinction between his own activities and professional dramatics:

> We . . . do it to recreate ourselves, our House, and the better part of the University . . . to practise our own style . . . to be well acquainted with Seneca or Plautus; honestly to embolden our path; to try their voices and confirm their memories; to frame their speech; to conform them to convenient action; to try what metal is in everyone, and of what disposition they are of . . .

The obsessive nature of Rainolds' attack upon the stage ought not to deflect attention from the evidence it suggests of considerable impropriety in Gager's productions, sheltering as they did under the cover of the Latin text and the broad humanist sympathies to which he appealed. As early as Grimald's *Archipropheta* (c. 1546/7) the spectacle of Herodias giving Salome a lesson in lascivious dancing indicates that more than mere Latin recitation was required of the university performers. According to Rainolds' informants (he would not attend the plays himself), Penelope's handmaidens in *Ulysses Redux* had not merely danced, but had sat undetected during the First Act amongst the women in the audience. By his own report, Gager himself is reduced to questioning the students after the performance to find out whether Melantho's desire in the text for kissing had had its physical counterpart on stage. However the sensuality of Gager's plays may have been enacted, undoubtedly the moral tone of the subsequent Italian comedies and their Latinized imitations sank to a level that scarcely justified the educational value claimed for them. By the turn of the century, in a play like Walter Hawkesworth's *Labyrinthus* (1602/3) for instance, much of the focus is on the embarrassment and titillation aroused by sexual encounters confused by both male and female cross-dressing, together with pre-marital intercourse and its infant product.[7]

As that essential separateness of university playing from the professional kind was itself mined from within by these developments of subject matter and its treatment, it was under assault also from without. The academic insularity that enabled both Gager and Rainolds and their adherents to take up the positions they did, depended on a university autonomy which despite the regular confirmation, and even extension of its powers, was precarious. Nothing, for instance, seems to have stopped the contamination of the university play by direct and regular acquaintance with the leading professional companies on tour. In 1575 the Vice-Chancellor of Cambridge appealed to the Privy Council to give him powers to ban itinerant playing on the grounds that it interfered with study. The Council replied charging him to forbid them within a five-mile radius, because the itinerants were 'light and decayed persons, who for filthy lucre are minded, and to seek nowadays to devise, and set up in open places shows of unlawful, hurtful, pernicious, and unhonest games' and, said the Privy Council, encouraged the spectators to become 'practisers of lewdness and unlawful acts'. Like many similar Elizabethan enactments it was ineffectual. The town authorities, hostile to university supervision, regularly accepted the players, and open conflict flared up in Cambridge in 1592, whilst at Oxford the problem of student attendance of these spectacles was such as to require a statute providing for the imprisonment of those students over eighteen who attended such performances, and public chastisement for those below that age.

Part of the universities' problem was that however much they asserted their need for the independent status of academe, they were locked inevitably into the Elizabethan system of royal patronage at what Gabriel Harvey described as 'the only mart of preferment and honour', the Court, and one which looked on the players with favour. In 1580, five years after the Privy Council had given permission for Cambridge to ban itinerants, two of its leading members, Burghley and Sussex, were busy recommending the Duttons' Oxford's Men to both universities. In 1587 the Vice-Chancellor of Oxford had the difficult task of turning away the company of his own Chancellor, the Earl of Leicester, which he did with a typical Elizabethan compromise which says much about the conflicting pressures of the time. He paid them twenty shillings, the full rate for a performance, to go away.

Some pressures, however, could not be resisted. The three visits of the Queen to the universities must have had a major influence, both on the encouragement of university drama, and on its development towards what ultimately became a single target of excellence. She

PERFORMANCE OF A UNIVERSITY PLAY

Figure 8.1 A vignette from the title-page of William Alabaster's *Roxana*, a Latin translation of an Italian original, performed c. 1590 at Cambridge, and illustrated in 1632. Leaving aside authenticity, proportion, and the absence of any suggestion of the lower halves of the spectators on the balcony, the tiny picture gives a vivid impression of figures in performance. The point of view seems to be thrown forward into close association with the action by a steeply raked auditorium.

134

visited them both early in her reign – Cambridge in 1564 and Oxford in 1566. The former visit gave advance notice of her values and her will in this matter. A 'great stage' which the University had caused to be set up in King's College hall was torn down and replaced, at the Queen's own expense, by a larger one in the Chapel, boarding over large sections of the nave and chancel, for a performance of Plautus' *Aulularia* on the Sunday, with scant respect for religious suscept-ibilities.[8] This was followed on the next two nights by a Latin tragedy, *Dido*, by Edward Halliwell, and an English comedy by Udall, *Ezechias*. Fatigued, the Queen forwent a fourth play, a Latin translation of Sophocles' *Ajax*.

At her first visit to Oxford two years later, Elizabeth absented herself from the first Latin play, a prose comedy, *Marcus Geminus,* but attended the second, James Calfhill's tragedy, *Progne*. The high point of her visit, however, seems to have been the two-part *Palamon and Arcite* written in English by Richard Edwards, now her Master of the Children of the Chapel Royal, who supervised the whole programme. The first part was performed on the Monday and the second delayed until the Wednesday. The crush of spectators outside the building caused a wall to collapse, killing three people, but after sending help Elizabeth ordered the play to proceed.

Two further matters indicate the royal influence on university drama. In 1592, when the ageing Queen paid a second visit to Oxford for a shorter programme of Latin comedies, her Revels Office supplied all the costumes and properties. At the end of her visit, according to Wood, the Queen summoned Rainolds and schooled him before the Heads of Houses 'for his obstinate preciseness, willing him to follow her laws, and not run before them' (*Annals,* ii. 251).

In assessing those pressures on university drama that helped to determine the particular quality of the representation of players in *The Second Part of the Return from Parnassus*, it is important to recognize the influence of the Inns of Court as a superior tier in the educational system: metropolitan, quasi-courtly, its members generally of a super-ior social standing, and many of them already graduates of the universities. Two references in the play suggest the greater worldliness attributed to the Inns by the university writer. The first is the scene in which the foppish Amoretto, now an Inns of Court man, spurns the humble scholar, Academico, in favour of selling his benefice to the ignorant Immerito. The second is an admiring reference to an Inns of Court poet –

Acute John Davis, I affect thy rhymes,
That jerk in hidden charms these looser times:
Thy plainer verse, thy unaffected vein,
Is graced with a fair and swooping train.   [sweeping]
(Martial and he may sit upon one bench,
Either wrote well and either loved his wench.)

(II. 253–8)

P.J. Finkelpearl comments, 'A reputation as a lover and satirist would seem to combine all that a young man in this milieu would hope for.'[9]

The peculiar circumstances of the pursuit of learning at the Inns of Court, as a kind of less regulated by-product of professional training, also offered challenge, as well as continuity, to the values of the university tradition. Carey Conley identifies a liberal pressure group at the Inns of Court rejecting the traditional university opposition to translation and concerned to make the classics more generally available.[10] Some would see in the championing of common law at the Inns the development of a more critical and political viewpoint, absent from the canon law taught at the universities.[11] This less inhibited, less traditional approach of the Inns to thought and culture, together with their closer geographical and social proximity to the Court, contributed to a more sophisticated, less suspicious treatment of the common player, which must have offered the universities an alternative model to their own.

One strand of university dramatic activity which helped to establish and legitimize a taste for satire, parody, and burlesque was the institution of the Christmas Kings, or Lords of Misrule, which, whatever its casual antiquity, became systematized in revised college statutes in the 1540s, and must have established certain expectations of the inversion of roles, influential both on subsequent texts and events. The best documented account is the revival of the practice in 1607, the *Christmas Prince* at St John's College, Oxford. There are many similarities with the grander activities of the Inns of Court, discussed below.

A second line of university humour, the topical satirical play, began in academic parody. The pedant of received Italian Comedy invited satire near to home, as displayed in a cluster of plays aimed at Gabriel Harvey, of which the only survivor, *Pedantius*, was performed at Trinity College, Cambridge, c. 1580/1. Topical plays became more vitriolic however when they were made to fuel the town-versus-gown hostility. Although in 1582/3 one Thomas Mudde was imprisoned for three days by the university authorities for writing a play attacking the

136

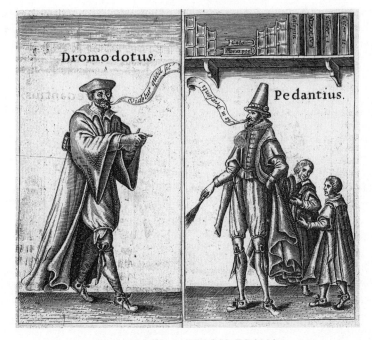

UNIVERSITY SATIRICAL DRAMA

Figure 8.2 Dromodotus and Pedantius from Edward Forsett's *Pedantius*, a much celebrated satire on Gabriel Harvey, written in 1581 and illustrated in 1631. Dromodotus is a scholastic pedant, whilst Pedantius (Harvey) has aspirations to be a courtier and man of affairs. Despite the time lapse, the illustration contains close reference to the play, and indicates Harvey's dress and appearance.

Mayor, by c. 1599/1600 a blind eye was evidently being turned to what was probably a much more savage attack on the townspeople in *Club Law*, performed at Clare Hall. The play represents on stage, in the thinnest of disguises, a selection of civic worthies who are charged with foolishness, corruption, and sexual immorality, before being humiliated in a plot loosely based on contemporary events. *The Second Part of the Return From Parnassus* itself includes personal topical satire on the Recorder of Cambridge, as well as on various authors and theatre practitioners.

There was a long-standing taste for burlesquing their social inferiors through self-consciously demeaning portrayals, apparent in *Gammer Gurton's Needle* performed by the students of Christ College at some time before 1575. In the lost *Riuales* by Gager at Oxford, the scholars had played yokel wooers, drunken sailors, and bawds. In *Narcissus, a Twelfth Night Merriment* (1603), the performers appear in the guise of gauche town lads, who come into the Hall wassailing. Only with difficulty are they prevailed on to stay and perform, when the Porter asks:

> What was that I took you all a gabbling t'other day in
> Mother Bunche's backside by the well there – when Tom
> at Hobses ran under the hovel with a kettle on's head?

This pretence of clodhopping simplicity introduces a play very similar in general tone to the 'Pyramus and Thisbe' burlesque in *A Midsummer Night's Dream*, and what is significant about this otherwise very slight play is that it contains so many specific echoes as to suggest more than a passing familiarity with that play, along with a number of others from the London stage. Like the anonymous *Caesar's Revenge* (c. 1592/6) at Trinity College, it helps to indicate the context of ambivalence towards the professional player in which the *Parnassus* plays are written, following as it does the experience of a whole generation of university graduates, including Marlowe, Lyly, Greene, Nashe, Peele, and Lodge, whose contribution had done so much to shape the London stage in the late 1580s and early 1590s.

Writing for the stage was widely represented as a moral defeat and a humiliation. Stephen Gosson, first playwright and then play-scourge, said, 'I was first instructed in the university, after drawn like a novice to these abuses', whilst *The Hog Hath Lost his Pearl* represents writing for the stage as the last refuge from penury.

Francis Meres, in *Palladis Tamia: Wit's Treasure* (1598) regretting the lack of modern patrons, such as the Roman poets had had, notes that it is by 'our witty Comedians and stately Tragedians . . . (O ingrateful and damned age) our Poets are solely or chiefly maintained, countenanced, and patronized'. Few writers were so charitable towards these new 'patrons'. Thomas Nashe and Robert Greene in particular bemoaned the rise to success and prosperity of the players allegedly at their expense, in a series of satirical pamphlets, designed, one imagines, as much for amusement as redress. Without the poets, says Nashe, in *To Gentlemen of Both Universities* (1589) the players would not have graduated to metropolitan prosperity and would still be living close to destitution and carrying 'their fardels on footback'. But the player, they said, did not remember his origins or his dependence upon the playwright. He forgot that his acting was no more than a 'mechanical

Figure 8.3 The title-role in George Ruggle's *Ignoramus*, a Latin satire on
Francis Brakin, the Recorder of Cambridge, and attacking lawyers,
performed before James I in 1615, and illustrated 1630. Like *Pedantius*, the
illustration relates closely to the text, but cannot have any connection with
its performance.

labour'. In *Francesco's Fortunes: Or the second part of Greene's Never Too Late* (1590) Greene girds at his contemporaries under the transparent disguise of Greece and Rome, when 'covetousness crept into the quality' and 'the Actors, by continual use grew not only excellent but rich and insolent'.

The pride of the players, said the poets, exhibited itself in the fine clothes they wore, which together with the grand manners they put on, smacked of social climbing, carrying their stage pretensions to regality or nobility onto the streets. Jonson purports to illustrate this in Histrio's demeanour and dress in *The Poetaster*. The Player, in Greene's autobiographical account in his *Groats-worth of Wit* (1592), mistaken for 'a gentleman of great living' and boasting that his share of the costumes is worth two hundred pounds, admits that 'men of my profession get by scholars their whole living'. However, the writers did not, they claimed, receive fair payment. The players, said Donald Lupton in *London and the Country Carbonadoed* (1632), 'are much beholden to scholars that are out of means, for they sell them ware the cheapest'. Modern studies are generally agreed that the income from writing for, the theatre compared well with other forms of graduate employ, and Alfred Harbage suggests that the writers' objections were really social; they did not like working for those they regarded as their inferiors.[12] The prejudice however was universally held. Writers continued to contrast the value of the text and its poor reward with the paucity of skill involved in performance and the prosperity of the players, whom the graduates in the *Parnassus* extract call 'those leaden spouts,/That nought do vent but what they do receive', whilst Samuel Rowlands asks:

> Will you stand spending your invention's treasure,
> To teach stage-parrots speak for penny pleasure,
> While you yourselves, like music-sounding lutes,
> Fretted and strung, gain them their silken suits?
>
> (*The Letting of Humour's Blood in the Head-Vein,* 1600)

More serious even than the conviction of being exploited was their growing apprehension of becoming surplus to requirements. As Kemp is made to say in the extract below, voicing the undiscerning prejudice of his fellows, 'Few of the university pen plays well. They smell too much of that writer Ovid and that writer *Metamorphoses* and talk too much of Proserpina and Jupiter. Why here's our fellow Shakespeare puts them all down.' Hence the Wits' most extreme rhetoric is reserved for the player-poets, whom we see parodied in *Histriomastix*. Nashe sounded the alarm with references to the players' 'idiot Art-masters, that intrude themselves to our ears as the Alchemists of eloquence, who (mounted on the stage of arrogance) think to outbrave better pens with the swelling bombast of a bragging blank verse'. Greene has Roberto's Player demonstrate his own abilities as an extempore playwright:

> The people make no estimation,
> Of Morals teaching education,
> Was this not pretty for a plain rhyme extempore?
> If ye will, ye shall have more.

Roberto tactfully declines the offer. Whether this satirical sketch is meant to be of a particular writer or some general indictment, clearly Shakespeare is in the forefront of their indignation; witness Greene's warning that his fellow poets too will be forsaken by the players.

The final insult was that the player-poets should be successful in peddling their wares. Joseph Hall in *Virgidemiarum*, 1597, laments:

> Too popular is tragic poesy
> Straining his toptoes for a farthing fee.

For all the vicious parody in *Histriomastix*, the vision of Chrisoganus, the scholar-poet, of a time when:

> I hope to see you starve and storm for books,
> And in the dearth of rich invention,
> When sweet smooth lines are held for precious,
> Then will you fawn and crouch to Poesy.

– can be no more than wishful thinking; the player-poets were to thrive, and to build on the experience of what Greene had dismissed as their 'mechanical labour'.

The extract from *The Second Part of the Return from Parnassus* opens with Burbage and Kemp, played of course by members of the college, criticizing university acting standards. Commentators are inclined to emphasize the author's contempt for the two professional players, and yet the sequence opens with what appear to be valid criticisms of bad and mannered acting.[13] There is no obvious sense here that Kemp does not understand the finer points of university acting, and this leaves open the possibility that his subsequent apparent blunders, concerning 'that writer *Metamorphoses*', and mistaking 'Studioso' for 'Otioso', are meant to be taken as deliberate jokes on his part. Furthermore the scholars seem to sense that banter is what is appropriate, perhaps required, in converse with him.

141

It is evident from the context outlined earlier that there are sensitive social antennae in use here, which take offence at the players' confident inversion of accepted inequalities:

> *Kemp*: Is't not better to make a fool of the world, as I have done, than to be fooled of the world, as you scholars are?

Kemp's conclusion in comparing himself with the scholars might be acceptable elsewhere, but here it exemplifies the self-satisfied 'worldly' wisdom which vitiates their learning and their virtue.

Just as Haddit, in the encounter in *The Hog Hath Lost his Pearl* below, attempts to reconcile his sense of social and educational superiority with his penury, so too the scholars try to cut Kemp down to size by suggesting that he is no more than a foolish jigger. He retorts by suggesting that he is their superior. He can practise to a high level a skill which they have now to begin to learn from the bottom.

Kemp humorously gives himself the status of a judge on circuit, and then an 'Alderman' of the playhouse. His line in comic justices is kept as a running joke on and off the stage; this combination of ignorance and power is but an extension of a general theme through this group of plays. And behind these comic assumptions is the cold reality of economic superiority, with Burbage calculating on how little he needs pay them and how much he can get out of them.

There follows a fascinating representation of an Elizabethan audition. We cannot be sure that it is in any way authentic or typical, and there have to be some serious doubts, but the authors of the three *Parnassus* plays do show considerable interest in representing performance style, as the clown episode in *Pilgrimage to Parnassus* shows. Burbage delivers a speech from *The Spanish Tragedy* and instructs the scholar to copy him. It would be of great interest to know whether this was common practice (he does not repeat it with the speech from *Richard III*) and indeed whether it was used as a training technique in rehearsal. In *Hamlet*, for instance, the same technique is adopted when he says 'Speak the speech, I pray you, as I pronounc'd it to you' (III.ii). We are to assume that Hamlet has just given a performance of a speech, presumably one of his insertions in 'The Murder of Gonzago', which he now instructs the players to copy.

The opportunities for parody and burlesque in *Parnassus* are perhaps not immediately apparent from the text, but it must be remembered that the performers are members of the College, ostensibly hostile to the common players, and that a speech repeated on-stage is almost always risible, especially since the lines are taken from *The Spanish*

Tragedy, first performed circa 1587, and a byword for the old-fashioned and pretentious amongst the intelligentsia by 1600; witness its use by the *pyrgi* in *The Poetaster*, and as a means of embarrassing Jonson in *Satiromastix* (I.ii. 351 and IV.i. 121).[14] On the other hand, it is unlikely that Kemp's monologue of the foolish justice could have been copied in reality, since it is presumably a spontaneous invention.

As a contribution to the general discussion about the relation between player and part, it is interesting to note that the players are made to use, as criteria of which parts will suit their prospective hired men, the voice for Hieronimo, the face for the Mayor, and the face and proportion of body for Richard III. Perhaps the final choice should alert us to the possibilities of satire here. Of all parts, Richard III is surely the last you would want to be offered because of 'the proportion of your body'! Nor, of course, in practice are these the sort of roles that would have been offered to hired men.

Indeed the whole passage should be treated with caution. There is no evidence that Kemp ever rejoined the Chamberlain's Men on his return from Italy and a number of reasons for assuming he did not.[15] Therefore the authenticity of his touring with Burbage after the performance of *The Poetaster* is highly dubious. This in turn casts doubt on the reliability of associating Shakespeare with the 'Purge', which has sparked off so much scholarly activity. It is safer to assume that the anonymous author's knowledge of London theatre personnel was no more than sketchy.

Asked by the players to follow them off to talk terms, the scholars remain on-stage to bemoan their fate at having fallen to the basest trade, when they should be properly recompensed for using their learning to record, and so preserve, virtue, much as Jonson says of 'Men-making poets' in his *Masque of Queens*. Presumably they then reject the players' terms, for in the next scene we see them reduced even further, to a level below players, that of itinerant musicians; the degradation with which Tucca threatened Histrio, reminiscent of the figure shown on the titlepage of the English version of Scarron's *Romans Comiques*, 1676.

THE SECOND PART OF
THE RETURN FROM PARNASSUS

Act IV Scene III

Enter BURBAGE and KEMP

143

Burbage: Now Will Kemp, if we can entertain these scholars at
   a low rate, it will be well; they have oftentimes a good
   conceit in a part.

Kemp: It's true indeed, honest Dick, but the slaves are somewhat proud, and besides, 'tis good sport in a part, to see   5
   them never speak in their walk, but at the end of the stage,
   just as though in walking with a fellow we should never
   speak but at a stile, a gate, or a ditch, where a man can go
   no further. I was once at a Comedy in Cambridge, and
   there I saw a parasite make faces and mouths of all sorts   10
   on this fashion. (*He grimaces by way of illustration*)

Burbage: A little teaching will mend these faults, and it may be
   besides they will be able to pen a part.

Kemp: Few of the university pen plays well. They smell too
   much of that writer Ovid and that writer *Metamorphoses*,   15
   and talk too much of Proserpina and Jupiter. Why here's
   our fellow Shakespeare puts them all down, aye and Ben
   Jonson too. Oh, that Ben Jonson is a pestilent fellow. He
   brought up Horace giving the poets a pill, but our fellow
   Shakespeare hath given him a purge that made him beray   20
   his credit.

Burbage: It's a shrewd fellow, indeed. I wonder these scholars
   stay so long. They appointed to be here presently, that we
   might try them. Oh, here they come.

Enter PHILOMUSUS and STUDIOSO

Studioso (*aside to Philomusus*): Take heart, these lets our clouded   25
   thoughts refine.
   The sun shines brightest when it 'gins decline.

Burbage: Master Philomusus and Master Studioso, God save you.

Kemp: Master Philomusus and Master Otioso, well met.

Philomusus: The same to you, good Master Burbage. What,   30
   Master Kemp, how doth the Emperor of Germany?

Studioso: God save you, Master Kemp. Welcome Master Kemp
   from dancing the morris over the Alps.

Kemp: Well, you merry knaves, you may come to the honour
   of it one day. Is't not better to make a fool of the world,   35
   as I have done, than to be fooled of the world, as you
   scholars are? But be merry, my lads you have happened
   upon the most excellent vocation in the world. For money,

they come north and south to bring it to our playhouse.
And for honour, who of more report than Dick Burbage   40
and Will Kemp? He's not counted a gentleman that knows
not Dick Burbage and Will Kemp. There's not a country
wench that can dance *Sellenger's Round,* but can talk of Dick
Burbage and Will Kemp.

Philomusus: Indeed Master Kemp, you are very famous, but   45
that's as well for (your) works in print as your parts in cue.

Kemp: You are at Cambridge still with 'size que', and be lusty
humorous poets, you must untruss.[16] I rode this my last
circuit purposely because I would be judge of your actions.

Burbage: Master Studioso, I pray you take some part in this   50
book and act it, that I may see what will fit you best. I
think your voice would serve for Hieronimo. Observe how
I act it and then imitate me.

Who calls Hieronimo from his naked bed?

Studioso: **Who calls, &c.**   55

Burbage: You will do well after a whole.

Kemp (To Philomusus): Now for you; methinks you should
belong to my tuition, and your face methinks would be
good for a foolish Mayor or a foolish justice of (the) peace.
Mark me: 60

**For as much as there be two states of a common-
wealth, the one of peace, the other of tranquillity; two
states of war, the one of discord, the other of dissen-
tion; two states of an incorporation, the one of Aldermen, the other Brethren; two states of a magistrate, the   65
one of governing, the other of bearing rule: now, as I
said even now, for a good thing cannot be said too
often: Virtue is the shoeing horn of justice, that is
Virtue is the shoeing horn of doing well, that is, virtue
is the shoeing horn of doing justly. It behoveth me and   70
it is my part to commend this shoeing horn unto you.
I hope this word 'shoeing horn' doth not offend any of
you, my worshipful brethren, for you being the worshipful headsmen of the town, know well what the
horn meaneth.[17] Now therefore I am determined not   75
only to teach, but also to instruct, not only the
ignorant, but also the simple, not only what is their
duty to their betters, but also what is their duty towards
their superiors.**

– Come, let me see how you can do. Sit down in the chair.　80
Philomusus: **Forasmuch as there be [2 states &c.] &c.**
Kemp: Thou wilt do well in time, if thou wilt be ruled by thy
　betters, that is, by myself, and such grave Aldermen of the
　playhouse as I am.
Burbage: I like your face and the proportion of your body for　85
Richard III. I pray (you) Master Philomusus, let me see you
　act a little of it.
Philomusus: **Now is the winter of our discontent**
Made glorious summer by the sun of York, [&c.]
Burbage: Very well, I assure you. Well, Master Philomusus and　90
　Master Studioso, we see what ability you are of. I pray
　walk with us to our fellows, and we'll agree presently.
Philomusus: We will follow you straight, Master Burbage.
Kemp: It's good manners to follow us, Master Philomusus and
　Master Otioso. (*Exeunt Burbage and Kemp*)　95
Philomusus: And must the basest trade yield us relief?
　Must we be practised to those leaden spouts,
　That nought do vent but what they do receive?

The scene continues with another sixty lines in the same vein,
bewailing the fate of the scholar to be ignored, and the blindness of the
powerful, who through not patronizing the writer, will not be
recorded for posterity.

　Studioso: Come Philomusus, let us break this chat.
　Philomusus: And break my heart, oh, would I could break that.
　Studioso: Let's learn to act that Tragic part we have.
　Philomusus: Would I were silent actor in my grave. (*Exeunt*)

A career in the theatre begun so inauspiciously, could not be expected
to last for long, and the very next lines in the play show them to have
descended even further.

Act V Scene I

PHILOMUSUS & STUDIOSO become fiddlers, with their consort

Philomusus: Tune fellow Fiddlers, Studioso and I are ready.
　They tune.
Studioso (*going aside sayeth*):
　Fair fall, good Orpheus, that would rather be

King of a molehill than a Kaiser's slave:
Better it is 'mongst fiddlers to be chief,
That at (a) player's trencher beg relief.   5
But is't not strange these mimic apes should prize
Unhappy Scholars at a hireling rate?
Vile world, that lifts them up to high degree,
And treads us down in grovelling misery.
England affords those glorious vagabonds,   10
That carried erst their fardels on their backs,
Coursers to ride on through the gazing streets,
Sweeping it in their glaring Satin suits,
And Pages to attend 'their masterships':
With mouthing words that better wits have framed   15
They purchase lands, and now 'Esquires' are named.

Glossary to the second part of *The Return from Parnassus*

IV   3   *conceit*: imagination, conception.
    11   *on this fashion*: like this.
    15   *Metamorphoses*: not a writer, but a work by Ovid.
    17   *Puts them all down*: 'surpasses them all' (Leishman).
    21   *Beray his credit*: 'befoul his reputation' (Leishman).
    25   *Lets*: hindrances, obstacles.
    29   *Otioso*: lazy, useless.
    43   Sellenger's Round: popular dance tune.
    46   *in cue*: in performance.
    47   *size que*: small portions, short commons.
    92   *presently*: straight away.
V   5   *trencher*: wooden plate.
    11   *Erst*: formerly.
    11   *Fardels*: bundles (on their backs, because too poor to afford a
          horse or cart).
    12   *Coursers*: superior kind of horse.

147

9

Histriomastix and the Inns of Court

The subplot of *Histriomastix* is a comprehensive indictment of the common player, and, granted its unfavourable bias, provides a rich seam of information about his day-to-day activities, as well as a general summary of current prejudices against him. We see a company formed, and are given the reasons for its formation, articles are drawn up and costumes commissioned, the players cry a current play, and have an impromptu reading of one in preparation, they sing-in the lord's banquet, perform snatches from two plays, and finish off with an improvisation on a theme; they negotiate with a playwright, rehearse, are pressed into the army, refuse to pay their bills, pawn their costumes, and are shipped off as undesirables. It is a rich piece of evidence which perhaps because of its negative bias has been undeservedly neglected.

Histriomastix cannot be assigned to the Inns of Court with the same degree of confidence as the other plays in this group can be assigned to their auspices, and we lack unambiguous evidence of both dating and authorship. None the less there are a number of factors, particularly the involvement of Marston, either as collaborator, author, or subject of parody, which suggest clear association of some sort with the Inns. At the very least, the play can be said to have their members in mind as an influential element in its intended audience.

The nominal function of the four Inns of Court was as a self-regulating training school and residence for lawyers. By Elizabethan times however, such was the value of a legal education on the one hand, and the prestige of their society on the other, that they became much more: they provided a training in the accomplishments of a gentleman, they constituted an important ladder to preferment and power, and, by their endeavours, they had a considerable influence on the cultural milieu of London.

Though the landowning fathers of many students recognized that a legal training was an important weapon in retaining power as well as gaining advancement, the majority of students, perhaps as many as five-sixths, regarded a spell at the Inns as no more than a necessary stage in their education, rather than as a preliminary to being called to the Bar.[1] The elaborate social life of the Inns, of which dramatic activities formed a considerable part, was itself an attraction, and though some no doubt concentrated upon it to the exclusion of their studies, as is alleged in various satirical accounts, their general tenor suggests such activities functioned for most students as a release from study, rather than as an alternative to it. Their characteristic modes include burlesque of legal protocol, jokes about the law, sexual innuendo expressed through legal phraseology and so on: all the recreations of those steeped in their studies, for which a modern equivalent might be the macabre high-jinks of the medical school.[2]

There were four Inns of Court; the Inner and Middle Temples, Gray's Inn and Lincoln's Inn; and subordinate to them were the Inns of Chancery, where non-graduate aspirants to the senior Inns prepared themselves. By 1600 the former had some one thousand residents and the latter about seven hundred. As well as contributing to the literature of the period, the Inns constituted a major element in its educated readership, as frequent dedications show. The geographical proximity of the Inns, the relative affluence of their members, and the practice, even amongst the conscientious, of breaking their studies for recreation (Prynne called them 'afternoons men'), made the Inns of Court perhaps the single most considerable and influential constituent of the private theatre audiences. With satirical progeny of their own, such as Davies and Marston, the Inns were no doubt receptive to the general tone of much of the Children's output, which from time to time acknowledged their presence. As Quomodo leaves the stage at the end of Act II scene iii of *Michaelmas Term* (1606), full of self-satisfaction at betraying his gull, he turns to speak directly to his audience: 'Admire me, all you students at Inns of Cozenage.'[3]

The surviving records of dramatic activity at the Inns themselves suggest a different emphasis from the pattern of the universities, both in performances by their own members and in the treatment of the professional player, who is less comprehensively taboo at the Inns, reflecting perhaps greater general familiarity with theatre-going and a more easy confidence in their own superiority. There are references to student performances from 1527, and the Bacon report on the Inns of 1540, suggests there was a general practice of student performances.[4]

The incorporation of revels and lords of misrule within the social life of the Inns was much more elaborate and integrated than at the universities, partly because of their acknowledged function in the training of lawyers and potential courtiers, and partly because dramatic means were acknowledged there as a tool in the politics of state. This was especially so in the early seventeenth century in the development of the revels into the processional masque, as an act of homage to the monarch, but it could be said to be anticipated in the earlier group of tragedies written and performed at the Inns. Even the earliest surviving account of a play at the Inns, that of the Gray's Inn performance of John Roo's play in 1526/7 which so upset Cardinal Wolsey, already shows this principle in action:

> The effect of the play was that lord governance was ruled by dissipation and negligence, by whose misgovernance and evil order, Lady Public weal was put from governance . . . the Cardinal . . . imagined that the play had been devised of him . . .[5]

Of the five extant plays written at the Inns, the first, Norton and Sackville's *Gorboduc*, performed before the Queen by the Inner Temple in 1561/2, is justly famous both for its introduction of blank verse to the stage and its sound political advice. Gascoigne's tragedy *Jocasta* (1566) a translation or adaptation from the Italian, is followed at Gray's Inn by his prose comedy adaptation of Ariosto's *Supposes*, which was an important step in the introduction of the New Comedy tradition to the English stage.[6] The genesis of the remaining two tragedies, *Gismonde of Salerne* (2. 1568) and *The Misfortunes of Arthur* (1588), both emphasize the characteristic of collaboration at the Inns in writing and production, which may well be a significant element in the composition of *Histriomastix*.[7]

G.Y. Gamble in his study of the tragedies stresses their innovative use of received medieval and classical material, and, in applying the lessons of the past to the present, the close relationship of the plays to the political and pedagogic concerns of the Inns. Their highly rhetorical style, he says, concentrated on stylized debate rather than action:

> these authors were educated to believe that by nature serious drama was instructive and instruction was made persuasive, and hence effective, by means of rhetoric.[8]

Visits of professional companies to the Inns are recorded from 1494, with a noticeable increase in frequency after 1560 when they are joined by records of children's companies. There may have been some falling off in the 1590s, but *Twelfth Night* was performed at the Middle Temple in 1602, and by 1605 the records of the Inner Temple show one and sometimes two professional performances each year, either on Candlemas or All Saints' Day, for the next ten years. Although in 1611 the Benchers solemnly abolished the practice it was reinstated within the year. The ambitiousness of some of the seasons of ostensibly amateur entertainment at the Inns has led commentators to speculate that they may have used the services of professionals. Although *The Comedy of Errors* was performed by Shakespeare's company of 'base and common fellows' at Gray's Inn in 1594 in circumstances that at least purport to have been spontaneous, certainly the services of five of the leading members of Prince Charles' Men were recruited for Middleton's *Masque of Heroes* at the Inner Temple in 1619.[9]

At the heart of the Inns of Court dramatic tradition, and perhaps of most significance in approaching the hypothesis of its auspices for *Histriomastix*, are the 'Revels'. The practice of feasting, often with elaborate rituals and additional entertainment, was widespread at the Inns. The expectations of lavish expenditure grew so much that by the seventeenth century men became daunted at accepting promotion to Reader or Serjeant for fear of its cost. In 1430 Lincoln's Inn had had four revels at different seasons, and in the sixteenth century to these was added the 'grand Christmassing'. Detailed accounts remain of the Christmas Revels at Gray's Inn in 1594/5, the *Gesta Grayorum*, and of *Le Prince d'Amour* at the Middle Temple in 1597/8, together with a long description of Christmas Revels at the Inner Temple in 1562.[10] In each case a Christmas Prince was chosen, who held court, made decrees, received ambassadors from the other Inns, and presided over an elaborate programme of masques, plays, disputations, mock trials, and other activities. There was sometimes also an anti-king.[11]

The tone of these events, what Evelyn called 'solemn foolery', is complicated by at least three different sets of values placed upon them. Like the University Lord of Misrule, the Christmas Revels were sanctioned and prescribed in statutes, and fines were levied on those who did not attend and participate.[12] There was an element of topsy-turvy ritualized inversion, intended to reaffirm the status quo. The elaborate ceremonial was thought good training for courtly preferment, and the array of mock-officers paralleled their Court equivalents in duties and behaviour. The 'law-sports' themselves, of impromptu trials and speeches of counsel, were all opportunities to further skills in argument. The *Gesta Grayorum* with parts for about 130 members is clearly seen as a participatory activity.

On the other hand, mockery of a system can destroy rather than strengthen it, and those helping to create selective social change do not always whole-heartedly embrace the principle of inversion, which is more attractive perhaps to a stable and confident hierarchy. There are examples of disorderly conduct. Money was demanded with threats of public humiliation. There was a custom of hunting in the hall and driving a cat and a fox into the fire to be burnt alive. The ruling Benchers tried unsuccessfully in 1595, for instance, to abbreviate the festivities. In 1627, a Temple lord of misrule, attempting to obtain a collection by hammering on citizens' doors, was apprehended by the Mayor and imprisoned.[13]

As with the later University plays, satire can be seen as the legitimate, if not always acceptable, heir of ritual inversion. Instead of confirming the status quo by traditional clowning, satire attacked whatever target it pleased, particularly if it were associated with authority. Eventually in 1599 satire passed the bounds of official tolerance and the Archbishop of Canterbury banned the publication of satires and epigrams. Finkelpearl suggests that the tone of the later *Prince d'Amour* at the Middle Temple in 1597/8 is similar to that of some Jacobean private theatre comedy:

> a world of amoral women, cuckolds, aphrodisiacs, whores and venereal disease, a world where the right end of true love is the maximum number of female conquests.[14]

He goes on to say, however, that such a view was combined, as a mixture and not a compound, with a dissatisfaction with such trifling, and held by those who also wrote love poetry of youthful idealism. Satire never entirely replaced the earlier love of the grotesque, and although the precise distribution of personnel in the masques at the Inns, as at Court, remains unclear, their anti-masques offered many opportunities for genteel comic self-abasement, from hogs to bawds.

As with the universities, and indeed with drama as a whole, the influence of the monarchy was to stimulate – and to some extent confuse – the values of the drama of the Inns of Court. There had long been an element of serious ostentation in the Christmas Revels. Henry Machyn records in his diary of 1561:

> The 27th day of December came riding through London a lord of misrule, in clean complete harness, gilt, with a hundred great horse and gentlemen riding gorgeously with chains of gold, and

their great horses goodly trapped, unto the Temple, for there was great cheer all Christmas.[15]

His description accords closely in tone to that of Gerald Legh, writing in the following year of the Inner Temple revels as being grand and ceremonious.[16] When the picture is extended forward in time to include the Stuart Masques from the Inns of Court, even though they continue to offer anti-masque opportunities for burlesque and the grotesque, the overall tone of the Inns of Court semi-dramatic pageantry, particularly in the processional masques of 1613, is one of courtly aspiration.

In 1595 the Prince of Purpoole, the Gray's Inn Lord of Misrule, pretended to go off on a military campaign to Russia, and his supposed return (which the Benchers tried to discourage) included not merely a procession of barges on the Thames and a Latin welcome from St Paul's School, but also the direct involvement of the Queen in the fiction of his royalty. She exchanged royal correspondence with him and allowed him a royal salute from the Tower artillery. After the masque of *Proteus and the Rock Adamantine* played before the Queen, which concluded the festivities and in which the mock Prince was chief masquer, she invited the performers to Court, allowed them to kiss her hand and invited the Prince to perform at the barriers with real courtiers. Such encouragement must have been very exciting and very unsettling, much as her condescension to the 'Lady Emilia' at Oxford in 1566, or Essex's invitation to two student actors from Queen's College, Cambridge in 1594/5 to perform a 'device' for the Queen's birthday. To engage in combat before her is to break through the fiction of armchair soldiers sending off knights to imaginary battles in the escapist fantasies of a sedentary profession, and to enter instead into a testing reality. Fortunately on this occasion the student Prince performed creditably and gained a prize. According to Sir Dudley Carleton, however, on a similar occasion in 1616 the Inns of Court men proved better trenchmen than swordsmen.[17] The traditional self-deflation of the Christmas monarch, put to severe test under Elizabeth by so much favour, is less apparent in the courtly exercises mounted by the Inns in the next two reigns. How far the lavish masques were motivated by emulation and how far they were required tribute it is sometimes difficult to say, since the political complexion of the Inns was more varied than the ostensible statements of loyalty taken at their face value might suggest.[18] The central legal issue of absolutism, put to the test under the Stuarts, was whether a monarch makes the law or rules under it. The triumph of common law, espoused by the Inns, contributed in some measure to the latter course and the establishment of constitutional monarchy.

Histriomastix presents a moral tale through a series of abstractions, each of which reigns over the land in turn. Peace encourages the Arts, but under Plenty people turn from them. This leads to the reign of Pride, of Envy, then of War, and finally of Poverty. Only when Peace returns and surrenders her throne to Astraea (Queen Elizabeth) can the sequence be concluded satisfactorily. The theme is illustrated through the fortunes and behaviour of aristocratic and citizen social groups, with occasional reference to the effects upon servants and peasants. The players make one or more appearances in each of *Histriomastix*'s six acts, and their fortunes are affected by each of the reigning abstractions in turn, but otherwise the inception, rise, and eventual banishment of their troupe forms a more or less self-contained story of its own, and is reprinted here in its entirety.

The tone throughout is unremittingly caustic and derogatory. Professional players, it suggests, are recruited from discontented tradesmen on the very periphery of acceptable society – a pedlar and makers of such trivial things as beards and fiddlestrings. Virtual illiterates ('Faith we can read nothing but riddles'), they turn to playing, it is said, because of the opportunities to pretend to be better than they are, to be 'Lords and Kings', when really they are rogues and cowardly knaves and ought to be treated as such. They seek social emulation through the stage, and thereby draw themselves, as Gosson puts it, 'within the compass of a lie'.[19] The anonymous author grounds his indictment of the common player on the time-honoured but dubious contrast between what the player pretends to be and what he is, as though it were somehow proof of dishonesty, rather than a description of all playing:

> *Belch*: I'll play the conquering king, that likes me best.
> *Gutt:* Thou play the cowardly knave – Thou dost but jest.

Again in the scenes with the soldiers, the falseness of playing is underlined by the alleged cowardice of the players in the field (a calumny not borne out, for instance, by their later conduct in the Civil War).[20]

Their names are chosen to emphasize their unsavoury grossness: 'Gutt' refers to the intestines used in his trade, but also means fat or greedy; 'Belch', as well as its obvious meaning, is a slang term for poor beer; 'Clout' means rags or clod; and 'Gulch' means a glutton or drunkard. There are frequent allegations of sexual immorality. Act Four finds them quarrelling because Belch is debauching Gutt's wife, whilst Clout uses homosexual wiles to obtain a present from his admirer, and when charged by the Constable with keeping punks instead of wives, Posthast is made to say with utter frankness, 'Who are not glad to bring such as they can get.'

The general dealings with all and sundry are represented as shiftless and dishonest. They take a baronet's name without permission, and later sing of their fly-by-night quality, of seeking a new master every week, and of not being able to keep the company together. Such groups break up into twos and threes and become (although they of course deny it) 'Coneycatchers that cozen mayors, and have no consort but themselves'. They abandon their performance before the Mayor because Lord Mavortius will give them a better reward. They try to avoid settling their score at the inn, or paying their share of the poor rate, and they offer Master Bougle drink as an alternative to payment. As their fortunes improve they become greedy and arrogant. When at the end they believe themselves to have the option of transportation or returning to their trades, the latter, they admit, is no longer tenable:

Posthast: Fall to work after playing – impossible!

In short, they are cheats and their presentation accords with the traditionalist objections to making a profession out of playing as a way of extorting something for nothing. In contrast to their shiftless, mercenary contrivings, the latter part of Act Two emphasizes the virtues of old-fashioned hospitality. Posthast's song at the end of the act, with its direct references to the Inns, evokes the boozy, companionable mood of mirth-in-hall. The players are part of a larger entertainment that includes neighbourhood morris dancers, and all the participants are well received, and urged to imbibe their 'skins'-full' before they begin. The players themselves have already had half-an-hour's start, and their first duty is non-dramatic, as they sing-in the meat course. Unlike the arrogant Italian guest, the English spectators, in the tradition of 'offerings', are fairly tolerant of the players faults:

Mavortius: Be patient for perhaps the play will mend.

Even when, to please their guest, they have broken off the lamentable performance, Philarchus is still prepared to defend traditional values:

By'r Lady, sir, I like not of this pride.

Give me the ancient hospitality:
They say, 'Tis merry in the hall, when beards wag all.'
The Italian lord is an Ass: the song is a good song.

Most reprehensible of all, in the eyes of the genteel playwright, is the common player's commitment to a popular audience. The sole legitimate criterion of success, the play says, ought to be whether they appeal to the gentry. Beneath them there are only 'thickskinned auditors' and 'the vulgar sense'. Posthast, despite his repeated emphasis on his gentility, is a satire on the player-poet, so castigated in the University Wits' pamphlets and elsewhere. There is a considerable amount of evidence to suggest he is a satire on Munday (although there is a passing reference to that other despised player-poet, in the line: 'when he shakes his furious Speare' [II. 273]).[21] Just as Jonson in his attack on Munday in The Case is Altered charges him with loyalty to 'stale stuff', and the 'old decorum', and to despising the new style of 'humours', so Posthast is praised by his fellows:

> Here's no new luxury or blandishment,
> But plenty of old England's mother words.

They reject the properly written plays of Chrisoganus in favour of their own 'stuff' which will 'serve the multitude'. Within the satirical cast of the piece, they are made to take satisfaction in the inferior homegrown quality of what they produce, bringing forth 'Bayard', the mud-besmattered cart-jade, in place of 'Bucephalus', the classical thoroughbred (IV. 162). We are given 'a flurt', as Gutt would have it, (or 'spurt' as Belch puts it) of a variety of offerings from their feeble repertoire, all satires on the popular genres.[22] Promising a heroic-romantic play on the classical love-story of Troilus and Cressida, they produce a pathetic piece of doggerel somewhere between 'Pyramus and Thisbe' and the execrable puppet play in Bartholomew Fair, with its similar coarse debasement of classical legend. Cressida's beauty, for instance, is compared to 'the crystal stream that runs along the street', which given the use by the Elizabethans of the channel in the street as an open sewer would have been neither sweet-smelling nor clear. In Act Two there are fragments of a maudlin educational morality in preparation, and the snatches of its performance later in the act are crude and foolish. The Lascivious Knight and Lady Nature sounds as though it might be a salacious down-market version of the hybrid morality, perhaps neglecting moral emphasis in favour of the more dubious possibilities inherent in the Lady Vanity-type of material seen above in

Sir Thomas More. In Act Four we find Gutt rehearsing a piece of rampum scrampum afflatus reminiscent of the Ancient Pistol –

> I'll tear their turrets tops,
> I'll beat their Bulwarks down . . .

This is similar presumably to the 'huffing parts' that attract Gulch, in the tradition made popular by imitations of *Tamburlaine*. Posthast's literary endeavours provide a succinct compilation of all that was considered worst in the writing of such as the 'scrivener's boy', the 'artist prentice', and the 'bold ballad monger', and all those Chrisoganus, the scholar-poet, judges to be without the necessary wit or education. The lines do not scan, there are feeble rhymes, sometimes where a rhyme is anticipated it fails to arrive, and the utter paucity of invention is signalled by the mere repetition of words to fill up the line: 'Oh, prodigal child, and child prodigal.'

Although lawyers do not have any particular prominence in the play, and criticism of them simply takes its place alongside other social groups, it could be argued that it is a rather special schema that contains lawyers, and yet omits for instance the clergy, traditionally the first estate. The legal references do not seem particularly numerous, compared with say the Gray's Inn *Masque of Mountebanks* (1618), but the names of the characters suggest at least a detailed knowledge of the Law. As Chambers first pointed out, there are some substantial speeches, particularly near the beginning, 'so full of the technical learning of the schools as to suggest an academic audience', although this is not in itself proof of particular auspices.[23]

Perhaps the best argument for locating *Histriomastix* at the Inns of Court remains the rather general one of the play's concern with government, a regular preoccupation of the Inns' dramatic fare. The play has an epic/moral spread across six reigns and all classes. There is a utopian air of wish-fulfilment in the final solution of banishing the players. Before the cycle is finally broken, Poverty is seen as a cleansing agent: 'Yet is poor Honesty rich Honour's ground': She dignifies her throne with 'deep Divines', scholars and philosophers, and hence part of the reformation of society is the banishment of the players who have contributed to her waste and corruption. There is a youthful idealism too in the Fourth Act realization of what Chrisoganus had threatened in his long speech of Act Three, which echoes the Nashe/Greene attacks on player-poets, with some of the hysterical jaundiced tone of the *Parnassus* plays. Not only, says the play, have the poets successfully blockaded the playhouses:

> the best Poets grown so envious,
> They'll starve rather than we get store of money.

– but, *mirabile dictu*, the playhouse audiences have finally come to be able to distinguish quality and to prefer it to rubbish:

> the gentlemen see into our trade.
> We cannot gull them with brown-paper stuff.

As with the Parnassus plays, it is sometimes difficult to know how far the hysterical tone of the condemnations is meant to be treated sympathetically. The players grudgingly admire Chrisoganus' delivery in his attack upon them:

Gutt: He beats the air the best 'ere I heard.

But they are unperturbed by the content:

Clout: Farewell the Muses, poor Poet adieu,
When we have need't maybe we'll send for you.

The players' replies are amusing and deflating, but are they also meant to be crass, self-satisfied, and presumptuous?

As well as the subject matter, the form is also suggestive of an institutional, and most probably an Inns of Court, entertainment. It requires, or certainly could be made to use, large numbers of performers. It has an almost studiedly primitive lightness of treatment consonant with such a tradition. Although, as has been suggested, there are similarities with other such burlesques, as for instance in the plays of Jonson and Shakespeare, a distinguishing characteristic of this play is the speed with which the jibes are made. Unlike say the full-blown rehearsal and performance of 'Pyramus and Thisbe' in *A Midsummer Night's Dream*, it proceeds with a series of little barbed squibs, before passing on rapidly to something else, prodigal of incident and performer resources. It is a style which allows many aspects and shortcomings of players to be touched on briefly. If a new character is required by the action, he can be summoned immediately, mid-speech, and discarded as soon as he has served his turn. Thus, unmotivated, the Constable arrives on cue, the Scrivener appears as soon as called and is dismissed once his function has been established, and even before he has had details of the contract he is to draw up. Master Bougle and his costumes are treated even more briefly. Within such a convention, the interruption after only eleven lines of the Troilus and Cressida play by the Juventus one suggests no more than an evening's entertainment, if it can be so described, telescoped into a few moments. The result is a series of cameo-like scenes that chart their fortunes incisively and with great rapidity.

HISTRIOMASTIX

Act I

The play begins in the reign of Peace, attended by the arts and sciences. A group of noblemen, led by Mavortius, determine to devote their energies to learning and put themselves under the tutelage of Chrisoganus, a scholar. They go off to study. In a sharp change of mood, a group of tradesmen enter with a drinking song and determine to turn player, because in peace time they are unsuccessful in their trades. They summon a scrivener to draw up a contract. They order costumes from Master Bougle, and decide to take the name of Sir Oliver Owlet's Men.

Enter INCLE, BELCH, GUTT, and POSTHAST singing

The nut-brown ale, the nut-brown ale
Puts down all drink when it is stale.
The toast, the nutmeg, and the ginger 114
Will make a sighing man a singer.
Ale gives a buffet in the head,
But ginger underprops the brain.
When ale would strike a strong man dead, 118
Then nutmeg tempers it again.
The nut-brown ale, the nut-brown ale
Puts down all drink when it is stale.

Incle: This Peace breeds such Plenty, trades serve no turns. 122
Belch: The more fools we to follow them.
Post: Let's make up a company of Players,
    For we can all sing and say,
    And so (with practice) soon may learn to play.
Incle: True, could our action answer your extempore.
Post: I'll teach ye to play true Politicians. 128
Incle: Why, those are the falsest subtle fellows lives.
Belch: I pray, sir, what titles have travelling Players?
Post: Why, 'proper fellows', they play Lords and Kings.
Incle: What parts would best become us, sir, I pray?
Belch: Faith, to play Rogues, 'till we be bound for running away.
Post: Content. Scrivener, ho! (*Enter a SCRIVENER*) 134
    You must tie a knot of Knaves together.

Scriv: Your appellations?
Post: Your names he means: the man's learned.
Belch: I, Belch, the Beard-maker.   138
Gutt; I, Gutt, the Fiddlestring-maker.
Incle: I, Incle, the Pedlar.
Post: I, Master Posthast, the Poet.
Scriv: Your nomenclature?   142
Post: O stately Scrivener! That's 'Where dwell ye?'
Omnes: Townsmen, townsmen all.
Scriv: The *Obligatories Condition*?
Post: Politician Players. (*Exit Scrivener*)   146
Belch: But whose men are we all this while?
Post: Whose but the merry Knight's, Sir Oliver Owlet's?
    There was never a better man to Players.
Gutt: If our 'parel be not point-device, the fat's i' th' fire.   150
Post: What a greasy phrase. This playing will furnish ye.
Belch: What ho, Master Bougle, a word.
Post: Here's half a dozen good fellows.
Clout: Soft, sir, we are but four or five.   154
Post: The liker to thrive.
Bougle: (*enters*): What saucy knaves are these?
Post: He speaks to you players; I am the poet.
Belch: As concerning the King and Clown.   158
Bougle: Will you have rich stuff indeed?
Post: 'Tis not to be dealt on without store of drink.
Bougle: Store of money you would say.
Post: Nay 'tis well said, for drink must clap up the bargain. Let's
    away. (*Exeunt*)   162

The act then returns to its former tone. Two lawyers and two
merchants, idle through Peace, discuss how they shall spend the
afternoon. A play is suggested, but dismissed as 'a deal of prating to so
little purpose'. Instead they go to the 'Academy' and hear a lecture
from Chrisoganus. Escorted by a harvest song, Peace resigns her throne
to her daughter, Plenty.

Act II

Under the hedonistic influence of Plenty, supported by Plutus, Ceres,
and Bacchus, the lords reject Chrisoganus and learning in favour of
pleasure. The Players' second scene finds them already in business,

advertising their play at the Market Cross. Posthast is hard at work on a new play and gives a brief reading from it. Invited to perform to Lord Mavortius, they abandon the performance they have been 'crying' and were due to give before the Mayor.

Enter COUNTRYMEN; *to them* CLERK OF THE MARKET. *He rings a bell, and draws a curtain, whereunder is a market set about a cross.*

Count: Where's this drunkard Clerk to ring the bell?
Clerk: Heigh ho, bottle ale has buttoned my cap.
Corn-buyer: What's a quarter of corn?   72
Seller: Two and sixpence.
Buyer: Tie't up, 'tis mine.

Enter a MERCHANT'S WIFE, *with a* Prentice, *carrying a hand-basket*

Wife: Ha' y' any potatoes?
Seller: Th'abundance will not quit-cost the bringing.
Wife: What's your Cock-sparrows a dozen?   77
Seller: A penny, Mistress.
Wife: There's for a dozen; hold.

Enter GULCH, BELCH, CLOUT, *and* GUTT. *One of them steps on the cross, and cries a play.*

Gulch: **All they that can sing and say,**   80
       Come to the Town-house and see a Play.
       At three o'clock it shall begin,
       The finest play that e're was seen.
       Yet there is one thing more in my mind: 84
       Take heed you leave not your purses behind.

Enter a BALLAD SINGER, *and sings a ballad.*

Ballad: What's your play's name? Masters, whose men are ye?
       How, the sign of the Owl i'th' Ivy bush? Sir Oliver Owlet's?
Gulch: 'Tis a sign ye are not blind, sir.   88
Belch: (shouting): The best that ever trod on stage! *The Lascivious Knight and Lady Nature!*

Enter POSTHAST

Post: Have you cried the play, Masters?
Omnes: Aye, aye, aye. No doubt we shall have good doings, but how proceed you in the new plot of the *Prodigal Child*?   92
Post: Oh, sirs my wit's grown no less plentiful than the time.

There's two sheets done in folio will cost two shillings
in rhyme.

Gutt: Shall we hear a flurt before the audience come?

Post: Aye, that you shall, I swear by the Sun. Sit down, sirs (*He
reads the prologue, they sit to hear it*)

When Author's quill in quivering hand,
His tired arm did take:
His wearied Muse bade him devise,   100
Some fine play for to make.
And now, my Masters, in this bravado,
I can read no more without Canadoe.[24]

Omnes: What ho! Some Canadoe quickly!   104

Enter VINTNER *with a quart of wine*

Post: Enter the Prodigal Child – fill the pot, I would say.

Huffa, huffa, who calls for me?
I play the Prodigal Child in jollity.

Clout: Oh, detestable good!   108

Post: Enter to him Dame Virtue:

My Son, thou art a lost child,
(This is passion, note you the passion?)
And hath many poor men of their goods beguiled:
Oh, prodigal child, and child prodigal . . .   113
Read the rest, sirs, I cannot read for tears.
Fill me the pot, I prithee, fellow Gulch.

Gutt: Faith, we can read nothing but riddles.   116

Post: My masters, what tire wears your lady on hear .head?

Belch: Four squirrel's tails tied in a true loves knot.

Post: Oh, amiable good, 'tis excellent!

Clout: But how shall we do for a Prologue for lords?

Post: I'll do it extempore.   121

Belch: Oh, might we hear a spurt if need require?

Post: **Why – Lords, we are here to show you what we are.**
     Lords, we are here although our clothes be bare.
     Instead of flowers in season,
     Ye shall gather rhyme and reason.   125
I never pleased myself better. It comes off with such suavity.

Gulch: Well, fellows, I never heard happier stuff;
Here's no new luxury or blandishment,
But plenty of old England's mothers words.

Clout: Is't not pity this fellow's not employed in matters of State?   130

But where's the Epilogue must beg the plaudite?

Post: Why man, **The glass is run, our play is done,**
Hence Time doth call, we thank you all.

Gulch: Aye, but how if they do not clap their hands?

Post: No matter, so they thump us not.   135
Come, come, we poets have the kindest wretches to our
Ingles.[25]

Belch: Why, what's an Ingle, man?

Post: One whose hands are hard as battledores with clapping at
baldness.

Clout: Then we shall have rare ingling at the *Prodigal Child*.   140

Gulch: Aye, an't be played upon a good night. Let's give it out for
Friday.

Post: Content.

Enter STEWARD

Stew: My masters, my Lord Mavortius is disposed to hear what
you can do.   144

Belch: What! fellows, shall we refuse the Town-play?

Post: Why, his reward is worth the Mayor and all the town.

Omnes: We'll make him merry, i' faith. We'll be there. (*Exeunt*)

This scene is followed by a brief exchange between the middle-class
characters, who have turned from learning to field sports.

Before the players' second entry in this act, a picture of generous
good-living is drawn, emphasizing the traditional virtues of hospitality.
The players are part of a larger entertainment, which also includes
morris dancers. Posthast attempts to beg a horse. The fly-by-night
quality of the troupe is picked up again in the song with which they
begin their performance, celebrating the tendency amongst such
touring groups to split. The players perform a brief scene from a
Troilus and Cressida play, and an unrelated one with Morality
characters. It is, as the Italian lord observes, 'base-brown-paper-stuff',
and Mavortius, despite his initial indulgence, terminates the performance because it is so bad. Posthast, apparently unperturbed, offers to
finish the evening with an impromptu song on a theme to be supplied
by the guests. They wryly choose drink and poets.

Enter USHER OF THE HALL, *and* CLERK OF THE KITCHEN

Usher: Master Clerk of the Kitchen, faith, what's your
daily expense?   172

Clerk: Two beeves; a score of Muttons;
　Hogsheads of Wine and Beer, a dozen a day.
Usher: Never was [an] Age more plentiful.
Clerk: Usher, it is my Lord's pleasure all comers be
　bounteously entertained.　　　　　　　　　　　　　　177
Usher: Aye, but it's my Lady's pleasure?
Clerk: What else? She scornes to wear cloth breeches, man.

Enter PORTER

Porter: A Morris-dance of neighbours crave admittance.
Clerk: Porter, let them in, man. (*Enter* Morris-dancers)　181
　Butler, make them drink their skins full.
Omnes: God bless the founder.
Clerk: Porter, are these Players come?　　　　　　　　184
Porter: Half an hour ago, sir.
Clerk: Bid them come in and sing. The meat's going up.
Usher: Gentlemen and yeomen, attend upon the Sewer.

Enter PLAYERS, *with them* POSTHAST, THE POET

Usher: Sir Oliver Owlet's men, welcome. By God's will,
　It is my Lord's pleasure it should be so.
Post: Sir, we have caroused like Kings:　　　　　　　190
　For here is plenty of all things.
Usher: Look about you, Masters; be uncovered.

Enter Sewer *with service, in side livery coats*

Players: **Brave lads, come forth and chant it, and chant it,**
　　　　for now 'tis supper time.
　　See how the dishes flaunt it, and flaunt it,
　　　　with meat to make up rhyme.　　　　　　196
　　Pray for his honour truly, and truly,
　　　　in all he undertakes.
　　He serves the poor most duly,
　　　　and duly, as all the country speaks.
Post: God bless my Lord Mavortius, and his merry men all.
　To make his honour merry we sing in the hall.
Usher: My masters, for that we are not only [for causes]　203
　Come new to the house; but also [for causes]
　I marvel where you will lodge.
Post: We hope [for causes] in the house, though drink
　be in our heads,

164

Because of Plenty we carouse for beef, and beer,
   and beds.   207
Usher: Said like honest men. What plays have you?
Belch: Here's a Gentleman scholar writes for us.
  I pray, Master Posthast, declare for our credits.
Post: For mine own part, though this summer season,
  I am desperate of a horse.
Usher: 'Tis well. But what plays have you?   213
Post: A gentleman's a gentleman that hath a clean shirt on, with
  some learning. And so have I.
Usher: One of you answer the names of your plays.
Post: *Mothern Gurton's needle* [a tragedy]   217
  The Devil and Dives [a comedy]
  A russet coat and a knaves cap [an Infernal]
  A proud heart and a beggar's purse [a pastoral]
  The widow's apron strings [a nocturnal].
Usher: I promise ye, pretty names.
  I pray, what ye want in anything, to take it out in drink,
  And so go, make ye ready, masters. (*Exeunt players*)   224

Enter LORD MAVORTIUS, PHILARCHUS, *with* LANDULPHO (*An Italian*
  Lord) *and other* Nobles *and* Gentles *to see the play*

Mavor: My lords, your entertainment is but base,
  Coarser your cates, but welcome with the best.
  Fellows, come cushions; place fair ladies here.
  Signor Landulpho, pray be merry, sir. . .   228

Usher: Room, my Masters, take your places.   244
  Hold up your torches for dropping there!
Mavor: Ushers, are the Players ready? Bid them begin.

Enter PLAYERS *and sing*

Some up and some down, there's players in the Town:
You wot well who they be.   248
The sum doth arise to three companies:
One, two, three, four, make we.
Besides we that travel, with pumps full of gravel,
Made all of such running leather,
That once in a week, new masters we seek,   252
And never can hold together.

Enter PROLOGUE

Prologue: **Phillida was a fair maid – I know one fairer than she.**
  Troilus was a true lover – I know one truer than he.
  And Cressida, that dainty dame, whose beauty fair
    and sweet,
  Was clear as is the crystal stream that runs along the street. 258
  How Troyl he, that noble knight, was drunk in love,
    and bade goodnight.
  So bending leg likewise, do you not us despise.
Land: Most ugly lines and base-brown-paper-stuff,
  Thus to abuse our heavenly poesy,
  That sacred offspring from the brain of Jove,
  Thus to be mangled with prophane absurds, 264
  Strangled and choked with lawless bastard words.
Mavor: I see (my Lord) this homespun country stuff
  Brings little liking to your curious ear.
  Be patient, for perhaps the play will mend.

Enter TROILUS *and* CRESSIDA

Troil: **Come Cressida, my Cresset light,** 269
  Thy face doth shine both day and night
  Behold thy garter blue
  Thy knight his valiant elbow wears,
  That when he shakes his furious Speare
  The foe in shivering fearful sort
  May lay him down in death to snort.
Cress: **Oh knight, with valour in thy face,** 276
  Here, take my screen, wear it for grace,
  Within thy helmet put the same,
  Therewith to make thine enemies lame.
Land: Lame stuff indeed, the like was never heard.

Enter a roaring DEVIL *with a* VICE *on his back,* Iniquity *in one hand, and*
Juventus *in the other*

Vice: **Passion of me, sir, puff, puff, how I sweat, sir;**
  The dust out of your coat I intend for to beat, sir.
Juven: **I am the prodigal child, I, that I am,**
  Who says I am not, I say he is to blame. 284
Iniqu: **And I likewise am Iniquity,**
  Beloved of many, alas, for pity.
Devil: **Ho! ho! ho! these babes of mine are all;**
  The Vice, Iniquity, and child Prodigal. 288

Land: Fie! what unworthy foolish foppery
　Presents such buzzardly simplicity.

Mavor: No more, no more, unless 'twere better,
　And for the rest ye shall be our debtor.　　　　　　292

Post: My Lords, of your accords,
　Some better pleasure for to bring,
　If you a theme affords,
　You shall know it,　　　　　　296
　That I, Posthast, the Poet,
　Extempore can sing.

Land: I pray, my Lord, let's ha' it; the Play is so good
　That this must needs be excellent.

Mavor: Content (my Lord) pray give a theme.　　　　　　301

Land: Your Poets and your Pots
　Are knit in true-Love knots.

Post: Give your scholar degrees, and your lawyer his fees,
　And some dice for Sir Petronel Flash:[26]
　Give your Courtier grace, and your Knight a new case,　　　　　　305
　And empty their purses of cash.
　Give your play-gull a stool, and my lady her fool,
　And her Usher potatoes and marrow;
　But your poet were he dead, set a pot to his head
　And he rises as pert as a sparrow.
　O delicate wine, with thy power so divine　　　　　　312
　Full of ravishing sweet inspiration,
　Yet a verse may run clear that is tapped out of beer,
　Especially in the vacation.
　But when the term comes, that with trumpets and drums
　Our playhouses ring in confusion,
　Then Bacchus me murder – but rhyme we no further –
　Some sack now, upon the conclusion!　　　　　　319

Mavor: Give them forty pence. Let them go. (*Exeunt Players*)
　How likes Landulpho this extempore song?

Land: I blush in your behalves at this base trash.
　In honour of our Italy we sport
　As if a synod of the holy Gods
　Came to triumph within our Theatres. . .　　　　　　325

Phil: . . . By'r Lady, sir, I like not of this pride.　　　　　　341
　Give me the ancient hospitality:

They say, 'Tis merry in the hall, when beards wag all.'
The Italian Lord is an Ass: the song is a good song.

Act III

Pride arrives as the new ruler, casting a mist in which the lords vanish.
She persuades the lawyers and merchants to break the sumptuary laws
and dress above their station. Mavortius sacks retainers who have given
good military service in order to afford selfish entertainment. A group
of ladies are seen tyrannizing tradesmen to supply their vanity.

Under the new reign, badness at first seems no impediment to the
players' success. Chrisoganus, rejected in Act II by the nobles, has
turned to writing plays. The players refuse his demand for ten pounds
per play, confident that Posthast's 'stuff' will satisfy their undiscrimi-
nating popular audience. Likewise when Mavortius' steward, sent to
summon them, is unwilling to offer more than four pounds for a
performance, they refuse him too.

Enter CHRISOGANUS, POSTHAST, GULCH, CLOUT, GUTT, *and* BELCH

Belch: Chrisoganus, faith, what's the lowest price?	
Chris: You know as well as I; ten pound a play.	180
Gulch: Our company's hard of hearing of that side.	
Chris: And will not this book pass? Alas for pride!	
I hope to see you starve and storm for books,	
And in the dearth of rich invention,	184
When sweet smooth lines are held for precious,	
Then will you fawn and crouch to Poesy.[27]	
Clout: Not while goosequillian Posthast hold his pen.	
Gutt: Will not our own stuff serve the multitude?	
Chris: Write on, cry on, yawl to the common sort	
Of thickskinned auditors: such rotten stuffs,	
More fit to fill the paunch of Esquiline,	
Than feed the hearings of judical ears.	192
Ye shades triumph, while foggy Ignorance	
Clouds bright Apollo's beauty! Time will clear	
The misty dullness of Spectators' Eyes:	
Then woeful hisses to your fopperies!	196
O age, when every Scrivener's boy shall dip	
Profaning quills into Thessalia's spring;	
When every artist prentice that hath read	
The pleasant pantry of conceits shall dare	
To write as confident as Hercules;	201

When every Ballad-monger boldly writes
And windy froth of bottle-ale doth fill
Their purest organ of invention –   204
Yet all applauded and puffed up with pride,
Swell in conceit, and load the Stage with stuff
Raked from the rotten embers of stale jests:
Which basest lines best please the vulgar sense,
Make truest rapture lose pre-eminence.
Belch: The fellow doth talk like one that can talk.
Gutt: Is this the well-learned man Chrisoganus?
  He beats the air the best that e're I heard.
Chris: Ye scraps of wit, base Echoes to our voice,
  Take heed ye stumble not with stalking high,
  Though fortune reels with strong prosperity. (*Exit*)   215
Clout: Farewell the Muses, poor Poet, adieu;
  When we have need, 't maybe we'll send for you.

Enter STEWARD

Stew: My Lord hath sent request to see a play.
Post: Your Lord? What, shall our pains be soundly
    recompensed
  With open hand of honour's frank reward?   220
Stew: Ye shall have four fair Angels, gentlemen.
Clout: Fair Ladies, mean you? We have four i' th' play.
Stew: Nay [my good friends], I mean in fair pure gold.
Gulch: Fie 'tis too much! Too long e're it be told.
Stew: 'Mas, these are single jests indeed,   225
  But I will double it once, ye shall have eight.
Post: But are you sure that none will want the weight
  To weight down our expense in sumptuous Clothes?
Belch: Well, pleasure's pride shall mount to higher rate;
  Ten pound a play will scarce maintain our state.
Stew: Fat Plenty brings in Pride and Idleness:
  The world doth turn a Maze in giddy round:
  This time doth raise what other times confound.
Post: O sir, your moral lines were better spent
  In matters of more worthy consequent.   235
Gulch: Well, whilst occasion helps to climb aloft,
  We'll mount Promotions highest battlement.
Stew: And break your necks, I hope. Climb not too fast;
  A heady course confusion ends at last.

Post: Preach to the poor. Look, Steward, to your compt,
  Direct your household, teach not us to mount.
Stew: Farewell, ye proud [I hope they hear me not]
  Proud Statute Rogues.[28] (*Exit, they follow*)   243

The aspiring lawyers, merchants, and their wives attend Lord
Mavortius' banquet. Denied his play, Mavortius orders a masque from
the courtiers, which fails to please. They fall to drinking and then
quarrelling. As they fall asleep, Envy appears and 'breathes amongst
them'.

Act IV

Full of Envy, the nobles wake to quarrel and threaten war, from which
the lawyers and merchants hope to profit. Chrisoganus has his second
long speech bewailing the fate of true scholars and attacking those who
benefit from Ignorance. This is immediately followed by the entry of
the players. The scene finds them in rehearsal. Mirroring the general
theme of the act, their unity is now threatened by envy and dissension.
Posthast is late, and will be fined accordingly. One player begs a sword
hilt from his admirer by 'ingling', and two others quarrel because one is
debauching the other's wife. Their future does not bode well, as the
'gentlemen see into our trade'; their poor dramatic fare has finally been
seen for what it is. Even the players themselves are now disenchanted
with Posthast's scripts.

    Enter BELCH, GULCH, *and* CLOUT *with an* INGLE

Gulch: Jack of the Clock-house, where's Master Posthast?
Belch: In my book for Slow-pace; twelve-pence on's pate for
  staying so late.   160
Gutt: Prologue begin (*Rehearse &c.*)
  Gentlemen, in this envious age we bring Bayard
  for Bucephalus. If mired, bogged, draw him forth
  with your favours. So, promising that we
  never mean to perform, our Prologue peaceth.   164
Gulch: 'Peaceth'? – what peaking pageanter penned that?
Belch: Who but Master Posthast.
Gutt: It is as dangerous to read his name at a playdoor
  As a printed bill on a plague door.   168
Clout: You wear the handsomest compassed hilt I have seen.
Ingle: Doth this fashion like my friend so well?

Clout: So well I mean to wear it for your sake.

Ingle: I can deny thee nothing, if I would (*Giving it to him*)   172

Gulch: Fie, how this Ingling troubles our rehearsal.
   Say on.

Gutt: Fellow Belch, you have found a haunt at my house:
   You must belch and breath your spirits somewhere else.   175

Belch: Jealous of me with your seat for Master John?

Gutt: When the door's shut, the sign's in Capricorne.

Clout: Then you might heave the latch up with your horn.

Gulch: This Cuckoldly coil hinders our rehearsal.[29]

Gutt: **I'll tear their turret tops,**   180
    I'll beat their Bulwarks down,
    I'll rend such Rascals from their rags,
    And whip them out of town.

Belch: **Patience (my Lord) your fury strays too far.**

Gulch: Stay, sirs, rehearse no farther than you are,
   For here be huffing parts in this new book.

Gutt: Have I e'er a good humour in my part?   187

Gulch: Thou hast ne'er a good one out of thy part.[30]

Belch: I'll play the conquering King, that likes me best.

Gutt: Thou play the cowardly knave; thou dost but jest.

Clout: Half a share, half a shirt. A Comedian,
   A whole share, or turn Chameleon.   192

Gulch: Well sirs, the gentlemen see into our trade.
   We cannot gull them with brown-paper stuff,
   And the best Poets grown so envious,
   They'll starve rather than we get store of money.

Gutt: Since dearth of Poets lets not players live by wit,
   To spite them let's to wars, and learn to use a spit.

Clout: O excellent ill – a spit to roast a rhyme!

Gutt: 'Twill serve you to remember dinnertime.   200

Belch: That's true, 'tis time, let's away. (*Exeunt*)

Act V

War reigns, with its attendants Ambition, Fury, Horror, and Ruin. The ravages of war show up the players' chosen trade as effete and superfluous. Much is made of the contrast between the realities of manliness required in times of stress and the falseness of playing.

   The players are pressed into the army, despite their claims to be a 'bone fide' troupe, 'a full company', and Posthast is unsuccessful in his attempt to bribe himself out.

Enter BELCH *setting up the bills. Enter to him a* CAPTAIN

Capt: Sirrah, what set you up there?
Belch: Text-bills for Plays.
Capt: What! Plays in time of Wars? Hold, sirrah!
 There's a new plot. (*Puts money into his hand*) 64
Belch: How many mean you shall come in for this?
Capt: Player, 'tis press money.
Belch: Press money, press money! Alas, sir, press me?
 I am no fit Actor for th'action. 68
Capt: Text-bills must now be turned to Iron bills. (*Exit*)
Belch: And please you, let them be dagger pies.

Enter AN OFFICER, POSTHAST, GULCH, GUTT, *and* CLOUT

Officer: Sir Oliver's men? The last Players took the Town's
 reward like honest men. 72
Gulch: Those were a couple of Coneycatchers that
 Cozen mayors, and have no consort but themselves.
 But we are a full company, and our credit
 With our Master known. 76
Officer: Meanwhile there's press-money for your reward.
Clout: No [I thank your worship]. We mean not to trouble your
 town at this time.
Officer: Well, Masters, you that are master-sharers
 Must provide you upon your own purses. 81
Gutt: Alas, sir, we Players are privileged:
 'Tis our Audience must fight in the field for us,
 And we upon the stage for them. 84
Post: Sir, as concerning half a score angels,
 Or such a matter, for a man in my place –
Officer: Those days are out of date.
Belch: Then more's the pity, sir. (*Exit Officer*)
Gulch: Well, I have a Brewer to my Ingle:
 He'll furnish me with a horse great enough.
Post: Faith, I'll e'en paste all my ballads together,
 And make a coat to hold out pistol-proof. 92
Clout: I marvel what use I should make of my Ingle,
 The hobby-horse seller.

Gutt: Faith, make him sell a whole troop of horse
   To buy thee one.   96
Belch: Sirs, if these soldiers light upon our playing 'parel,
   They'll strut it in the field, and flaunt it out.
Post: Well, sirs, I have no stomach to these wars.
Gutt: Faith, I've a better stomach to my breakfast.
Clout: A shrewd morning's work for Players!
Omnes: Let's be gone. (*Exeunt*)   102

The war is treated in a series of short scenes. The lords vaunt their
anger, and spurn Chrisoganus as he attempts to reconcile them. A mob
of common people threaten anarchy and indiscriminate violence. The
lawyers and merchants sit in their shops and quake. There is a brief
scene of the pressed players on the march, the soldiers brutally pointing
the difference between their stage bravado and their actual cowardice,
as their fine apparel is taken from them.

Enter a CAPTAIN *with* Soldiers: *The soldiers having most of the players'*
   apparel: and bringing out the players amongst them

Soldier: Come on, Players. Now we are the Sharers
   And you the hired men. Nay, you must take patience.
   'Slid, how do you march?   240
   Sirrah, is this you would rend and tear the Cat
   Upon a Stage, and now march like a drowned rat?
   Look up and play the Tamburlaine, you rogue you. (*Exeunt*)

The Act ends with a dumb-show in which all the factions fight, with a
choric conclusion from Chrisoganus.

Act VI

Poverty now reigns, and the lords, brought low, submit themselves to
Chrisoganus and his instruction. The middle classes realize their folly,
and the poor starve.

In the players' final scene their light-fingered, self-indulgent progress is brought to a halt. In the sterner domain of Poverty, they are
brought, literally, to account. Posthast attempts to joke himself out of a
tavern bill, which includes a sharers' dinner. The hostess appeals for
help to the Constable, and the players are made to pawn their only
valuables, the stage costumes. After this, they are faced with either
paying their share of the poor relief, or being shipped off to an
unknown destination as undesirables, and it is this latter course which is

finally followed. The Constable echoes Posthast's earlier judgement, that, after playing, they are spoilt for honest work or returning to their trades. They are herded off to the ship, and the last that is heard of them is a wry joke: 'It's an ill wind blows a man thus clean out of ballading' (Posthast).

Enter POSTHAST *with his hostess*

Host: Post me no posting. Pay me the shot.   187
    You live by wit; but we must live by money.
Post: Goody Sharpe, be not so short.
    I'll pay you, when I give you money.
Host: When you give me money! Go to, I'll bear no longer.
Post: What, and be under fifty?   192

Enter CONSTABLE

Host: Master Constable, ho! These Players will not pay their shot.
Post: Faith, sir, War hath so pinched us we must pawn.
Const: Alas, poor Players! Hostess, what comes it to?
Host: The Sharers' dinner six pence apiece. The hirelings [   ]
    pence.   196
Post: What! Sixpence an Egg, and two and two at an Egg.
Host: Faith, Famine affords no more.
Post: Fellows, bring out the hamper. Choose somewhat out o' th'
    Stock. (*Enter the* PLAYERS)
    What will you have this cloak to pawn? What think you it's
    worth?   200
Host: Some four groats.
Omnes: The pox is in this age! Here's a brave world, fellows.
Post: You may see what it is to laugh at the Audience.
Host: Well, it shall serve for a pawn. (*Exit*)   204
Const: Soft, sirs, I must talk with you for tax-money
    To relieve the poor; not a penny paid yet.
Post: Sir, (at few words) we shared but fifteen pence last week.
Const: But 'tis well known that each maintains his Punk,
    And taverns it with drunken suppers still.
Omnes: Alas, they are our wives.   210
Const: Ye are not all married.
Post: Who are not glad to bring such as they can get?
Belch: Before I'll give such a precedent, I'll leave playing.
Gulch: Faith, and I too. I'll rather fall to work.

Post: Fall to work after playing? Impossible!

Const: Sirs, will you hear the truth?   216

Gutt: Sir, you may choose.

Const: But you must all choose whether you'll be shipped, and set ashore no man knows where, as the Romans did, or play for the maintenance of the poor, and yourselves kept like honest men.

Omnes: We choose neither.

Post: Saving your sad tale, will you take a pot or two?

Const: The dearth of Malt denies it.

Clout: It's a hard world if the Constable despise it.

Gulch: Must we be shipped in earnest, or do you make us sheep in jest?

Const: *Ecce signum.*

Post: Constable, do you know what you do?

Const: Aye, banish idle fellows out o' th' land.   228

Belch: Why, Constable, do you know what you see?

Const: Aye, I see a Madge howlet, and she sees not me.

Post: Know you our credit with Sir Oliver?

Const: True, but your boasting hath cracked it.   232

Gutt: Faith, I must fall to making fiddle strings again.

Belch: And I to curl horse tails to make fools beards.

Post: I'll boldly fall to balItading again.

Const: Sirs, those provisos will not serve the turn.

What ho, Sailors, ship away these players   237

Enter Sailors

Sailor: The wind blows fair, and we are ready, sir.

Const: No matter where it blows. Away with them.

Post: It's an ill wind blows a man thus clean out of balItading.

(*Exeunt*)

In a brief concluding scene, Peace returns and Poverty vanishes. There appear to be alternative endings. In one, Peace resigns her throne to Astraea (Queen Elizabeth). In the second, probably older, version, the other reigning abstractions submit their sceptres to Peace, 'sitting in Majesty'.

175

Glossary to *Histriomastix*

I 140 *inkle*: narrow tape sold by pedlars.
   150 *'parel*: costumes.
        point device: just so.
   152 *bougle*: bead.
II 76 The glut makes them not worth transporting.
  117 *tire*: headdress.
  131 *plaudite*: applause.
  138 *Battledore*: bat or beetle used in laundry and tennis.
  173 *beeves*: plural of beef.
  187 *Sewer*: waiter.
  192 *be uncovered*: remove hats.
  226 *cates*: food.
  248 *wot*: know.
  260 *bending leg*: bow.
  269 *cresset light*: beacon; metal vessel containing grease or oil in
        which a wick burned; hence sexual innuendo.
  277 *screen*: veil.
  283 *juventus*: youth.
  290 *buzzardly*: stupid.
  307 *gull*: credulous person.
  319 *sack*: Spanish white wine or sherry.
III 189 *yawl*: howl.
  221 *Angels*: ten-shillings coins.
  224 *told*: counted.
  227 *want*: lack.
  240 *compt*: accounts.
IV 159 *Jack of the Clock-house*: mechanical figure which strikes a bell.
  160 *pate*: head.
  162 *Bayard*: carthorse.
  163 *Bucephalus*: heroic steed.
  164 *peaceth*: pieceth(?).
  165 *peaking*: mean-spirited, skulking.
  169 *compassed*: shaped or designed.
  176 Gutt suspects Belch of debauching his wife.
  177 *Capricorne*: zodiacal sign of He-goat.
  179 *coil*: uproar.
  186 *huffing*: swaggering.
  198 *spit*: slang term for sword, giving rise to a pun.
V   62 *Text-bills*: play posters.

68 *action*: pun on acting and warfare.

69 *Iron bills*: pole-weapon and farm implement.

70 *dagger pies*: named after celebrated inn in Holborn (see *The Devil is an Ass*, I.i. 64–6).

72 Referring to their earlier failure to perform before the Mayor.

73 *Coneycatchers*; cheats.

74 *cozen*: cheat.

97 *light upon*: find.

101 *shrewd*: rotten, bad, harmful, unfortunate.

VI 187 The post of the alehouse where the tally of credit was kept.

187 *shot*: reckoning. The hostess is demanding he settle the bill.

196 There seems to be a number missing here.

208 *punk*: harlot, mistress.

223 *dearth*: high price, scarcity.

225 *shipped*: the pun is weakened by modernizing the text; the original is 'shept'.

226 Ecce signum: 'behold the sign'. Presumably the Constable gestures to the ship.

230 *Madge howlet*: the Barn Owl; associations include its strange cry and supposed cowardice.

236 *provisos*: conditions, or here, alternatives.

10

Apprentice drama and
The Hog Hath Lost his Pearl

The Hog Hath Lost his Pearl, written by Robert Tailor and printed in 1614 as being 'Divers times Publicly acted, by certain London Prentices', is an indication of yet another seam of amateur drama, which, with its confrontation between the impecunious scholar poet, Haddit, and the unscrupulous player, Master Changecoat, continues the practice of common player disparagement well beyond the period represented by the other plays in this study.

Haddit's threat to invoke an apprentice riot is, in a manner, a self-reference by the performers. On the holiday of Shrove Tuesday there was something of a tradition in which gangs of apprentices went on the rampage and attacked brothels, theatres, and other resorts of the leisured class in the suburbs. A pitched battle was fought at the Cockpit with the players in 1617, and much damage done.[1] It is probably to this recurrent event that Edmund Gayton refers in 1654, when he recalls the reactions of an audience at the refusal of the players to humour their fickle tastes, when, as well as throwing missiles such as tiles and laths: 'as there were mechanics of all professions, who fell everyone to his trade', they 'dissolved a house in an instant, and made a ruin of a stately fabric'.[2]

However, as well as being associated with the Shrovetide disturbances, there seems to have been a significant minority of apprentices with more genteel pretensions than their rowdy fellows, sufficient to attract a Common Council order in 1582 to curb those apprentices who 'did affect to go in costly Apparel and wear Weapons, and frequent Schools of Dancing, Fencing and Music', and apprentices are regularly mentioned as theatre-goers.[3] Although for gentry to enter city trade was still considered by many as demeaning, it had its proponents. John Stowe (*Survey*, 1598) thought it preferable for impoverished younger sons to go into trade rather than to stay in the country and turn to 'naughty Courses for a Subsistence'.[4] The traditional definition of a

gentleman as one who does not work with his hands, and the sixteenth-
century reality that gentry did go into trade, are nicely accommodated
in Thomas Fuller's formulation in *Holy State*: 'Gentry therefore may be
suspended perchance, and asleep during the apprenticeship, but it
awakens afterwards.'[5] Apprenticeship as an entry to the powerful and
profitable guild system could be more nominal than actual, with a
system of patrimony and with the cost of entry to some apprenticeships
well out of the reach of the ordinary family.[6]

The satirical comedy *Eastward Ho!* (1605), performed at Blackfriars
by the Children of Her Majesty's Revels, exploits the conflicting views
on gentility and apprenticeship. The virtuous genteel apprentice,
Golding, espouses the view that:

> Whate'er some vainer youth may term disgrace,
> The gain of honest pains is never base;
> From trade, from arts, from valour, honour springs;
> These three are the founts of gentry, yea of kings.
>
> (I.i. 143–6)

His fellow-apprentice, Quicksilver, on the other hand, is just such a
'vainer youth', and has what he regards as the ambitions of a
gentleman. He wishes to be idle, drunken, and quarrelsome, and his
reformation as a kind of tongue-in-cheek prodigal is one of the themes
of the play.

It is presumably apprentices with genteel aspirations who hired the
private theatre of Whitefriars in order to perform a play which is
highly critical of the popular theatre, with its 'idle-headed', garlic-
loving audiences and shifty, ignorant players. An account of the first
performance of *The Hog Hath Lost his Pearl* is contained in a letter from
Sir Henry Wotton to Sir Edmund Bacon, dated 1612/13:[7]

> On Sunday last at night, and no longer, some sixteen Apprentices
> (of what sort you shall guess by the rest of the Story), having
> secretly learnt a new play without book, entitled, *The Hog Hath
> Lost his Pearl*; took up the White Friars for their Theatre: and
> having invited thither (as it should seem) rather their Mistresses
> than their Masters, who were all to enter *per buletini* for a note of
> distinction from ordinary Comedians. Towards the end of the
> Play, the sheriffs (who by chance had heard of it) came in (as they
> say) and carried some six or seven of them to perform the last Act
> at Bridewell;[8] the rest are fled. Now it is strange to hear how
> sharp-witted the City is, for they will needs have Sir John

Swinnerton, the Lord Mayor, be meant by the Hog, and the late Lord Treasurer by the Pearl.

This was not, however, the end of the affair. The title-page of the 1614 edition indicates that this was not the only performance, but that it was 'Divers times Publicly acted', and the Prologue, which seems to have been written for subsequent performances and with an eye to publication, hints at the events described above as part of the difficulties of getting the play performed, and notes in triumph that they have been overcome:

> Our long-time-rumoured Hog, so often crossed
> By unexpected accidents, and tossed
> From one house to another: still deceiving
> Many men's expectations, and bequeathing
> To some lost labour: is at length got loose. . .
> Hath a knight's licence, and may range at pleasure. . .

It would seem that Swinnerton's allegations that the play contained personal satire had not been upheld, but that the first performance was interrupted because the apprentices lacked a licence from the Master of Revels. In the Prologue they deny 'Grunting at state affairs, or invecting/ Much at our city vices'. Certainly the play itself, as printed, does not offer much obvious opportunity for personal application, and the Hog/Swine references in the Prologue, it is hinted, have been added subsequently to annoy their enemies. In the previous year Swinnerton had lost a case against the customs officers in which he had alleged corruption, 'but upon ripping up the matter they went away acquitted'. The Lord Mayor had to be content with being 'commended for his good meaning to the king's service'.[9] It may be that he was known to be rash.

More to Swinnerton's taste would have been *Hector of Germany* by Wentworth Smith, a patriotic play performed in the same year, 1613, to celebrate the visit of Frederick V, Count Palatine of the Rhine, and dedicated to the Lord Mayor. Its title-page announces that 'it hath been publicly Acted at the Red-Bull, and at the Curtain, by a Company of Young men of this City'. Given the coincidence of date, it is highly likely that both plays were performed under the same auspices and, when 'publicly acted', at the same theatres.[10] 1613 seems to have been a period of unprecedented activity amongst the apprentices.

Whatever ambitions seethed in the apprentice breast, as burlesqued in *The Knight of the Burning Pestle* (c. 1607/8), whose apprentice grocer,

Ralph, can 'fetch you up a couraging part' in the grocer's garret, and numbers amongst his repertoire Hotspur, Mucedorus, and, inevitably, Hieronimo, nevertheless the Prologue to *Hector* modestly distinguishes its performers as amateurs, and relies upon traditional educational values for their defence:

> If you should ask us, being men of Trade,
> Wherefore the Players faculty we invade?
> Our answer is, No ambition to compare
> With any, in that quality held rare;
> Nor with a thought for any grace you give
> To our weak action, by their course to live:
> But as in Camps, and Nurseries of Art,
> Learning and valour have assumed a part,
> In a Cothurnal Scene their wits to try,
> Such is our purpose in this History.

The play has two more or less independent plots. The romantic plot concerns Albert, who, in a moment of weakness, whilst waiting to aid his friend Carracus in an elopement, lies with the intended bride. She, in an age of voluminous clothes, poor lighting, and pervasive theatrical convention, mistakes him for her lover. The revelation of the crime sends all three wandering in various states of hypertension and disguise, fortuitously in the same part of the forest, to eventual repentance and reconciliation.

In the plot from which the play takes its title, the usurer Hog is tricked of his money and of Rebecca, his daughter, by Haddit, aided by his relation, Lightfoot, who stage a bedroom vision for Hog, in which the Player has a small part. Explaining their plan to Rebecca, she asks,

> *Rebecca*: . . . but how many have you made instruments herein?
> *Haddit*: Faith, none but my cousin Lightfoot and a player.
> *Rebecca*: But may you trust the player?
> *Haddit*: Oh, exceeding well. We'll give him a speech he understands not . . .

The main scene which contains the Player, included here, is largely extraneous to the rest of the play, except in so far as it helps to substantiate the character of Haddit. As one of gentle birth now reduced through prodigality to the base trade of writing for players, and at its lowest and seamiest end, the penning of jigs, he is suitably witty and arrogant in his dealings with the shifty Master Change-coat.

The jig was an afterpiece to the main play in which the chief Clown and his associates, probably in two pairs, performed a brief bawdy tale, mainly through dancing and singing. C.R. Baskervill identifies and prints only four extant stage jigs within the period that match this description, but they give some indication of the content and treatment of a dramatic phenomenon that is subject to frequent reference.[11] *Rowland's Godson* tells of a trick by which a mistress safeguards her adulterous relationship with a servant. In *Singing Simpkin*, a wife hoodwinks a bully and saves her clownish lover, but is outwitted by her elderly husband. In *Atwell's Jig*, the bed-trick is used to cure an errant husband. *The Black Man* is a low farce in which the clownish hero joins forces with the tinker of the title to retrieve his sweetheart from two raffish gentlemen. All are in verse, and use a variety of tunes; *Atwell's Jig*, for instance, identifies each new tune in the text. Only the first of the group lacks a moral ending, but the subject matter generally is adulterous, and *Singing Simpkin* in particular has more than its fair share of smutty innuendo.

David Wiles traces the origins of the jig in seasonal rituals which survived the Reformation by attaching themselves to the morris tradition, forming a burlesque wooing dance between a fool and a man/woman and occupying 'an ambiguous terrain somewhere between patriotism and subversion'.[12] The term 'jig' was also used of a lively dance and has active sexual connotations. In the theatre it encouraged audience participation and provided an opportunity for bawdy extemporization. The form gained the particular displeasure of the Middlesex magistrates in 1612, who claimed that 'cut-purses and other lewd and ill-disposed persons in great multitudes do resort thither at the end of every play many times causing tumults and outrages'.[13] The playhouses particularly notorious for their jigs were the 'northern circuit', The Curtain, The Red Bull, and The Fortune.

The tone adopted by Haddit towards writing for the players is in the general tradition developed by the University Wits. It echoes in particular the semi-autobiographical style of *Greene's Groats-worth of Wit* (1592), in which Roberto describes his descent through being lodged by the player 'in a house of retail . . . conversing with bad company . . . falling from one vice to another', becoming 'an Arch-playmaking-poet', learning 'the legerdemains of nips, foysters, coney-catchers, crossbiters, lifts, high Lawyers, and all the rabble of that unclean generation of vipers'.

The scene between Haddit and Master Change-coat reveals the seedy dog-eat-dog nature of writing for the stage. Part of its interest lies in the contest for supremacy between the two men, as each alternates two modes of address towards the other. Master Change-coat, as his name suggests, does so as a matter of course, having no integrity or self-respect. His opening gambit is to fawn and pretend an elaborate deference to Haddit, as gentleman and poet, but, suspecting that his intended purchase might be too literary for his customers, he asks to read it, and perhaps, as Haddit suggests, to memorize it. He is at his sharpest as they approach negotiating a price, when he treats Haddit more frankly as an aspiring and down-at-heel seller of a doubtful commodity in a buyer's market, presuming to correct Haddit's metre and syntax. His first offer is low, and when challenged, he doubles it, but 'more', he says, 'for your love than otherwise'.

Haddit too sees it as a contest for cash, and if successful as easy money; 'there be money to be gotten by foolery', and he alternates his manner to get the best price. He begins and ends with an elaborate pretence of being a dedicated scholar, which entitles him to express the superiority he feels, and coincides with his own poverty, but from time to time he ameliorates this with sufficient real or assumed enthusiasm to maintain the Player's interest, as towards the end when describing his latest and probably fictitious project. Either in earnest or in jest, Haddit suggests that even jigs can bear their allegories. The four ropes of onions, he says, represent four kinds of 'livers', punning on moral behaviour and the normal accompaniment to onions. Similarly, 'hangers-on' refers both to parasites and to the stalks themselves. The grandiloquence of his concluding promise, to disclose 'so rare a hidden and obscure mystery' at 'some convenient time', which alerts the Player to the possibility that it is too highly written, perhaps indicates his intentions are satiric. He is rueful perhaps that only such crass stuff is sufficiently popular to be bought, and that he has no outlet for more sophisticated literature.

Suspicious that the Player will not at first raise his price because he has already memorized sufficient to set the playhouse poet on, and that even his offer of 'besides much drink at free cost, if the play be liked' is no more than a pre-rehearsed technique for cheating authors, Haddit threatens him with an apprentice riot. At this threat, the Player doubles his offer, and they are reconciled, the Player indicating he will pay more in future if he is given first option on Haddit's work. The episode closes with a series of comments on the triviality of the exercise.

THE HOG HATH LOST HIS PEARL

From Act I Scene I

Enter ATLAS, a serving man to Haddit, 'a youthful gallant'

Atlas: Here's the player would speak with you.
Haddit: About the jig I promised him. My pen and ink! (*Atlas brings them.*) I prithee, let him in. There may be some cash rhymed out of him.

Enter CHANGE-COAT, a player

Player: The Muses assist you, sir. What, at your study so   5
  early?
Haddit: Oh, chiefly now, sir; for *Aurora Musis amica*.
Player: Indeed, I understand not Latin, sir.
Haddit: You must then pardon me, good Master Change-coat;
  for I protest unto you, it is so much my often converse that,   10
  if there be none but women in my company, yet cannot I
  forbear it.
Player: That shows your more learning, sir. But, I pray you, is
  that small matter done I entreated for?
Haddit: A small matter! You'll find it worth *Meg of Westminster*,   15
  although it be but a bare jig.[14]
Player: O Lord, sir, I would it had but half the taste of
  garlic.[15]
Haddit: Garlic stinks to this. If it prove that you have not more
  whores than e'er garlic had, say I am a boaster of my own   20
  works, disgrace me on the open stage, and bob me off with
  ne'er a penny.
Player: O Lord, sir, far be it from us to debar any worthy
  writer of his merit. But I pray you, sir, what is the title
  you bestow upon it?   25
Haddit: Marry, that which is full as forcible as garlic. The
  name of it is, *Who buys my four ropes of hard onions?* – by
  which four ropes is meant, four several kinds of livers; by
  the onions, hangers-on – as at some convenient time I will
  more particularly inform you in so rare a hidden and   30
  obscure mystery.
Player: I pray, let me see the beginning of it. I hope you have
  made no dark sentence in't; for I'll assure you, our audience

184

commonly are very simple, idle-headed people, and if they
should hear what they understand not, they would quite   35
forsake our house.

Haddit: Oh, ne'er fear it; for what I have writ is both witty to
the wise, and pleasing to the ignorant: for you shall have
those laugh at it far more heartily that understand it not,
than those that do.   40

Player: Methinks the end of this stave is a foot too long.

Haddit: Oh no, sing it but in tune, and I dare warrant you.

Player: Why, hear ye. (*He sings*)
And you that delight in trulls and minions,
Come buy my four ropes of hard St Thomas onions.   45
Look ye there; **Sir Thomas** might very well have been left
out. Besides, **hard** should have come next to **onions**.

Haddit: Fie! no; the dismembering of a rhyme to bring in
reason shows the more efficacy in the writer.

Player: Well, as you please. I pray you, sir, what will   50
the gratuity be? I would content you as near hand
as I could.

Haddit (*aside*): So I believe! (*Aloud*) Why, Master Change-coat, I
do not suppose we shall differ many pounds. Pray, make
you offer. If you give me too much, I will, most doctor-of-   55
physic-like restore.

Player: You say well. Look you, sir, (*Gives him two coins*) there's
a brace of angels, besides much drink of free-cost, if it be
liked.

Haddit: How, Master Change-coat! 'A brace of angels,   60
besides much drink of free-cost, if it be liked!'
I fear you have learned it by heart. If you have
powdered up my plot in your sconce, you may home,
sir, and instruct your poet over a pot of ale the
whole method on't. But if you do so juggle, look   65
to't. Shrove Tuesday is at hand, and I have some
acquaintance with bricklayers and plasterers.

Player: Nay, I pray, sir, be not angry; for as I am a true stage-
trotter, I mean honestly. And look ye, more for your love
than otherwise, I give you a brace more.   70

Haddit: Well, good words do much. I cannot now be angry
with you, but see henceforth you do like him that would
please a new-married wife: show you most at first, lest
some other come between you and your desires. For I

protest, had you not suddenly shown your good nature, 75
another should have had it, though it had been for nothing.

Player: Troth, I am sorry I gave you such cause of impatiency;
but you shall see hereafter, if your invention take, I will not
stand off for a brace more or less, desiring I may see your
works before another. 80

Haddit: Nay, before all others; and shortly expect a notable
piece of matter, such a jig whose tune, with the natural
whistle of a carman, shall be more ravishing to the ears of
shopkeepers than a whole consort of barbers at midnight.

Player: I am your man for't. I pray you, command all the 85
kindness belongs to my function, – as a box for your friend
at a new play – although I procure the hate of all my
company.

Haddit: No, I'll pay for it rather. That may breed a mutiny in
your whole house. 90

Player: I care not. I ha' played a king's part any time these ten
years; and if I cannot command such a matter, 'twere poor,
'faith.

Haddit: Well, Master Change-coat, you shall now leave me, for
I'll to my study. The morning hours are precious, and my 95
Muse meditates most upon an empty stomach.

Player: I pray, sir, when this new invention is produced, let me
not be forgotten.

Haddit: I'll sooner forget to be a jig-maker. (*Exit player*) So,
here's four angels I little dreamt of. Nay, and there be 100
money to be gotten by foolery, I hope fortune will not see
me want. . .

Glossary to *The Hog Hath Lost His Pearl*

7 *Aurora Musis amica*: The Goddess of the Dawn is the friend of the
Muse.

28 *several*: different.

33 *dark sentence*: obscure meaning.

44 *trulls and minions*: female and male prostitutes.

51 *as near hand*: as closely.

63 *sconce*: head.

69 *trotter*: one who seeks out business.

78 *if your invention take*: if what you have written is successful.

79 *brace of angels*: £1.

83 *carman*: carter, carrier.

11

Heywood, Massinger, and the defence of playing

Any sustained defence of the popular stage was slow in coming. In 1577 'T.W.' had begun the attack with his sermon, and Northbrooke published his condemnation. Stockwood gave his sermon in 1578, Gosson published his first attack in 1579, and 'Anglo-phile Eutheo' followed in 1580. When Gosson published his *Plays Confuted in Five Actions* in 1582, although Stubbes and Babington were not to publish until the following year, the bulk of this particular broadside had already been fired, with, according to Gosson, scarcely a reply.

Apart from a rather slight extant pamphlet by Lodge (c. 1579) thought to be the suppressed *Honest Excuses* mentioned by Gosson, we have only the latter's uncorroborated and hostile evidence of the players' activities in their defence up to this time. They scoured both universities, he says, to find a champion, but without success. They revived two of his own plays, and performed the allegorical *Play of Plays and Pastimes*, in defence of playing, paraphrasing Horace and urging moderation upon the character of Zeal, and they published a work called *Strange News out of Affrick* ridiculing Gosson. Ten years passed before two defences appeared in print, in 1592, one brief but pithy in 'The Complaint of Sloth', part of Nashe's *Pierce Penniless His Supplication to the Devil*, and the more diffuse, less telling, *Kind-Hart's Dream* by the publisher Henry Chettle. Both however glance at the issue, rather than treat it head-on, and it was not until Thomas Heywood, the actor and playwright, published his *Apology for Actors* in 1612 (probably composed about 1607), and after the bulk of the derogatory representations had been performed, that the 'quality' can be said to have found a sustained and sincere champion, even if much of his material is derivative, and some of it jejune.

Massinger's play, *The Roman Actor* (1626), is much indebted to Heywood's prose work, and, like it, constitutes a summary of all the arguments in defence so far raised, and more or less irrespective of quality. A later work in dialogue, *The Muses' Looking-Glass* by Thomas Randolph (1630), purports to be a defence of the stage, but its restricted purpose, 'To show/How Comedy presents each single vice/ Ridiculous' cannot be said to add much that is new. It was not until the delayed publication of Sir Richard Baker's *Theatrum Redivivum* that an adequate reply was made to Prynne's monumental statement of the opposition case in *Histrio-mastix* (1633), but not before the opposition had effectively closed the theatres for eighteen years. When they re-opened, and Baker's work was published (in 1662), it was in a very different theatrical context, beyond the scope of the present study.

The most obvious reason why there was no sustained rebuttal of the preachers' condemnation during the earlier part of the period must have been that it was not thought necessary. The players continued to perform, to be popular, and to make money. Much of the hysteria evident in the attacks comes from frustration at their failure to influence the players' noble and royal patrons. Confirmation that the players continued to perform in spite of civic and clerical opposition, simply because they were popular, comes from an unexpected quarter in an Anglo-Italian phrasebook by John Florio, 1578, which contains the dialogue:

> *Gent*: Where shall we go?
> *Lady*: To a play at the Bull, or else to some other place.
> *Gent*: Do Comedies like you well?
> *Lady*; Yea sir, on holy days.
> *Gent*: They please me also well, but the preachers will not allow them.
> *Lady*: Wherefore, know you it?
> *Gent*: They say, they are not good.
> *Lady*: And wherefore are they used?
> *Gent*: Because every man delights in them.
>
> (John Florio, *First Fruits*, 1578)

If 'every man delights in them', what have the players to fear?

It is probable that the players' most successful reply to their critics was indirectly through their own medium, the plays, which abound with straight-laced and spoil-sport puritans such as Jonson's Zeal-of-the-Land Busy in *Bartholomew Fair*, with his abortive attack on the puppets, and the pastors of Amsterdam in *The Alchemist*. Randolph's two choric observers in *The Muses' Looking-Glass* are Blackfriars' Puritans, selling haberdashery and feathers respectively. It was an irony that nonconformity should flourish, shielded from City jurisdiction, in the same liberties as the players, and it helped to give substance to the charge of hypocrisy. 'Know', says Beeston, 'I am none of these/ That in-ly love what out-ly I detest'.[1] Middleton has a strong line in sectarian hypocrites, as in Penitent Brothel in *A Mad World, My Masters*, the promoters and gossips in *A Chaste Maid in Cheapside*, and Oliver the Puritan in *The Mayor of Queenborough* who is tormented by being made to watch a play. Even Shakespeare invokes the Puritan spirit in Malvolio, a 'time-pleaser', and gives lines to Sir Toby Belch that sum up much popular feeling:

> Dost though think, because thou art virtuous, there shall be no more cakes and ale?
>
> *(Twelfth Night* II.iii. 108–10)

Given the hostility towards players discussed above, it is not perhaps surprising that the playwrights in general offer little defence on behalf of those who bring their creations to life. Where playing is defended, it is often of amateur drama, sharply distinguished both by those who refer back the older tradition of spontaneous mirth in the hall, and by those who justify its use in education. Nothing says more for the differences between our conception of the creative interaction of playwright and performers today, and the much more rigid demarcation then, than the distinction so frequently made between defending plays on the one hand and attacking players on the other. Sidney, in his *Apology for Poetry* (composed c. 1583), can dismiss the players: 'Our Comedians think there is no delight without laughter' and talk of the play-texts being 'pitifully abused' in performance; and yet his description of the value of tragedy seems strongly conceived in terms of the effects of performance, 'stirring the affects of admiration and commiseration.' He and his contemporaries avoided inconsistency by asserting the superiority of classical acting from which the present had declined:

> The action of the theatre, though modern states esteem it but ludicrous, unless it be satirical and biting, was carefully watched by the ancients, that it might improve mankind in virtue.

The relative standing of contemporary acting and the eventual claims for its superiority over any other, foreign or classical, becomes a major issue in later pro-theatre writing, and was much more feasible to sustain after another thirty years of artistic consolidation and experiment in the permanent playhouses.

Thus the early defence of plays in the Elizabethan period is very largely divorced from playing and concentrates principally on the traditional justification of didacticism from Donatus, expressed later by Heywood as showing 'what in our lives and manners is to be followed, what to be avoided'. The formulation by Robert Wilmot in his *Tancred and Gismunda* (1591) 'the exaltation of virtue and the suppression of vice', is echoed in literally dozens of prologues in the period.[2] Although the didactic formula was more appropriate to some of the earlier moral interludes, the later and better plays, after say 1580, continue to invoke it as their *raison d'être*. Very frequently the evident disparity between the actual content and its didactic justification was met by reference to Horace's dictum that comedy aims to mingle delight with profit. Poets, says Sidney, 'delight to move men to take that goodness in hand, which without delight they would fly as from a stranger'. Finally, a few playwrights, like Marston in his Prologue to *The Dutch Courtesan* (1604), dispensed with claiming profit altogether:

> And if our pen in this seem over-slight,
> We strive not to instruct but to delight.

The vast majority however continued to assert the didactic function of drama, often in terms of a moral 'mirror', a formulation attributed by Donatus to Cicero, that 'a Comedy is the imitation of life, the glass of custom, and the image of truth'.[3]

Heywood in his *Apology for Actors* (published 1612) accepts the didactic function of drama with enthusiasm, and even improves upon it, with his stress on the immediate power of representation not merely to modify people's views but to make them confess murders and even to frighten away Spanish invaders. Heywood's main theme however is the joint claims to dignity for the acting profession given by its antiquity and its continued association with monarchs. Much of his argument is anticipated in the brief, racy, but incisive defence of playing by Nashe in his *Pierce Penniless His Supplication to the Devil* (1592) the product of a sharper mind but a more wayward sympathy. Nashe it is who gives Heywood his cue, not merely for the association of playing and the monarchy, which was commonplace, but more particularly for the justification of playing as the inculcator of honour, the nobleman's virtue. In a famous passage he identifies his enemy in class terms as bourgeois, acquisitive of both money and power, and materialist; against which are set, by implication, the positive virtues of the courtier and gentleman:

All arts to them are vanity; and, if you tell them what a glorious thing it is to have Henry V represented on the stage, leading the French king prisoner, and forcing both him and the Dauphin to swear fealty, 'Aye, but' (they will say) 'what do we get by it?'

The lines are thus drawn by Nashe between Court and city.

Playwrights before Heywood, for instance Edwards, Lodge, and Chapman, had derived justification from the authority of the ancients, but Heywood sets out to write an entire history to show a continuous tradition, and from the players' point of view. His treatment of the post-Roman period is necessarily scanty, and of the Greeks to a large measure fictitious. However it is the glory of the Romans themselves which is his principal justification, and he collects an impressive amount of information about them, especially their theatres. He never satisfactorily matches the grandness of their building with the poverty of their material, nor with the unsavouriness of imperial life. He shows a, by our standards, disturbing lack of interest in the ethics of their use of theatre, for instance as a pretext for the rape of the Sabine Women, or in distinguishing theatrical from other sort of events, as when in the middle of an enthusiastic account of Roman theatre buildings he recounts that eighteen elephants were killed in a single entertainment.

One of Heywood's main themes is the royal esteem in which actors were held. He traces a continuous line of noble patrons from Hercules, through Achilles, Theseus, Alexander, to Julius Caesar, and jumps rather speedily to modern times. Whilst noting contemporary foreign patrons, he asserts, 'But in no country are they in that eminence that ours are: so our most royal and ever-renowned sovereign, hath licensed us in London.'[4] So much did the Roman Emperors honour the theatre, says Heywood, that in the Golden Age they regularly took the stage themselves, from Julius Caesar, who acted many parts in his own theatre, through a sinister roll of fame including Caligula, Nero, Vitellius, Domitian, and Commodus.

Heywood in his roundabout way is asserting a political reality of great significance to the fortunes of the professional player. Elizabeth, in having, as Heywood describes it, 'favourably tolerated' the players under the pretext of their rehearsing, performing, and keeping in readiness 'for her majesty's solace', protected them from the preachers and city authorities and allowed them to consolidate and develop their craft. In consequence, by the turn of the century they had achieved heights perhaps never equalled. On the other hand, the more active involvement of her successors, James and Charles, had a stronger influence on both content and attitude, which, together with the polarization of audiences and the related development of indoor playhouses by the adults from 1609, led to an ultimately deleterious identification of theatre with the monarchy in its gradual isolation from a substantial body of the nation. Players are not rogues, says the author of *An Excellent Actor* (1615) in reply to Cocke's hostile 'character', for 'Rogues are not to be employed as main ornaments to his Majesty's Revels'.

The early Jacobean defenders of the stage show signs of moving towards an aesthetic of stage representation which goes beyond the simple didactic debate. Heywood regards what he calls 'Action' as being superior both to Oratory, 'a kind of speaking picture', and to Painting, 'a dumb oratory', in that it combines the virtues of both. Positive examples 'can no way be so exquisitely demonstrated, nor so lively portrayed, as by action'. Randolph in *The Muses' Looking Glass* (1630) follows Heywood in pointing out that 'Men are not won by th'ears so well as eyes'. Francis Bacon in *The Advancement of Learning* (1603) had observed the especial capacity of theatre to stimulate the imagination and sympathies of the individual through participating in a group experience – 'the minds of men in company are more open to affections and impressions than when alone.' Randolph also makes explicit what is implicit in Heywood's book, that 'action' operates by affecting the emotions of the onlooker, in having Comedy say to Tragedy, 'You move with fear; I work as much with shame – / A thing more powerful in a generous breast.'

It is perhaps unfortunate that Heywood's observations on the power of 'action', once again following Nashe, are so often illustrated in terms of the stage representation of martial virtue. Not only does this inevitably restrict modern sympathy, but it also exposed his flank, since it confirms by implication the argument of his adversaries. If Vice is more ubiquitously represented than Virtue, then, by this argument, more harm is done by the theatre than good.

To analyse Heywood's arguments one by one is to do less than justice to the overall context. Heywood is modest and reasonable in his general tone; he says in his opening poem to the City Actors, 'I rather covet reconcilement than opposition'. From time to time, beneath the grand assertions of antiquity, royal favour, didacticism, reformation, and inspiration, all no doubt necessary to ward off the continued attack on the stage, there can be perceived in Heywood's work a gentler theory of 'moderate recreation'. Heywood and his friends in a sense anticipate our modern stress on the audience constructing its own meaning. As John Taylor puts it in his commendatory poem:

> For plays are good or bad, as they are used,
> And best inventions often are abused.

The first act of *The Roman Actor* (1626) has as its chief object a set-piece defence of playing in the by now familiar terms of a moral mirror in which, by their representation, vice is castigated and virtue encouraged. It may well have been occasioned in part by *A Short Treatise Against Stage-Plays* presented to Parliament in the previous year, 1625. Massinger served a long apprenticeship with Fletcher as his collaborator, and *The Roman Actor* is his first play after the latter's death, and the beginning of a long association with the King's Men as their chief dramatist. It had an elaborate publication, and is perhaps his own clarion call in which he asserts the value of his endeavours.[5]

Massinger follows Heywood in representing Roman civilization and drama as superior to anything that followed, and in suggesting, by tracing a close parallel between Imperial Rome and their own time, an unbroken tradition of playing; which gives dignity to the present, and makes intrinsic the special relationship between player and ruler. In doing so Massinger faces as best he can the problem that the ruler in his story is a vicious and corrupt tyrant.

From the end of the eighteenth century, the defence of the stage from Act One was performed as a separate afterpiece under the title *The Drama's Vindication*. More recently however, as part of the rehabilitation of Massinger as a political thinker, Martin Butler has questioned the sincerity of Massinger's protestations.[6] He points to the three inner plays, each of which, he says, undercuts the case for the positive value of plays. Certainly the first of these, in Act Two, might seem at first sight to offer some support for this view. When the freedman Parthenius is unsuccessful in persuading his father, Philargus, to give up his miserly ways, Paris the player suggests they show him a play, *The Cure of Avarice*:

> *Paris:* . . . Your father, looking on a covetous man
> Presented on the stage, as in a mirror,
> May see his own deformity, and loathe it.

(II.i. 97–9)

This proposal has of course strong echoes of *Hamlet* and Heywood's *Apology*. In Philargus' case, however, although he has identified at every point with the stage miser, *The Cure of Avarice* fails to reform him. It is left to Caesar to cure his avarice by execution, which provides a motive for the freedman's subsequent revenge. However there is no implication in the dialogue that the miser's lack of repentence constitutes a defeat for the stage; it seems rather that it is an indication of his foolish obduracy. Covetousness, traditionally the final and most powerful sin, is shown to be able to withstand even the power of the stage. Nor can the theme be said to be borne out in the subsequent inner plays, which, as the next chapter suggests, can be seen rather as exploring than condemning the ambiguity of the stage.

Were Massinger as Butler suggests, 'deliberately writing the most anti-theatrical play of the English Renaissance', it is difficult to believe that the King's Men would have tolerated such a strategy from their newly-appointed house dramatist. And if that were the case, why is the Defence so long? And why is it universally praised by those present on-stage? Surely if Massinger's intention had been to question it, then he would have done so at the same time, by means of an ironic commentator, or some disparity of action and sentiment? Not only has such an interpretation escaped all commentators and theatre-goers since Massinger's time, but his close friends and contemporaries who wrote the dedicatory poems for its publication likewise accepted the play as a noble defence of the stage. Thomas Jay, for instance:

> And when thy Paris pleads in the defence
> Of Actors, every grace, and excellence
> Of Argument for that subject, are by Thee
> Contracted in a sweet Epitome.

Thus if it was Massinger's original purpose to undercut the claims made by Paris for the positive value of playing, then he singularly failed to communicate his intentions.

THE ROMAN ACTOR

From Act I Scene III

Aret: Cite Paris, the tragedian.
Paris: Here.
Aret: Stand forth.
  In thee, as being the chief of thy profession,
  I do accuse the quality of treason,
  As libellers against the stage and Caesar.
Paris: Mere accusations are not proofs, my lord: 35
  In what are we delinquents?
Aret: You are they

That search into the secrets of the time,
And, under feigned names, on the stage present
Actions not to be touched at; and traduce
Persons of rank and quality of both sexes,   40
And, with satirical and bitter jests,
Make even the senators ridiculous
To the plebians.
Paris: If I free not myself,
  (And in myself the rest of my profession)
  From these false imputations, and prove   45
  That they make that a libel, which the poet
  Writ for a comedy, so acted too,
  It is but justice that we undergo
  The heaviest censure.
Aret: Are you on the stage,
  You talk so boldly?
Paris: The whole world being one,   50
  This place is not exempted: and I am
  So confident in the justice of our cause,
  That I could wish Caesar (in whose great name
  All kings are comprehended) sat as judge,
  To hear our plea, and then determined of us.   55
  If to express a man sold to his lusts,
  Wasting the treasure of his time and fortunes
  In wanton dalliance, and to what sad end
  A wretch that's so given over does arrive at;
  Deterring careless youth, by his example,   60
  From such licentious courses; laying open
  The snares of bawds, and the consuming arts
  Of prodigal strumpets, can deserve reproof;
  Why are not all your golden principles,
  Writ down by grave philosophers to instruct us   65
  To choose fair virtue for our guide, not pleasure,
  Condemned unto the fire?
Sura: There's spirit in this.
Paris: Or if desire of honour was the base
  On which the building of the Roman Empire
  Was raised up to this height; if to inflame   70
  The noble youth with an ambitious heat
  T'endure the frosts of danger, nay of death,
  To be thought worthy the triumphal wreath

By glorious undertakings, may deserve
Reward or favour from the commonwealth,   75
Actors may put in for as large a share
As all the sects of the philosophers;
They with cold precepts (perhaps seldom read)
Deliver what an honourable thing
The active virtue is. But does that fire   80
The blood, or swell the veins with emulation
To be both good and great, equal to that
which is presented on our theatres?
Let a good actor in a lofty scene,
Show Alcides honoured in the sweat   85
Of his twelve labours; or a bold Camillus
Forbidding Rome to be redeemed with gold
From the insulting Gauls; or Scipio
After his victories imposing tribute
On conquered Carthage: if done to the life,   90
As if they saw their dangers, and their glories,
And did partake with them in their rewards,
All that have any spark of Roman in them,
The slothful arts laid by, contend to be
Like those they see presented.

Rust: He has put   95
  The consuls to their whisper.

Paris: But 'tis urged
  That we corrupt youth, and traduce superiors.
  When do we bring a vice upon the stage,
  That does go off unpunished? Do we teach,
  By the success of wicked undertakings,   100
  Others to tread in their forbidden steps?
  We show no arts of Lydian pandarism,
  Corinthian poisons, Persian flatteries,
  But mulcted so in the conclusion that
  Even those spectators that were so inclined   105
  Go home changed men. And, for traducing such
  That are above us, publishing to the world
  Their secret crimes, we are as innocent
  As such as are born dumb. When we present
  An heir that does conspire against the life   110
  Of his dear parent, numb'ring every hour
  He lives as tedious to him, if there be

Among the auditors one whose conscience tells him
He is of the same mould – we cannot help it.
Or, bringing on the stage a loose adult'ress, 115
That does maintain the riotous expense
Of him that feeds her greedy lust, yet suffers
The lawful pledges of a former bed
To starve the while for hunger; if a matron,
However great in fortune, birth or titles, 120
Guilty of such a foul unnatural sin,
Cry out, 'Tis writ by me' – we cannot help it.
Or, when a covetous man's expressed, whose wealth
Arithmetic cannot number, and whose lordships
A falcon in one day cannot fly over, 125
Yet he so sordid in his mind, so griping
As not to afford himself the necessaries
To maintain life; if a patrician,
(Though honoured with a consulship) find himself
Touched to the quick in this – we cannot help it. 130
Or, when we show a judge that is corrupt,
And will give up his sentence as he favours
The person, not the cause; saving the guilty,
If of his faction, and as oft condemning
The innocent out of particular spleen; 135
If any in this reverend assembly,
Nay e'en yourself my lord, that are the image
Of absent Caesar, feel something in your bosom,
That puts you in remembrance of things past,
Or things intended – 'tis not in us to help it. 140
I have said, my lord, and now, as you find cause,
Or censure us, or free us with applause.

Lat: Well pleaded, on my life! I never saw him
Act an orator's part before.

12

Ambiguities

A Player . . . His profession has in it a kind of contradiction, for none is more disliked, and yet none more applauded . . .

(John Earle, *Microcosmography*, 1628)

Some measure of ambivalence towards theatre both by those who watch and whose who are engaged in it is inherent in the activity. At one moment it can encapsulate what is significant about experience; within the individual psyche, in personal relationships, or concerning man and the universe; at the next that sympathy and identification, so laboriously constructed and so intimately engaged, is betrayed, deliberately by farce, or unintentionally by incompetence, and we are reminded that theatre is only pretence, only 'playing'. The expression of mixed feelings towards theatre goes back at least as far as St Augustine, who, within a general condemnation in his *Confessions*, reviews his own early enthusiasm for the art.[1]

Consciousness of the ambiguities inherent in playing perhaps in part accounts for the paucity of its defence in the Elizabethan period, and for a certain degree of disingenuousness that creeps in from time to time. It is all very well to justify a play in terms of being a 'mirror', but it all depends on what that mirror is made to reflect. 'A Play's a brief Epitome of time', John Taylor claims in his contribution to the host of dedicatory poems appended to Heywood's *Apology*:

> Where man may see his virtue or his crime
> Laid open, either to their vices' shame,
> Or to their virtues' memorable fame.

This evenhandedness however is not reflected in the examples he gives. Starting off with 'stabbing, drabbing, dicing, drinking, swearing', he spends the remaining twenty-six lines of the poem on examples of vice,

198

without a single positive example of virtue; a catalogue that runs remarkably parallel with that of his opponents. His principal, Heywood, is careful to draw attention to the power of the stage to inculcate (mainly martial) virtue by example, but his emphasis can hardly be said to be reflected in the general run of plays. As Stephen Gosson points out in *Plays Confuted in Five Actions* (1582), 'When the soul of your plays is either mere trifles, or Italian bawdry, or wooing of gentlewomen, what are we taught?' Gosson's question was hard to answer. The defenders could insist that vice was always shown to be punished, as Thomas Nashe, in *Pierce Penniless* (1592) 'for no play they have, encourageth any man to tumult or rebellion, but lays before such the halter and the gallows: or praiseth or approveth pride, lust, whoredom, prodigality, or drunkenness, but beats them down utterly', or they could argue as Chettle does, that 'vice cannot be reproved, except it be discovered'. Discovery through representation, however, may incite an emulation which no amount of moral commentary will dissuade. Both critics of the theatre and its defenders are agreed upon its power to influence by example; the defenders perhaps foolishly accepting the battleground laid out by their adversaries. Critics of playing point to the deleterious effects of promulgating vice, and the defenders to the positive power of representing virtue. On a simple head-count, much more vice is represented than virtue, no doubt because, like ourselves, they found it more interesting. Elizabethan dramatists claimed much the same moral purpose as do our modern Sunday newspapers: to cleanse society by a fearless and sustained exposure of vice; and perhaps, to answer their puritan detractors, were under more pressure to do so. We however are entitled to give them similar credence, especially when their exposure becomes more than usually sustained. The amount of time some playwrights spend with fallen women, and others in the corrupt courts of their version of Renaissance Italy, ought to alert us to the special characteristics of their moral censure.

Modern criticism has on the whole given the opponents of theatre an unsympathetic treatment, perhaps because of their often hysterical bigotry, their prolixity, and the sense they sometimes give of their own conscious, but unacknowledged, vulnerability to the theatre's siren call; as for instance William Prynne, in *Histrio-Mastix* (1633), quoting Cyprian:

He who is most womanish and best resembles the female sex, gives best content. The more criminous, the more applauded is he; and by how much more obscene he is, the more skilful is he accounted. What cannot he persuade who is such a one?

Undoubtedly the theatres were places of sexual stimulation. A great many plays feature either prostitutes or loose women of other classes, such as Julia in *The Duchess of Malfi* (V.ii), attempting to hold up the object of her desire with a pistol until he should satisfy her. The stage directions often require explicit display of lustfulness, such as that for Domitia in *The Roman Actor*, (IV. ii) '*courting Paris wantonly*'. Shakespeare gives cues for stage action in Ulysses' lines on Cressida:

> There's language in her eye, her cheek, her lip,
> Nay, her foot speaks. Her wanton spirits look out
> At every joint and motive of her body.
>
> (*Troilus and Cressida* IV.v. 55–7)

Even Juliet, that paragon of maidenly modesty, is shown aching for love and for the night: 'though I am sold,/Not yet enjoy'd' (*Romeo and Juliet* III.ii) and in her love reluctant on the morn to let her lover go. She is gentle and romantic, but determined in her sexuality.

On occasion these representations must have been doubly immodest because played by male performers, who could be more shamelessly explicit, and who were themselves, through what Prynne described as 'meretricious, effeminate lust-provoking fashions of . . . apparel', the means of further sexual stimulation. The Victorian view, retailed in our own century by Granville-Barker, that the boys simpered modestly on-stage, and that the sexual attractiveness of the characters was not discussed until they had left, not only ignores a lot of explicit stage directions and the performance implications of the texts, but also much of the potential of the performance situation, as contemporary drag acts show, albeit they may seem to us in dubious taste.[2] Whether on the other hand the result of the representation of blatant sexuality was a mass exodus from the theatres into the bawdy houses, which Prynne elaborately shows to be 'Cosin-germanes' and so paired as to be conveniently adjacent, or even as Stubbes claims, after the 'wanton gestures . . . bawdy speeches' and 'kissing and bussing' of transvestite performance, 'everyone brings another homeward . . . and in their secret conclaves (covertly) they play the Sodomites, or worse', is perhaps another matter.[3] Whatever else it was, all-male performance was an accepted convention of long standing, and such charges are not borne out by the general cultural estimation in which plays were then held. Jonson, although himself a maligner of the players as bawds in *The*

Poetaster, in *The Devil is an Ass* (II.viii) has his characters recount, apparently without opprobrium, the transvestite capers of one Dick Robinson, a contemporary boy-player, entertaining a gossips' feast dressed as a lawyer's wife, which is presented as a relatively innocent activity. In either event, if is difficult to believe that, tricked out in the erotic fashions of the Court in which gender is so elaborately differentiated, performers who possessed the necessary skills and beauty, did not on occasion, like the self-liberated androgynous heroines they were so often called upon to play, exploit their ambiguity to upset and challenge, as well as charm, the expectations of their beholders:[4]

> *Rosalind*: If I were a woman, I would kiss as many as had beards
> that pleas'd me . . .
>
> (Epilogue to *As You Like It*)

'What cannot he persuade who is such a one?' What no authority inside or outside the playhouse could do was to control or legislate for whatever happened in the individual moment onstage. It is the spontaneous potential of the theatre-form that the more faithfully an experience is simulated, the more potent it is to be betrayed.

Opponents of the stage can be seen to have addressed themselves to the central ambiguities, or as they would regard them, the dangers, of the mimetic process itself; of how an actor creates a role; albeit their conclusions were narrow and often alarmist. Does acting consist of pretending to be someone; that is to say a conscious amalgam of observation, practice, and technique? Or is it 'becoming' someone, with the emphasis on identification and intuition, and with skill in so far as it is identified operating at a largely automatic level? Although the discussion in the first chapter of this study suggested a model for Elizabethan theatre in which technique appeared to be firmly in control, anyone who has acted will recognize that 'pretending' and 'becoming' can never to be completely separated out, and that the creative process has many analogies with the *hungan* of Voodoo worship who opens himself as a vessel for the descending god, or for that matter with the shoplifter's defence of, 'Something came over me; I wasn't quite myself'.[5] The deliberate confusion by the renegade playwrights Gosson and 'Anglo-phile Eutheo', of real evil and its stage imitation, until both activities are made to carry the same moral opprobrium, may not be very helpful, but John Rainolds, that implacable critic of all mimetic representation, popular or educational, is less easily gainsaid when he suggests that the repeated impersonation of vice cannot but impair the character of those who perform:

> chiefly when earnest and much meditation of sundry days and weeks, by often repetition and representation of the parts, shall as it were engrave the things in their mind with a pen of iron, or with a point of a diamond.
>
> (John Rainolds, *Th'overthrow of Stage Playes*, 1599)

It is after all the principle of the Stuart Masque as practised by Jonson that the characters of the performers shall be affected by enactment:

> As music them in form shall put,
> So will they keep their measures true . . .
> Till all become one harmony,
> Of honour and of courtesy . . .
>
> (Ben Jonson, *Love Restored*, 1612)

Jonson goes on to assert that once they have learned these virtues, the effect will be permanent.

The plays themselves not infrequently echo their opponents' confusion of part and person. Kemp, for instance, in the adults' own representation of him in *The Travels of Three English Brothers*, bases his mockery of Harlequin on the latter's failure to see the impropriety of allowing his wife to act, which makes him in reality the cuckold he pretends to be on-stage.

Massinger's *The Roman Actor* explores in its player scenes some of the ambiguities inherent in the process of watching stage plays. Whereas its first half deals with the conventional defence of playing, even if in the end somewhat wryly, the second half ventures into the much more interesting area of the private satisfactions that playing has to offer. It does so in terms of illicit attempts by members of a decadent society to make theatre serve needs outside itself. Both the Emperor and Domitia, his mistress, are so taken with the ideal fictions that players create that they vainly hope by consorting with them either to carry the world of the play into their own lives (as Domitia commands Paris to be a stage lover to her) or to exalt execution by entering the play to do it (as does Caesar).

In their confusions of theatre and the real world however, they touch on some of the central ambiguities of all playing; the relationships between part and performer, for instance, and the source of the imaginative creation of a role. The issues they raise also have a general application to the way in which stage fictions are received by their audiences, and the relationship between the stage fiction and the private inner life of the individual spectator. Plays can embody fears and desires, provide escapism and fantasies, and, by temporarily releasing the individual observer through his identification with the stage characters from the obligations of social position or sexual role, they can enable a surrogate exploration of alternatives to present behaviour. Watching the performer, as performer, adds an extra dimension to the voyeurism inherent in viewing the enacted fiction. There is an incipient eroticism in the very process of self-display and its reception; the performer dominates the relationship, and yet at the same time becomes the creature of his audience; hence his ambiguous social position in most societies.

In Act III scene ii, Caesar is unable to derive the satisfaction he intends from torturing two honourable Stoics, and as they are sent off to execution, Domitia enters to cheer him, she says, with her production of *Iphis and Anaxarete*. In reality she has two quite different ends in view. Indeed each of the three inner plays is intended by those who initiate it to serve some instrumental function, to achieve some influence on real life, under the cover of innocent recreation. Mainly, in this classic lamentation of unrequited love, she wishes to see the actor, Paris, displayed as a lover, but it provides also an opportunity to humiliate the haughty princess, Domitilla, by making her act out on-stage the less admirable aspects of her own character.

The opening of the inner play of *Iphis and Anaxarete* makes clear how far it is Domitia's own private theatricals. She has even been responsible for Paris' make-up:

> The seeming late-fallen, counterfeited tears
> That hang upon his cheeks, was my device.

The play begins at her command and the actors wait upon her direction. In asides to Caesar, Domitia praises first Paris' 'shape', and then his acting, but as the scene continues, despite her own direct association with the mechanics of the performance, she becomes more and more taken up with the illusion:

> *Domitia*: Does he not act it rarely?
> Observe with what feeling he delivers
> His orisons to Cupid; I am rapt with't.

(175–7)

This is not perhaps so much the result of the excellence of the

203

performance, as a sign of her own instability, and the influence that lust has upon her judgement. She is not genuinely deceived by what she sees, but rather self-stimulated by a fantasy of her own contriving. The player Latinus enters as the Porter to Anaxarete, before whose gate the hapless Iphis is lamenting.

> *Latinus*: **Ha! who knocks there?**
> *Domitia*: – What a churlish look this knave has! –
> *Latinus*: **Is't you, sirrah?**
>   **Are you come to pule and whine? Avaunt, and quickly:**
>   **Dog-whips shall drive you hence else.**
> *Domitia*: – Churlish devil!
>   But that I should disturb the scene, as I live
>   I would tear his eyes out.
> *Caesar*: 'Tis in jest, Domitia.
> *Domitia*: I do not like such jesting; if he were not
>   A flinty-hearted slave, he could not use
>   One of his form so harshly. How the toad swells
>   At the other's sweet humility!
> *Caesar*: 'Tis his part:
>   Let 'em proceed.
> *Domitia*: A rogue's part, will ne'er leave him –
>
> (III.ii.205–15)

And the play proceeds. In this first outburst at least Domitia had taken cognisance that it was, as Caesar says, 'in jest'. At its climax however, as Paris prepares to represent the suicide of Iphis, Domitia is so carried away by what she has created that involuntarily she enters the play:

> *Paris*: . . . **As a trophy of your pride, and my affliction,**
>   **I'll presently hang myself.**
> *Domitia*: – Not for the world!
>   Restrain him, as you love your lives!
> *Caesar*: Why are you
>   Transported thus, Domitia? 'tis a play

Domitia then pleads indisposition and instructs Paris to attend her on the morrow for his reward.

When he obeys her summons, Domitia demands that Paris play the lover to her. She argues that if he can play such a part on-stage, he must have the qualities within him:

>   thou, whom oft I have seen

> To personate a gentleman, noble wise,
> Faithful, and gamesome, – and what virtue else
> The poet pleases to adorn you with,
> . . . must be really, in some degree,
> The thing thou dost present.

He replies by countering that he can play weak and vicious characters, and that were her argument true, it would apply equally to them:

> How glorious soever, or deformed,
> I do appear in the scene, my part being ended,
> And all my borrowed ornaments put off,
> I am no more, nor less, than what I was
> Before I entered.

Both speeches, of course, mask concerns of a more immediate nature; Paris is trying to extricate himself from the prospect of treasonous fornication, on which the Empress is bent. Domitia, baulked of so simple a transition to love-making, goes on to appeal to his sense of gratitude and then to resort to threats, but the issue she raises is not so easily settled. There is weight in her argument, that what you do not in some sense possess within yourself you cannot show, which refuses to be put aside completely in any discussion of the nature of acting. Earlier she had given a new twist to type-casting by making Domitilla take a part that would display her essential haughtiness. Though Paris talks of 'weak and vicious' characters, we never see him play any; his doctor is a moralist, his lover devoted, and in his final performance he is called upon to play himself, the upright and loyal servant. (Perhaps Domitia's failure in the intimate drama she has conceived is because she has cast him against type?) There is an incipient type-casting too in the parts of the cantankerous miser and the churlish porter allotted to Latinus. Earlier, Domitia had blamed him for the churlishness of the character he played, and said of him as porter, 'A rogue's part, will ne'er leave him', suggesting that playing somehow rubbed off.

Caught between his fear of Domitia's vengeance and his loyalty to Caesar, Paris compromises with a kiss. Caesar observes this, and, discovered, Paris falls to the floor in shame and abasement. Domitia however is unrepentant, and Caesar, oscillating between his desire for revenge and his continued fascination with Domitia, delays sentence on her and sends her off to confinement.

Left alone with Caesar, Paris sues for a speedy execution, and the Emperor laments the need to destroy such nobility. He commands a performance of a play, *The False Servant*, with a plot identical in substance to their situation, and himself takes the part of the injured husband, killing Paris 'in earnest', and thus ennobling his death. There is no sense here of a 'real' death on-stage being ironic and deceitful, as in, say, Middleton's marriage masque in *Women Beware Women*. Rather the scene takes its tone from Heywood's description of condemned men in Ancient Rome suing as an alternative to other forms of execution to be killed on-stage by 'princely actors'.

Perhaps the most interesting moment in terms of the scene's juxtaposition of art and life is when Caesar hesitates before his entry into the inner play. Paris, despite his own feelings, and his companions' mystification, is playing a familiar role, but Caesar, in crossing the boundary forbidden by convention, must demean his own status by accepting a cue from one set apart by *infamia* who has momentarily become his fellow, and speak the prescribed words of the play. He is perhaps the least prepared and roughest of the royal players. He rejects the false beard, the property sword, and finally the words themselves; only the 'action' stays in his mind, the necessary thrust of the sword.

It simply will not do to categorize this scene as a condemnation of the stage. Much more complex attitudes are at work as to the power of playing, in its ability to ennoble life and to probe its deepest recesses, as well as to debase, demean and falsify.

The discussion in Chapter 3 suggested that Shakespeare's plays likewise exhibit a recognition of the indivisible mixture of the positive and negative aspects of playing. Bottom may be foolish and egocentric, and Falstaff ultimately an advocate of anarchy and self-indulgence, but both men exhibit the boundless energy and resilience of playing in such a way as to prevent our total condemnation of them. Hamlet charts the many and various stages of his own ambivalence towards the players. It is true that the prince tends to be more enthusiastic about the playwriting – as with the unnamed Trojan play, which he finds 'well-digested in the scenes, set down with as much modesty as cunning' – than he is about the performers; there is a little of the tetchy dramatist trying to school the players as to how they should speak his own lines. However too many conclusions ought not perhaps to be drawn from Lucianus and his 'damnable faces'. Shakespeare too was a player, though tradition has it that he was not very good and retired early from direct performance. Whatever the truth of this, it is clear that he had a long and a more-or-less continuous association with a close group of leading players for upwards of twenty years. Any pronouncements on his attitude to playing that fail to take account of this workaday context, based on selective readings of particular stage utterances, are on very shaky ground.

Clearly much of his criticism of players in *Hamlet* is of bad actors, those who rant and strut and are insensitive to the meaning of the words, rather than of players in general. Hamlet is, after all, entrusting them with a matter of great importance. Some of the other references too may be to inferior actors – the 'strutting player' of *Troilus and Cressida*, the 'poor player' of *Macbeth*, the scurrilous mimes of *Antony and Cleopatra* and the bumbling amateurs of *Love's Labour's Lost* and *A Midsummer Night's Dream*. There is no reason why we should expect Burbage and his fellows to dismiss their own calling, except perhaps in terms of *sprezzatura*, that special sort of self-depreciation that comes from confident knowledge of one's own worth; the tone perhaps that Prospero adopts of his masque, 'Some vanity of mine art'. If this is so, then their undervaluing of playing is not meant to be taken too literally.

Player-references in Shakespeare are sometimes used to chart his supposed disillusionment with the stage.[6] Whilst it is likely that with the passage of time he would lose some of his early idealism, a much more potent factor is the dramatic and social context within which these supposed condemnations of the stage were spoken. In the movement from the patriotic histories and optimistic comedies of the 1590s to the tragedies and bitter comedies of the 1600s there is an overall darkening of attitudes to life in general that echoes the spirit of the time. Macbeth's 'poor player/ That struts and frets his hour upon the stage/ And then is heard no more' and its close association with the tale 'Told by an idiot, full of sound and fury,/ Signifying nothing', is said on news of his wife's death. To expect a reasoned view of anything as trivial as theatre at such a moment is on a par with the apocryphal inquiry of poor Mrs Lincoln. The key point in respect of context is that the slighting references to the stage, in *Hamlet*, in *King Lear*, in *Macbeth* and in *Antony and Cleopatra*, occur at moments in the performance when the activity of playing is actually being demonstrated at its noblest.

Ben Jonson, on the other hand, was not a company dramatist, and constantly shifted his allegiance according to his choleric personality and artistic principles. However, once again, there has been a tendency to make judgements on his attitude to the stage without sufficient regard to his status as a practitioner, or as a satirist. There is no shortage of statements in Jonson's writings which appear to denigrate theatrical activity. In 1605, imprisoned for his part in *Eastward Ho!*, he writes to the Earl of Salisbury:

> The cause (would I could name some worthier) though I wish we had none known worthy our imprisonment, is, a (the word irks me, that our Fortune hath necessitated us to so despised a course) a play, my Lord.

For all the apparent contempt for plays expressed here, the passage tells us more about how Jonson best thought to make his plight sympathetic than it does about his actual views. It is a skilful, one might almost say artful, piece of self-depreciation. After all, he was in prison because he chose to write plays, had been doing so for a considerable time – indeed he had been imprisoned before, over the *Isle of Dogs* – and was to continue to write plays, and risk further imprisonment.

In assessing Jonson's views of theatre it is important to separate his attitudes towards contemporary styles of dramaturgy, towards his audiences, and in respect of current antagonisms within the theatre fraternity, on the one hand, from any wider evaluation of the activity, and also from his very evident dislike of unacknowledged dishonesty in ordinary life, on the other.

Jonson frequently expressed his contempt for popular dramatic modes, from the 'ill customs of the age' attacked in the Prologue to the revised *Every Man in His Humour*, through the general indictment of the current theatre as 'nothing but ribaldry, profanation, blasphemy' in the Dedication to *Volpone*, to the 'tales, tempests and such like drolleries' of *Bartholomew Fair*. The attack on Munday as Antonio Balladino in *The Case is Altered* may serve as *locus classicus* for his views of the public stage, whilst his 'Expostulacion with Inigo Jones' serves a similar purpose in attacking the false priorities of spectacle over 'sense' in the Court Masque.

Similarly Jonson's stormy relationship with his audiences is too well authenticated to need much illustration. It reaches its extreme in the sick old man's despair at the failure of *The New Inn*:

> Come, leave the loathèd stage,
> And the more loathsome age,
> Where pride and impudence, in faction knit,
> Usurp the chair of wit:
> Indicting and arraigning every day
> Something they call a play.

Whilst Jonson's plays are full of tricksters and hypocrites, their presence provides doubtful evidence for hostility to the theatrical process itself. In his discussion of culpable role-players in Jonson's plays, Jonas Barish excepts Brainworm in *Every Man in His Humour*, whose antics, he says, 'spring purely from play, on the success of which neither his economic security nor his sense of his own reality depends'.[7] As the most player-like of Jonson's deceivers, so Brainworm is the most free of opprobrium.

The satirical charge at the centre of Jonson's plays is not against theatrical mimesis, but against contemporary gulls and dupes who present a false picture of themselves in everyday life, often through some personal inadequacy, and so carry stage behaviour onto the street. An oft-cited passage is from *Timber, or Discoveries*:

> I have considered our whole life is like a play: wherein every man, forgetful of himself, is in travail with expression of another. Nay, we so insist on imitating others, as we cannot, when it is necessary, return to ourselves . . .
>
> (II.1105–11)

This however will not serve to show Jonson's alleged contempt for the stage, since the comparison here is to the discredit of Life, rather than the Stage. It is at heart a denial of the adequacy of the Play Metaphor, which so excited his contemporaries. To forget oneself on-stage temporarily 'in travail with expression of another' is precisely what is recommended of actors in varying degrees in all ages. Its uncontrolled use in ordinary life is an entirely different matter. The behaviour of the unsatisfactory apprentice courtier in *Cynthia's Revels* is reprehensible because, in a non-theatrical situation, he behaves like an actor, without genuine spontaneity, (and, being 'unperfect', is not even a good actor):

> There stands a Neophyte glazing of his face,
> Pruning his clothes, perfuming of his hair,
> Against his idol enters; and repeats
> (Like an unperfect prologue, at third music)
> His part of speeches, and confederate jests,
> In passion to himself.
>
> (III.iv)

In the Induction to *Every Man Out of His Humour*, Jonson distinguishes those who genuinely have a particular bias of personality from those who merely pretend to it as a fashion and as a way of dignifying themselves:

> [*Asper*] when some one peculiar quality
> Doth so possess a man, that it doth draw
> All his affects, his spirits, and his powers,
> In their confluctions, all run one way,
> This may be truly said to be a humour.
> But that a rook, by wearing a pied feather. . .
>   . . . should affect a humour!
> O, it is more than most ridiculous.

In Jonson's great comedies the failure of the dupes to recognize their own natures, and therefore the illegitimacy of their ambitions, lays them open to being deceived by others. Those who then exploit them are seen as being qualitatively superior, as the less despicable, and more honest in their dishonesty, because, as quasi-theatrical, they are conscious of the roles they assume.

Even Jonson's very evident quarrels with so many of his fellow practitioners need to be seen in the context of what might be called 'Abuse as Entertainment'. There are implications in the evidence that the whole 'War of the Theatres', the so-called *Poetomachia*: poet-versus-player, adults-versus-children, and poet-versus-poet, was no more than a contrivance to make money. In his *Apologetical Dialogue*, Jonson, impugning the motives for writing *Satiromastix*, describes his opponents as:

> Fellows of practised and most laxative tongues,
> Whose empty and eager bellies, in the year,
> Compel their brains to many desperate shifts

– and later in a more contrived mood of generosity:

>   What they have done 'gainst me,
> I am not moved with: if it gave them meat,
> Or got them clothes, 'tis well; that was their end.

In *The Poetaster* Jonson makes Histrio say:

> Oh, it will get us a huge deal of money (Captain) and we have need on't; for this winter ha's made us all poorer than so many starved snakes. Nobody comes at us; not a gentleman, nor a –

There is even corroboration in *Satiromastix*, when in his Epilogue Tucca asks the audience to clap because of 'this cold weather', but the main drift of Dekker's remarks is to suggest, perhaps disingenuously, that the

War is for the amusement of the audience, for 'sport'. The same implication is to be found in *Hamlet*: the theatre folk are taking, perhaps being forced to take, to pugilism in order to stimulate trade:

> *Rosencrantz*: Faith, there has been much to-do on both sides;
> and the nation holds it no sin to tar them to controversy.
> There was for a while no money bid for argument, unless
> the poet and the player went to cuffs in the question.

This is not to say that real passions were not aroused, even in simulated combat, nor that old scores were not settled. No doubt some people were hurt, very possibly including Jonson, judging by the fury of his rhetoric in the *Apologetical Dialogue*. However in general there appears to have been a relish for controversy, such that Dekker, himself closely associated with the theatre, could take up cudgels on either side at whim. Even some of the most prominent and abusive anti-theatre pamphleteers seem to have been motivated more by a mixture of ambition and cupidity than by genuine indignation. The renegade playwright 'Anglo-phile Eutheo', having risen to an hysterical denunciation of the players, could then return to writing for them, as Gosson puts it, 'like ye dog to his vomit'.[8] Marston has a character in *What You Will* (1601, III.i.1840) observe, 'What's out of railing's out of fashion'. Dekker talks in his opening address to *Satiromastix* of 'this lamentable merry murdering of Innocent Poetry', and in the Epilogue, through the person of the irrepressible Captain Tucca, he promises that 'if you set your hands and Seals to this, Horace will write against it, and you may have more sport', and they will 'untruss him again, and again, and again'. This anticipation of present insults provoking further replies and therefore the opportunity of further insults smacks very much of the tradition of 'flyting', made popular by the Scots in the sixteenth century, as a kind of context in which the participants alternately directed abusive verse at one another.[9] Formalized abuse has a long history, back at least as far as the Fescennine jesting of the *Ludi Romani*, with its possible fertility origins. Similar phenomena are to be found in many forms of popular comedy, from Aristophanes and the Fabula Atellana, through to the inventive abuse of comedians in our own time.

This skirmishing may not have been to everyone's liking. Certainly there is a widely expressed, if not always sincere, distaste for satire, and what Chapman, in the Prologue to his *All Fools*, calls 'personal application'. John Davies, himself a satirist, affects in *Witte's Pilgrimage* to criticize the *Poetomachia* and the misuses to which the children are put. On the other hand, in *The Raven's Almanacke*, Dekker's prognostications for 1609 include 'Another civil war', presumably amongst the adults, and the tone of the extended military metaphor that follows suggests that his enthusiasm for theatrical pugilism is unabated.

R.B. Sharpe pointed out that when the abuse appeared to be personal, as elsewhere in this tradition, it was often literary and derivative.[10] The model for much of the verse satire of the 1590s was Juvenal. As Antony Covatta suggests, 'Elizabethan satirists did not write out of a deeply offended sensibility', instead they 'responded to an increasing fascination with classical satire by trying their hand at writing imitations'.[11]

Although the coney-catching pamphlets of the 1590s are often used to provide testimony of contemporary hostility to players, they make treacherous evidence for the earnest searcher after hard facts. Their re-working of traditional material, their exaggeration, their fantasy, their partisan calumnies and casual distortions, are all overlaid by a racy, idiomatic style and a contrived sense of immediacy and reality, a journalistic style of the 'here' and 'now' that gives them the appearance of an authenticity which they do not possess. (The City Comedies make some of the same claims, with equal spuriousness.)

Nor is repetition of a particular assertion necessarily evidence of independent corroboration. Often sufficient allowance is not made for the Elizabethan habit of pursuing an argument by aggregation. When a writer takes up the cudgels in an argument, he automatically invokes those of his predecessors. No point is forgotten, however trivial its origin. Nashe, for instance, tells of a player taxed by Augustus with being the subject of brawls and quarrels, who replies that the Emperor should be pleased the people were so occupied, 'for otherwise they would look into thee and thy matters'. The same anecdote turns up in Heywood, as a reply *by Cicero*, this time to *Julius Caesar*. Heywood likens the didactic function of the stage representation of Vice to the Persian practice of making servants and captives drunk in order to encourage temperance in their own children. Randolph is still peddling the same story in 1630, only of Spartans and Helots.[12] Even more frequent examples of the same process could be cited from the puritan opposition, leading to that great exhaustive compilation, Prynne's *Histrio-Mastix*.[13]

However things are made worse on the pamphleteers' side by what is sometimes a lack of genuine loyalty – the writer is really only interested in keeping the controversy going – combined with a mischievous taste for the disingenuous espousal of the opposite case. Thomas Nashe's *Pierce Penniless His Supplication to the Devil* (1592), for instance, has a mixture of seriousness and playfulness, combined with an interest in the alien world of London lowlife, a fascination mixed with distaste; all of which largely seems to have escaped those in his own time who regurgitated his arguments in subsequent defences of playing, as well as commentators more recently who have taken his remarks as genuine evidence. At one point in his pamphlet, the opponents of the theatre, after having been identified first as the mercenary bourgeoisie, and then republicans, have become no more than the tapsters and brothel-keepers who cannot stand the competition of the theatres for the same sort of customer. Whether it is taken as insult or flattery that the theatre audience is made up exclusively of alcoholic whoremasters, surely it cannot be true? The same joke is taken up and developed by Chettle in *Kind-Heart's Dream* of the same year, in which Peter Pandar complains to Tarlton that the theatres are carrying out a deliberate plan to steal his customers by revealing his trade secrets in their plays: 'for no sooner have we a trick of deceit, but they make it common, singing Jigs, and making jests of us, that every boy can point out our houses as they pass by.'

Defending the playhouses by these associations is to echo the preacher's slur, but with more of the carefully contrived tone of the dissolute gallant, stooping to take his pleasures, and finding plays marginally more interesting than the stews. It is surely a comic pose?

Elsewhere in his pamphlet, Nashe links his praise of the display of martial virtue and his interest in the seamy side of London life with the preposterous argument that theatres are justified because they keep discharged soldiers, no doubt a contemporary problem, off the streets. He recommends, again surely with his tongue firmly in his cheek, that it is good 'policy', the Elizabethan term for unsavoury manipulation, to tolerate plays, as 'light toys to busy their head withal', and so prevent sedition as well as vice. He later links the captains with courtiers and gentlemen of the Inns of Court, who without plays would also fall to vice in the afternoons, 'the idlest time of the day'.

Nashe's *jeu d'esprit* becomes part of the orthodox defence echoed in the dedicatory poems of Heywood's theatrical colleagues printed with the *Apology for Actors*. The actor Richard Perkins in his poem adopts the *persona* of a bored gallant whose 'tired spirits must have recreation', arguing for the superiority of plays over drabbing, gaming and drinking, whilst Taylor, in the same collection, confuses the issue by branding his critics as hypocritical 'suburb sinners':

> Thus when a play nips Satan by the nose,
> Straight all his vassals are the actors' foes.

It is left to the more reasonable Heywood to assert a less racy and more moderate image for the activity: 'Many amongst us, I know, to be of substance, of government, of sober lives, and temperate carriages, house-keepers, and contributory to all duties enjoined them. . .'.

Issues about the value and purpose of dramatic representation remain in the forefront of Elizabethan writing for and about the theatre, both sides agreeing on the power of its influence. The fashion for including players as characters in the plays is both a product, and an intensification, of their awareness of the moral ambiguities of playing. Had not the Children's Theatre actively sought comparison with the adults, most probably it would have been obliged to suffer it in less favourable circumstances. In many ways the Elizabethans viewed playing with a more sophisticated ambivalence than is often encountered today; balancing the freedoms and perspectives it could offer against its potential for distortion and self-indulgence. Unlike Heywood's simple and optimistic model, or our current enthusiasm for Applied Drama, their plays illustrate that to apply drama to life was to use an uncertain and a two-edged weapon.

Above all, in discussing Elizabethan dramatic self-reference it is important to acknowledge its function as humour. Both plays and pamphlets were designed to entertain, and, like much of our own modern satirical writing, they were not too scrupulous about the justness of their attacks. This does not gainsay the seriousness or sincerity of many of the objections to players, but it ought to condition our response to their use on-stage and in coney-catching literature.[14]

If the writers for the theatre are themselves ambivalent towards the value of playing, what of the performers? Since by its nature the theatrical process is always available to be seen as ridiculous, it often defends itself by frank acknowledgement through self-parody. Institutional drama too mocked itself and others of the same kind. The Children mocked their own earlier styles, such as those of Lyly. The anonymous author of the *Second Part of the Return from Parnassus* begins by making fun of the popular Italian Comedy style of much university drama, and the rest of the play may be tinged by self-parody. In 1607 the chief movers of the Revels at St John's College, Oxford, found themselves invited to a play, *Yuletide*, at Christ Church, in which

Christmas Princes themselves were an object of mirth. In this context, attacks on the hardened professional entertainers are only to be expected.

Any interpretation of even the most apparently serious attack upon the players has to be conditioned by the context in which that attack is uttered. Performing an attack upon playing is to create a rich area of ambiguity, since the traditional objections to playing, whether invoked or implicit, cohere most thickly around mimesis itself. However much the amateur or institutional performer may signal as his target the social inferiority of players, or the baseness of making a living by performance, these objections threaten to condemn both victim and attacker.

The satirizing of players by theatrical means necessarily involved a shrinkage of scope, from the moral to the social or technical. Not only did the parodists forgo by their performance the right to attack mimesis in principle, but they also closed off the metaphorical function of stage imitation. Whilst they could show the soldier, the puritan or the doctor to be player-like, by pointing the contrasts between their protestations and their actions, and showing them to be cowards, hypocrites, or quacks, for them to accuse the player of deception was not to condemn him, but merely to define his art. The puritan could argue that the better the performance, the closer the player showed his kinship to that paramount actor, the Devil, but the institutional performer could only insinuate rather lamely that the professionals were upstarts who acted badly, and were thereby foolish and despicable. In fact contemporary testimony, corroborated by the acting demands of the texts themselves, suggests that by the turn of the century the professional player had achieved a high standard of performance. *Histriomastix*, in particular, sounds more like the received prejudices of an earlier age getting a, perhaps semi-humorous, airing. As recently as the 1560s, the Inns of Court, for instance, had taken the lead in theatrical innovation in language, subject matter and the relationship of actor and audience, but by the 1580s and 1590s the initiative had passed firmly to the professionals, so that the influence was reversed. Inns' formal drama declined as the professional drama became more worthy of attention; whilst at the universities the most successful strain of satirical drama was performed in English, and took on many of the other characteristics of the popular stage.

The criticism of players through their representation, especially around the turn of the century, can also be seen as another manifestation of a growing interest in the professional theatre and its workings.

The dramatic parodies of the adult repertory in *The Poetaster* are akin to those of Euripides and Aeschylus in Aristophanes' *The Frogs*, as a kind of early dramatic criticism. The general effect of this body of player-representations, whether ostensibly disparaging or not, is to draw attention inwards, to the fascination with the process of theatre. The ambivalence of satire is often due to its ridiculing the things it finds attractive.[15]

13

Conclusion

The phenomenon of the player-role is part of an historical process which proceeds quite rapidly in the late sixteenth and early seventeenth centuries. It can be seen in the broader context of dramaturgy as a series of mediating techniques, but from a social perspective it is a recognition, at least partly acknowledged, of changing circumstances; made more evident by the existence of two, for a time, antagonistic forms of theatre, and by a growing self-consciousness within the theatrical process which the Children's Theatre stimulated. The representation of itinerants, and of clowns and extemporization, is also in part, however scornful the context, a nostalgic farewell to a passing age; whilst the bombastic and tardy defence of the players perhaps reflects shifts in the stage's relations with the monarchy.

Part of the scorn with which the common player is represented in some of the extracts reviewed is stimulated by an awareness of the decline of the amateur, educational drama and the values it had enshrined. One obvious factor in this process of change is the popularity of the common players at Court, and more broadly with the aristocratic and the intellectual sections of society, a number of whose members by the late 1580s are also directly involved in the popular theatre, either as patrons or practitioners. The amateur performance of plays had long been acknowledged as an essential part of the school curriculum and hence the educated classes in general had gained a taste for plays. Since the distinctions between professional and amateur, in subject matter and intention, were diminishing much more rapidly than the institutions admitted, and only the method of reward, for instance, seems at Court to have distinguished one from another, the privileged classes provided a ready-made audience for both, and discriminated according to quality rather than auspices. As Kemp is made to say with some satisfaction in *Return from Parnassus*, 'He's not counted a gentleman that knows not Dick Burbage and Will Kemp.'

The universities can be said to have produced the institutional model in most extreme contrast to the despised public stage, but it was one full of paradoxes which made it very precarious. It purported to resist change, and, as so often in Elizabethan theatrical activity, an apparently immutable standard was asserted. In the same way as the adult players continued to claim to be liveried household servants, and the choir schools, as they made handsome profits for their investors, pretended to be rehearsing for her Majesty's solace, so too the universities claimed that performances were necessarily educational, because they were in Latin. Each apparently held firm to a traditional value, which actually concealed a process of adaptation. As the century wore on, religion, banned on the public stage, became too sensitive a topic for amateur plays, especially as so many of the scholarly consciences in the puritan movement increasingly took exception to playing *per se*, and so the way was left open for the ascendancy of Roman Comedy as the principal model for university drama; and the enemy was admitted within the gates. The academic dramatic tradition distinguished itself very confidently from contemporary professional playing, and yet paradoxically it imitated professional plays from a former age. Even the veneration due to antiquity could hardly justify later translations of contemporary Italian imitations of Roman Comedy. At a time when serious academic plays were being written at the Inns of Court in English, the language of performance become more and more dubious as an educational justification.

Another potent influence, both in seeing off much of the amateur drama and in narrowing the gap between what remained and the professional stage, was the rapid change in the conception of play-form. The establishment of regular, and eventually purpose-built, playing venues encouraged new attitudes to theatre-going and a longer more free-standing play-form than the older briefer 'interlude'. Except for the Masque, which was clearly marked off as a separate form, and used at least some professional resources, amateur dramatic traditions were in decline as casual and shapeless.[1] Queen Elizabeth showed a marked preference for formal plays rather than 'offerings', in a process which is perhaps anticipated in her father's reign by the establishment of the post of Master of Revels, quickly supplanting the older Lord of Misrule.[2] In some ways the older forms of drama were more difficult for the authorities to control. However much an institution may perceive festive licence and ritualized inversion as confirming its order and legitimacy, it can never have total confidence in its ability to make them serve a purely positive function. Beneath the whole activity of institutional drama, and notwithstanding the humanist enthusiasm for reviving classical values, one senses from time to time a much older, amoral, anarchic spirit set to mock anything.

Probably the single most important factor in confusing concepts of institutional and professional was the rise of the choristers' theatre. Even in the earlier period of the 1580s, the audience may not have been as exclusively composed of the aristocratic and those who aspired to that state, busily acting out a 'counter-performance' to assert their supposed social identity, as Shapiro suggests, but certainly the opportunity of seeing what had been prepared for the monarch must have been influential in legitimizing theatre-going amongst the educated and the privileged.[3] Its revival at the turn of the century was more frankly commercial, but it explicitly made play for a quality audience, to attract which, under its veneer of chapel auspices and court patronage, it had a new cutting edge and a greater degree of skill and sophistication.

It is difficult to overestimate the importance of the Children in redefining the nature of the activity of theatre at the turn of the century. As the adult theatre had held a mirror up to nature, so they too in turn offered a reflection of the adults; mocking, distorted, but powerful in its contribution to a new self-awareness. They did not perhaps invent the term 'common player', but they gave its use a sharper application in contradistinction to themselves; 'the common stages - so they call them -', as Rosencrantz is made to put it.[4] The-play-within-the-play goes back some time, and is prominent in Kyd's *The Spanish Tragedy* (c. 1587), players of a sort appear as early as 1497 in Medwall's *Fulgens and Lucres*, and Shakespeare has professional players in his *dramatis personae* from the early 1590s, but it is significant that the bulk of physical representations of the player on-stage, as well as satirical and metaphorical references to them within plays, stem from this period of direct confrontation.

In whatever manner the Children's Theatre was seen or purported to present itself, like the adults it catered to the tastes of its audience; it dealt in commercial entertainment and was judged in respect of whether it was successful in this. From our standpoint this seems an obvious goal, but it represents a clear break with its antecedents. To most of the amateur, institutional traditions such satisfactions had been secondary to other didactic, educational, or socially cohesive functions. To achieve these other aims, inhibitions had been placed on certain parts of the mimetic process; there had been restrictions on the rank and identity of both performer and auditor, on the style of performance, on subject matter (especially of religious drama), and on the language in which the text was written. Once these had each in turn been brought into question, the tendency was to move towards a common standard; to cast according to ability rather than merit or status; to sacrifice decorum to immediacy and excitement; to fuse text and action; to amuse rather than to edify, and to appeal to a broader audience. It clearly offended the Merchant Taylors that payment of the egalitarian penny should entitle members of an audience to ignore the traditional rights to respect, and the best seats, of the 'Masters of this Worshipful Company and their dear friends'.[5] The genteel apprentice *The Hog Hath Lost his Pearl* was first performed at Whitefriars before an invited audience of the performers' friends, but the Prologue, written presumably for later performances at The Curtain and The Red Bull, indicates that they now aspire to a popular audience, and are prepared to risk being pelted with 'apples, eggs or stones' in the process.

Not surprisingly one of the pressures on the beleaguered institutional drama to acknowledge its kinship with professional drama came from opponents of the stage. As with Rainolds' extension of the charge of *infamia* to university drama, so too Henry Clifton in his deposition against Evans and the others in 1600 alleging their misuse of the Queen's warrant for impressing choristers, ignores the much-vaunted superiority of the Chapel and its supposed opportunities for educational and social advancement. He describes his son as being threatened with becoming a 'base mercenary interlude player, to his utter loss of time, ruin and disparagement'. This was a view of the Chapel Children during Elizabeth's reign, at a time when the Children's Theatre may well have been at its most distinctive, which the ruling of the Star Chamber upheld.[6]

There were substantial losses as well as gains in this transition of emphasis from amateur to professional. Any educational or recreational drama since 1600, albeit that it may recognize its own separate objectives, has had to contend with principles of excellence drawn from the professional stage. Since in the process amateur drama is always likely to be compared to its disadvantage, this must have contributed to the withdrawal of large sections of the population from the satisfactions and opportunity for self-expression such activity formerly afforded. The late sixteenth-century Chester Banns assert that their mystery plays are 'not to get fame or treasure', and that if 'better men and finer heads' are now dissatisfied by the standard of performance of 'crafts men and mean men', then they should go elsewhere. However the embattled tone of this disclaimer indicates how hard it was to stand against the prevailing tide. A full hundred years earlier the York regulations of 1476 were enforcing common standards of artistic competence on all their pageants.[7]

On the more positive side, it could be argued that institutional drama had existed by wearing a series of blinkers, and that in its decline the inhibitions were banished one by one until, in the ascendancy of the professional player, theatre attained its true nature; it became more truly *dramatic* as content, attitude, performer and venue blended into a single indivisible union.

Many of the modern misunderstandings about these plays arise from a desire to reverse this process and to separate out the serious, intellectual, conceptual elements in the plays, as though they had some validity independent of their performance context.[8] Even before the recent enthusiasm to rehabilitate Massinger as a serious political thinker, the stress upon him as a moralist is echoed generally in commentaries, often as though dramatic technique or character consistency in his plays should be considered as subordinate to a didactic purpose.[9] (Nor is this treatment peculiar to Massinger.)[10] The issue is not whether Massinger's plays contain political references. Undoubtedly they do. The question is whether the play exists *for* the political statement, or whether it incorporates political issues, as it incorporates many other things, for purposes of its own. Martin Butler is inclined to the former position:

As a political playwright, Massinger comes close behind (Brome) . . . . In play after play of this decade, politics is not just an occasional or ephemeral issue but is the basic, fundamental concern and the principal determinant of dramatic form . . .[11]

I would argue, on the other hand, that plays make very poor propaganda; that their determinants are *dramatic*; that they devour everything that enters their maw and transform it in terms of their own concerns – for what 'works' – into the personalized, and confrontational. Massinger's interests are in writing a piece of theatre, and in doing so he uses whatever comes to hand that seems appropriate and topical. Politics here, classical or contemporary, are made to contribute to a world of heroic assertion in which all issues and all characters are made satisfyingly black or white.[12] The moral observation in the play rarely rises about the commonplace, however lucidly expressed, and is made suspect by a revealing lack of consistency –

which both Butler and Howard, seeking for coherence in political rather than theatrical terms, recognize, but cannot explain.

How much real conviction, for instance, is expressed in Domitilla's speech (III.i.53f.) in which she declines on behalf of the princesses to employ Stephano to assassinate Caesar, on the grounds that it is a decision for the 'Immortal powers' who 'Protect a prince, though sold to impious acts', when it is the very same princesses who later kill him? One suspects that morality is invoked to sustain the plot, which has to run for another three acts, rather than vice versa.

The early presentation of Caesar is less an attack upon monarchy, and less a moral or political statement, than it is an exercise in theatrical Grand Guignol. (Indeed if taken seriously it has sentiments that would put the censored parts of the *The King and the Subject* quite in the shade.)[13] Consider, for instance, the excessive nastiness of Caesar's treatment of the wronged husband (II.i.174). Because Lamia very naturally regrets the loss of his wife, Domitia, Caesar resolves to take his 'revenge' by having her sing at a window and so provoke Lamia and thus justify his punishment:

> *Caesar*: I will blend
> My cruelty with some scorn, or else 'tis lost;   175
> Revenge, when it is unexpected, falling
> With greater violence; and hate clothed in smiles,
> Strikes, and with horror, dead the wretch that comes not
> Prepared to meet it. – (*Enter* LAMIA *with the* GUARD)
> Our good Lamia, welcome . . .

'Hate clothed in smiles' is an aesthetic of stage villainy inherited from the Machiavel, producing a frisson more to do with theatricality than morality. Can we really envisage this speech in the mouth of Charles Stuart? If Lowin played Falstaff, Volpone, and Mammon, as James Wright reports in *Historia Histrionica* (1699), we may imagine with what thespian relish he tackled Caesar's entry in I.iv; triumphantly returning from the wars, assertive, arrogant, and plucking his choice of bed-fellow from before her husband and his fellow senators, and creating her Empress on the spot.

The Roman Actor in a sense marks the end of this study. It is the only play of the period to have a professional player at its centre. It offers three inner plays, extensive stage activity, and the most elaborate defence of playing ever to be spoken onstage. Act Four is largely given over to the confusions of stage fiction and reality. It is the one play that can be set unreservedly in support of the stage against the much more numerous uncomplimentary representations of players, and yet it fails to satisfy. Its central figure is a blank. Its famous defence, having engaged gear, switches off the brain, suffering from what T.S. Eliot called 'cerebral anaemia'. As a representation of theatre practice, it is not so much that it hovers uncomfortably between Ancient Rome and Caroline London, but rather that the players live on an ideal plane entirely lacking in the authenticity of either. There are references to contemporary details, of prologues and payments, but the attitude to the representation of playing oscillates from elaborate excuses for the perfectly normal convention of truncating inner plays, to the arbitrary inconsistencies of casting Domitilla, and the summary preparation of *The False Servant*.

In terms of the value of player-representations as an indication of performance practice, the distinctions which earlier plays made between their inner plays and the surrounding action have largely disappeared. All the characters speak in the same tone, and the whole play has come to exist in an unreal, stage world, where 'real' values no longer constrast with those of acknowledged pretence. Consider, for instance, how impoverished are the associations when Paris encourages his fellows before their trial (I.i.50f.):

> Nay droop not fellows; innocence should be bold.
> We, that have personated in the scene
> The ancient heroes and the falls of princes
> With loud applause, being to act ourselves,
> Must do it with undaunted confidence

To 'act ourselves' now means the same as to 'be ourselves'. When life can become stage posturing without reproof, then the special value of playing has been lost, and both are to be condemned. It is perhaps no accident that the Senate defence of playing should have enjoyed its main popularity as a solo turn when the Theatre cultivated the grand gesture and was most cut off from the real world.[14] In the hands of Massinger, even the defence of playing is no more than further material for heroic assertion. That dual awareness of the value of the stage and of its triviality, grounded in an honest assessment of human nature, which had enriched the Elizabethan concept of theatre and enlivened its representation of players, has quite disappeared.

In the particular kind of stage representations of players surveyed in the foregoing pages, the function of playing is an important issue, occasioned in part by the new dignities and challenges arising from the transition from itinerant to metropolitan status. In subsequent eras, as the theatre settled into being an accepted and predominantly middle-class entertainment, it ceased to be so pressing to attack or defend it. Elizabethan theatre was an imperfect theatre. The early denizens of the purpose-built theatres had continued the tradition of 'multiple unity' with their gallimaufreys and hodge-podges; with more stress upon the individual coherence of its elements than upon the total whole in both dramaturgy and performance.[15] The gradual establishment, as the period wore on, of working concepts of a more sophisticated unity, in which Shakespeare seems to have played a significant part, may have elevated the theatre as an art-form, but at the expense of the dissonant qualities: on the one hand, the unassimilated performance elements such as clowning, doubling and improvisation; and on the other, a healthy scepticism about the value of playing, which the anti-player controversy had helped to stimulate.

Appendix A
Henslowe's inventory of properties, 1598

(Taken from R.A. Roakes and R.T. Rickert (eds) *Henslowe's Diary*, 1961, modernized, and re-arranged into categories. Property items from his list of clown costumes of the same year have also been included.)

SCENIC 3-D PROPERTIES: Rock; cage; 3 tombs; Hell's Mouth; flight of stairs; bedstead; beacon; bay tree; wooden canopy: chariot; little altar; two mossy banks; stable; tree of golden apples, Tantalus's tree; two coffins; wheel and frame in *The Siege of London*; frame for the heading in *Black John*; cauldron for *The Jew of Malta*;

POSSIBLE SCENIC CLOTHS OR CUT-OUTS: the city of Rome; two steeples; rainbow; the cloth of the sun and moon;

PAINTED SIGNS ETC.: sign for *Mother Redcap*; Tasso picture; shield with three lions;

WEAPONS AND ARMOUR: eight lances; three clubs; one wooden hatchet; one leather hatchet; nine iron shields; one copper shield; four wooden shields; seventeen foils; shin armour; one small shield; helmet with a dragon; gilt spear; long sword;

MUSICAL INSTRUMENTS: a chime of bells; three trumpets, a drum, treble viol, bass viol, a bandora, a cittern, two rackets; three timbrells; sackbut;

HAND PROPERTIES: orb; golden sceptre; two cakes; golden fleece; Neptune's trident; crosier; wooden mattock; Cupid's bow and quiver; Mercury's caduceus; elm bowl; philtre; hobby horse; flag;

FALSE LIMBS ETC.: Mahomet's head; Phaeton's limbs; Argos's head; Kent's wooden leg; Iris's head; four Turks heads;

ANIMAL PROPERTIES/COSTUMES: lion skin; bear skin; boar's head; Cerberus's three heads; snake; bull's head; dragon in *Dr Faustus*; lion; two lion's heads; great horse with his legs; black dog;

COSTUME PROPERTIES: Neptune's garland; eight masks; bridle in

225

Tamburlaine; two fans of feathers; fan; Mercury's wings; chain of dragons; pair of embroidered gloves; Pope's mitre; three Imperial crowns; plain crown; ghost's crown; crown with a sun;

UNIDENTIFIED: 'hecfor for the play of Faeton, the limes dead' (heifer?).

Appendix B
Henslowe's wardrobe inventory, c. 1602

(Modernized from R.A. Foakes and R.T. Rickert (eds) *Henslowe's Diary*, 1961)

CLOAKS: Scarlet with two broad gold laces with gold buttons of the same down the sides; Black velvet; Scarlet, edged with silver braid, and silver buttons; Short velvet cape-cloak embroidered with gold and golden spangles; Light-blue satin with gold laces; Purple satin with a raised border of velvet and silver-twist; Black tufted;[1] Damask (of rich ornamented silk) with a velvet border; Long black taffeta; Coloured and interwoven with beads for a boy; Scarlet with gold buttons faced with bue velvet; Scarlet faced with black velvet; Red with gold braid; Black interwoven with beads.

GOWNS: Henry VIII gown; Black velvet with white fur; Crimson striped with gold, faced with ermine; Embroidered cloth of gold; Red silk with gold buttons; Cardinal's; Women's; Black velvet; Embroidered; 'With gold'; Cloth of gold belonging to Cavendish; Black velvet laced and drawn-out[2] with shite sarsenet (soft, silky material); Black silk with red flush;[3] Cloth of silver for Parr (an actor); Yellow silk; Red silk; Angel's silk; Two blue calico (cotton).

ANTIQUE SUITS (historical costumes): Coat of crimson velvet cut in panes[4] and embroidered with gold; Cloth of gold coat with green bases;[5] Cloth of gold coat with orange-tawny bases; Cloth of gold and silver coat with blue silk and tinsel; Blue damask coat (for) the Moor; Red velvet horseman's coat; Yellow taffeta pd (padded?); Cloth of gold horseman's coat; Cloth of baudekin[6] horseman's coat; Orange-tawny horseman's coat ornamented with lace; Daniel's gown; Blue embroidered bases; Will Summer's Coat (Henry VIII's jester); White embroidered bases; Gilded leather coat; Two head-dresses set with stones.

JERKINS AND DOUBLETS: Crimson velvet (padded?) with gold buttons and

227

braiding; Crimson satin case (outer-covering) decorated all over with gold braid; Velvet doublet with a diamond pattern, decorated with gold braid and spangles; Doublet of black velvet slashed with silver tinsel; Ginger coloured doublet; White satin (doublet) slashed on a white background; Black velvet doublet with gold braid; Green velvet; Black taffeta doublet slashed on black velvet; decorated with beads; Plain black velvet doublet; Old white satin doublet; Red velvet doublet for a boy; Carnation velvet doublet decorated with silver braid; Yellow spangled case; Red velvet with blue satin sleeves and case; Cloth of silver jerkin; Faustus' jerkin [and] his cloak.

FRENCHHOUSE:[7] Blue velvet embroidered with gold panes [and with] blue satin scalings; Silver panes decorated with carnation satin and silver braid; Guise's (*Massacre at Paris*); Rich panes with long stockings; Gold panes with black striped scalings of canis (?); Gold panes with velvet scalings; Gold panes with red striped scalings; Black beaded; Red panes with yellow scalings for a boy; Priam's hose; Spangled hose.

VENETIANS (knee-breeches): Purple velvet slashed in diamond shapes, decorated with spangles; Red velvet decorated with Spanish gold; Purple velvet embroidered with silver slashed with tinsel; Green velvet decorated with Spanish gold; Black velvet; Green striped satin; Cloth of gold for a boy.

Henslowe's costume lists of 1598 consist of one similar to the above, plus one which he describes as 'Inventory of the Clowns' Suits and Hermits' Suits, with divers other suits, as followeth'. This includes garments for the following:

senators; Neptune; Firedrakes; janizaries; torchbearers; friars; soldiers; Robin Hood and his men; Maid Marion; knaves; shepherds; priests; Danes; Moor's armour; Hercules' armour; fools; Merlin; clowns; Eve; pedant; dunces; ghost.

Appendix C
The Cradle of Security

In the city of Gloucester the manner is, as I think it is in other like corporations, that, when the players of interludes come to town, they first attend the Mayor to inform him what nobleman's servants they are, and so to get licence for their public playing; and if the Mayor like the actors, or would show respect to their lord and master, he appoints them to play their first play before himself and the Aldermen and Common Council of the city; and that is called the 'Mayor's play', where every one that will comes in without money, the Mayor giving the players a reward as he thinks fit to show respect unto them.

At such a play my father took me with him, and made me stand between his legs, as he sat upon one of the benches, where we saw and heard very well. The play was called *The Cradle of Security*, wherein was personated a king or some great prince, with his courtiers of several kinds, amongst which three ladies were in special grace with him; and they, keeping him in delights and pleasures, drew him from his graver counsellors, hearing of sermons and listening to good counsel and admonitions, that, in the end, they got him to lie down in a cradle upon the stage, where these three ladies, joining in a sweet song, rocked him asleep that he snorted again: and in the meantime closely conveyed under the cloths wherewithal he was covered a vizard, like a swine's snout, upon his face with three wire chains fastened thereunto, the other end whereof being holden severally by those three ladies who fall to singing again, and then discovered his face that the spectators might see how they had transformed him, going on with their singing. Whilst all this was acting, there came forth of another door at the farthest end of the stage two old men, the one in blue with a serjeant-at-arms' mace on his shoulder, the other in red with a drawn sword in his hand and leaning with the other hand upon the other's shoulders; and so they two went along in a soft pace round about by the skirt of the stage, till at last they came to the cradle, when all the court was in greatest jollity;

and then the foremost old man with his mace struck a fearful blow upon the cradle, whereat all the courtiers, with the three ladies and the vizard, all vanished; and the desolate prince starting up bare-faced, and finding himself thus sent for to judgement, made a lamentable complaint of his miserable case, and so was carried away by wicked spirits. This prince did personate in the moral the Wicked of the World; the three ladies Pride, Covetousness and Lechery; the two old men, the End of the World and the Last Judgement. This sight took such impression in me that, when I came to man's estate, it was as fresh in my memory as if I had seen it newly acted.

(Robert Willis, *Mount Tabor, Private Exercise of a Penitent Sinner*, 1639)

Appendix D
Itinerant players at work

The four charts below are designed to illustrate the working practices of itinerants in the 1570s. The title-pages of *The Tide Tarrieth No Man* and *Cambises* indicate how the characters are to be divided (although the latter has some mistakes). *Common Conditions* and *All for Money* specify only the number of actors to be used, and I have made conjectural assignments of parts.

The smaller the company the more frequently each performer appears. The four players sharing the thirty-two parts of the 1,572-line *All for Money* are on-stage respectively for 1,138, 925, 1,177 and 1,115 lines, with as little as twenty-one lines for changing character, and the play exhibits the typical alternation of good and bad characters by the same actor. The plays differ in the importance given to changing time, and thereby perhaps to character differentiation. *The Tide Tarrieth No Man*, is remarkable for the frequency with which the actors return to earlier roles, which has its own implications for performance style. All four plays use a Vice role to hold the play together; in *The Tide Tarrieth No Man*, for instance, he hardly leaves the stage. The same play also demonstrates that the Vice was not infrequently doubled with serious parts. Responsibilities however are more evenly shared than in later larger companies. The single exception is Player Eight in *Cambises*, with two appearances and twelve lines. This seems an indication of a young dependant rather than a company member, suggesting strongly that this text is not a speculative publication, but a play written for a particular company, and only subsequently published.

Brackets indicate subsequent appearances by the same character.

CONJECTURAL CASTING AND APPEARANCES OF EACH PLAYER

All for Money by Thomas Lupton, 1578

	1	2	3	4		1	2	3	4		1	2	3	4		1	2	3	4		1	2	3	4
00		x			500	x	x	x	x	1000	x		x		1500		x	x	x					
25		x			525	x	x	x	x	1025	x		x	x	1525	x		x	x					
50		x			550	x	x	x	x	1050	x		x		1550	x	x	x	x					
75		x			575	x				1075	x	x	x		1575									
100	x				600		x	x		1100	x	x	x		1600									
125	x		x		625			x	x	1125	x		x	x	1625									
150	x		x	x	650		x	x	x	1150	x		x	x	1650									
175	x		x	x	675		x	x	x	1175	x	x	x		1675									
200		x			700		x	x	x	1200	x	x	x		1700									
225		x		x	725		x	x	x	1225	x		x	x	1725									
250	x	x		x	750		x	x	x	1250	x		x	x	1750									
275			x	x	775		x	x	x	1275	x		x	x	1775									
300			x	x	800	x	x	x	x	1300	x		x		1800									
325	x	x	x	x	825	x	x	x	x	1325	x	x	x		1825									
350	x	x			850	x	x	x	x	1350	x	x	x		1850									
375	x	x	x	x	875	x		x	x	1375	x	x	x		1875									
400	x				900		x			1400	x		x		1900									
425	x				925	x	x			1425	x				1925									
450	x			x	950	x	x			1450		x		x	1950									
475	x	x	x	x	975	x	x	x		1475		x		x	1975									

(This table is only approximate)

Player one
Theologie 99–202
Mischievous helpe 257–86(?)
Sinne the Vice 330–604
Neyther money nor learning 811–89
(Sinne) 930–1439
Godly admonition 1526–72

Player two
Prologue 1–98
Money 203–86
Prest for pleasure 324–413
Gluttonie 485–584
Money without learning 657–877
(Money) 908–1000
Moneyles 1074–113
Nichol neuer out of the lawe 1179–224
Mother Croote 1315–95
Dives 1462–525
Humilitie 1547–72

Player three
Science 127–202
Pleasure 279–350
Damnation 389–413
Pryde 485–584
Learning with money 605–907
All for money 985–1412
(Damnation) 1498–525
Charitie 1547–72

Player four
Arte 153–202
Adulation 231–350
Swift to sinne 385–413
Satan 446–584
Learning without money 618–907
Gregorie graceles 1024–43
Wiliam with the two wiues 1134–74
Sir Laurence 1231–302
Judas 1440–525
Vertue 1547–72

Cambises by Thomas Preston c. 1570

	1	2	3	4	5	6	7	8
00					x			
10					x			
20					x			
30					x			
40	x	x	x	x				
50	x	x	x	x				
60	x	x		x				
70	x	x		x	x			
80	x	x		x	x			
90	x	x		x	x			
100	x	x		x	x			
110					x			
120					x	x		
130					x			
140					x			
150					x			
160	x	x	x		x			
170	x	x	x		x			
180	x	x	x		x			
190	x	x	x		x			
200	x	x	x		x			
210	x	x	x		x			
220	x	x	x		x	x		
230	x	x	x		x	x		
240		x	x		x	x		
250		x	x		x	x		
260		x	x		x	x		
270		x				x		
280		x					x	
290					x			
300					x			
310				x	x			
320		x		x	x			
330		x		x	x			
340							x	
350	x			x	x			
360	x	x		x	x			
370	x	x	x		x	x		
380	x	x	x		x	x		
390	x	x	x		x	x		
400	x	x	x		x	x		

	1	2	3	4	5	6	7	8
410	x				x			
420	x				x	x		
430	x		x		x	x		
440	x		x		x	x		
450	x		x		x	x		
460	x		x		x	x		
470	x		x		x	x		
480	x							
490	x	x	x					
500	x	x	x					
510	x	x	x					
520		x	x					
530	x	x	x				x	
540	x	x	x				x	
550	x	x	x				x	
560	x	x	x				x	
570	x					x	x	
580	x					x	x	
590	x					x	x	
600						x		
610						x		
620			x	x	x	x		
630		x	x		x	x		
640		x	x		x	x		
650	x	x	x	x	x	x		
660	x	x	x	x	x	x		
670	x			x		x		
680	x			x		x		
690						x		
700						x		
710	x	x			x			
720	x	x		x				
730						x		
740						x		
750	x				x	x		
760	x				x	x		
770	x				x	x		
780	x				x	x		
790	x				x	x		
800	x				x	x		
810	x				x	x	x	

	1	2	3	4	5	6	7	8
820	x				x	x	x	
830						x	x	
840		x						x
850		x						x
860		x			x		x	x
870	x	x	x	x	x		x	x
880	x		x	x		x		
890	x		x	x		x		
900	x		x	x		x		
910	x		x	x		x		
920	x		x	x		x		
930	x		x	x		x		
940						x		
950						x		
960						x		
970					x	x		
980					x	x		
990						x		
1000						x		
1010	x	x	x	x	x	x	x	
1020		x	x	x		x	x	
1030		x	x	x		x	x	
1040		x	x	x		x	x	
1050		x	x	x		x	x	
1060		x	x	x			x	
1070		x	x	x			x	
1080		x	x	x			x	
1090		x	x	x			x	
1100	x	x	x	x	x		x	
1110	x	x			x		x	
1120	x	x	x		x		x	
1130		x	x	x				
1140		x	x			x		
1150		x	x	x		x		
1160		x	x	x		x		
1170		x	x	x		x		
1180	x	x	x	x	x			
1190					x			
1200					x			

(This table is only approximate)

234

Player one
Counsel 37–112
Huf 160–248
Praxaspes 353–417, 420–524, 535–601
Third Lord 654–92
Murder 710–31
Lob 754–826
Lord/musician (?) 873–937; 1010–?
(Murder) 1101–26
(Third Lord) 1181–92

Player two
Lord 37–112
Ruf 160–292
Common's Cry 357–64
Common's Complaint 373–412
(Lord) 489–569
Smerdis 622–68, 706–31
Venus 843–80
1st Lord 1010–92

Player three
Knight 37–60
Snuf 160–265
Small Hability 325–40
Proof 373–412
Execution 434–74
(Knight) 489–569
Attendance 622–68
(Knight) 873–937
2nd Lord 1010–12, 1118–92

Player four
Cambises 37–112, 353–69, 654–92, 873–937, 1010–12, 1153–92
Epilogue

Player five
Prologue 1–36
Sisamnes 75–125, 307–38, 353–474
Diligence 622–68
Cruelty 710–31
Hob 754–826
1st Lord (musician) 861–?
Preparation 964–93
(Musician) 1010–?
(Cruelty) 1101–26
(1st Lord) 1181–92

Player six
Ambidexter 126–265, 292–338
Trial 373–412
(Ambidexter) 602–705, 732–838
(* Ambidexter) 938–1057, 1127–80

Player seven
Meretrix 221–92
Shame 341–52
Otian 420–74
Mother 573–601
Marian May-be-Good 813–42
Lady (Queen) 861–937, 1010–26

Player eight
Child 535–601
Cupid 843–80

(*) At this point no-one is free to play the unassigned Maid (861–937) except Ambidexter, or he could double with Venus, thus releasing Player two to play the Maid.

Common Conditions (Anonymous), 1576

	1	2	3	4	5	6		1	2	3	4	5	6		1	2	3	4	5	6
00						x	675		x	x				1350				x		
25		x	x	x			700	x	x	x				1375				x		x
50			x	x	x		725						x	1400				x		x
75			x	x			750				x		x	1425			x	x		x
100	x		x	x			775				x		x	1450			x	x		x
125	x		x	x			800				x		x	1475			x	x		x
150	x						825				x		x	1500		x				
175	x						850				x		x	1525	x	x				
200		x			x	x	875						x	1550	x	x				
225		x			x	x	900	x	x	x				1575			x		x	
250		x			x	x	925	x	x	x				1600			x		x	
275		x			x	x	950	x	x	x				1625			x		x	
300	x		x	x			975	x						1650	x	x	x			
325	x		x	x			1000	x		x	x	x	x	1675	x	x	x			
350	x		x			x	1025	x		x	x	x	x	1700	x	x	x			x
375	x	x	x		x	x	1050		x				x	1725	x					x
400	x	x	x			x	1075						x	1750	x			x	x	x
425	x		x				1100		x					1775	x			x	x	x
450				x			1125		x	x	x	x	x	1800		x	x		x	x
475					x		1150		x	x	x	x	x	1825		x	x		x	x
500		x					1175		x	x	x	x	x	1850	x	x	x	x	x	x
525		x					1200	x		x				1875	x		x	x	x	x
550	x	x					1225	x		x				1900						
575	x	x					1250	x						1925						
600	x						1275		x					1950						
625			x				1300		x			x		1975						
650		x	x				1325		x			x								

(This table is only approximate)

Player one
Common Conditions, the Vice, 98–210, 295–449, 549–623, 694–731, 894–1047, 1209–74, 1524–83, 1654–810, 1859–88

Player two
Tinker 211–94, 363–427
Lamphedon 510–609, 644–722, 910–75
Mountegos 1048–86
(Lamphedon) 1101–208, 1275–350, 1502–76, 1638–26, 1811–88

Player three
Clarissa 21–155, 295–449, 624–722, 910–75
Pirate 995–1047, 1125–94*
(Clarissa) 1209–49, 1423–90, 1584–1726, 1811–888

Player four
Sedmond 21–155, 295–363, 450–77, 760–884

*NB: Players Three and Six may only be required for the musical entry at 1125

Pirate 995–1047, 1125–94
(Sedmond) 1351–501
Lord 1751–96, 1859–88

Player five
Galiarbus 31–71
Tinker 211–94, 363–427
(Galiarbus) 478–509
Pirate 995–1047, 1125–94
Cardolus 1293–350
Leostines 1584–646, 1751–96, 1811–88

Player six
Prologue 1–20
Unthrift 211–94, 363–427
Sabia 732–893
Boy Pirate (leaves early?) 995–1000?
(Sabia) 1048–100
(Pirate) 1125–94*
Lomia 1379–491, 1698–796
Lord 1811–88
Epilogue 1889–904

The Tide Tarrieth No Man by George Wapull, 1576

	1	2	3	4		1	2	3	4		1	2	3	4
00	x				675	x	x	x	x	1350	x	x	x	x
25	x				700			x		1375		x		
50			x		725			x	x	1400			x	x
75			x		750			x	x	1425			x	x
100			x		775		x	x	x	1450		x		
125			x		800	x				1475	x	x		
150	x	x	x	x	825			x		1500	x	x		
175	x	x	x	x	850			x	x	1525	x	x	x	x
200	x	x	x	x	875			x	x	1550	x	x	x	x
225	x	x	x	x	900			x	x	1575	x	x	x	x
250	x	x	x	x	925			x	x	1600	x	x	x	x
275	x	x	x	x	950			x		1625	x			
300	x	x	x	x	975	x		x		1650	x	x		
325			x		1000	x	x	x	x	1675	x	x		x
350			x	x	1025	x	x	x	x	1700	x	x		
375			x	x	1050			x		1725	x	x		
400			x	x	1075		x			1750			x	
425	x	x	x		1100		x			1775	x		x	x
450	x	x	x		1125		x	x		1800	x	x	x	x
475	x	x	x		1150	x		x	x	1825	x			x
500	x	x	x		1175	x		x	x	1850	x	x		x
525	x	x	x	x	1200	x		x		1875				
550			x	x	1225	x	x	x		1900				
575		x	x		1250	x	x	x	x	1925				
600		x	x		1275	x	x	x	x	1950				
625		x	x		1300	x	x	x	x	1975				
650		x	x		1325	x	x	x	x					

(This table is only approximate)

238

Player one
Prologue 1–56
Hurtful Helpe 159–316, 428–551, 664–97
The Tenant 794–835
(Hurtful Helpe) 968–1061, 1139–362
Faithful Few 1468–751, 1776–879

Player two
Painted Profit 159–316
No Good Neighbour 428–551
Courtier 588–697
(Profit) 764–89, 996–1061
(Courtier) 1082–134
Wastefulness 1221–392
Christianity 1440–636
(Wastfulness) 1661–737
Correction 1813–27
(Christianity) 1858–79

Player three
Courage, the Vice 57–793, 836–1081, 1117–362
Debtor 1393–439
(Courage) 1521–620, 1752–827

Player four
Fayned Furtherance 159–316
Greediness 341–421
(Furtherance) 520–62, 664–97
(Greediness) 726–89
Wilful Wanton 856–951
(Furtherance) 996–1061
(Greediness) 1139–98
(Wanton) 1247–362
Sergeant 1393–439
(Greediness) 1521–620
Despair 1682–709
Authority 1776–879

Appendix E
The articles of the 'Purge' from
Satiromastix V.ii

[1] *Imprimis*, you shall swear by Phoebus and the half a score Muses lacking one: not to swear to hang yourself, if you thought any man, woman or child, could write plays and rhymes as well-favoured ones as yourself.

[2] You shall swear not to bombast out a new play, with the old linings of jests, stolen from the Temple's Revels.

[3] Moreover, you shall not sit in a gallery when your comedies and interludes have entered their actions, and there make vile and bad faces at every line, to make gentlemen have an eye to you, and to make players afraid to take your part.

[4] Besides, you must forswear to venter on the stage, when your play is ended, and to exchange courtesies, and compliments with gallants in the Lord's rooms, to make all the house rise up in arms, and to cry 'That's Horace, that's he, that's he, that's he that pens and purges humours and diseases'.

[5] Secondly, when you bid your friends 'to the marriage of a poor couple'; that is to say: your wits and necessities', *alias dictus*, 'to the of rifling of your Muse': *alias* 'your Muse's up-sitting': *alias* a 'Poet's Whitsun-ale'; you shall swear that within three days after, you shall not abroad, in book-binder's shops, brag that your 'viceroys', or 'tributory kings', have done homage to you, or paid quarterage.

[6] Moreover and *imprimis*, when a knight or gentleman of worship does give you his passport to travel in and out to his company, and gives you money for God's sake; I trust in Jesus, you will swear (tooth and nail) not to make scald and wrymouth jests upon his knighthood, will you not?

[7] Thirdly, and last of all saving one, when your plays are misliked at Court, you shall not cry 'mew' like a pussy-cat, and say you are glad you write out of the courtiers' element.

[8] In briefness, when you sup in taverns, amongst your betters, you shall swear not to dip your manners in too much sauce, nor at table to fling epigrams, emblems, or play-speeches about you (like hailstones) to keep you out of the terrible danger of the shot, upon pain to sit at the upper end of the table, at the left hand of Carlo Buffone; swear all this, by Apollo and the eight or nine Muses.

Notes

Introduction

1 Included in the 6th edition of Sir Thomas Overbury's *The Wife*, 1615, and attributed to Webster.

2 B. Harris, *The Malcontent*, New Mermaid edition, London, Benn, 1967, p.xv; M. Wine, *The Malcontent*, Regent Renaissance edition, London, Arnold, 1965; P.J. Finkelpearl, *John Marston of the Middle Temple*, 1969; G.K. Hunter, *The Malcontent*, Revels edition, London, Methuen, 1975; M. Scott, *John Marston's Plays*, 1978.

3 T.F. Van Laan, *Role Playing in Shakespeare*, 1978, p. 220.

4 Heckling spectators also emerge from the body of the audience in *The Knight of the Burning Pestle* and *Apollo's Shroving*. Other plays which have inductions that confuse actors and spectators include *The Staple of News*, *The Isle of Gulls*, *The Careless Shepherdess*, and *What You Will*.

5 See. R. Nelson, *Play Within Play*, 1971, p. 3f. For a discussion of the nature of theatrical illusion.

6 For a discussion of 'Drama as Offering' see M.C. Bradbrook, *The Rise of the Common Player*, 1962, p. 243f.

7 Middleton, Prologue to *No Wit, no Help like A Woman's*, 1613: Some in wit and some in shows/ Take delight and some in clothes/ Some for mirth they chiefly come,/ Some for passion – for both some;/ Some for lascivious meetings, that's their arrent;/ Some to detract and ignorance their warrant. J. Limon, *Gentlemen of a Company: English Players in Central and Eastern Europe, 1590–1660*, 1985, p. 13, quotes a translation of a Frankfurt poem of 1597 in which 'Nubile maids and lecherous dames' at a play paid their money mainly to watch 'what, with his tight-fitting hose/ The well-bred tumbler did disclose'.

8 E.K. Chambers, *The Elizabethan Stage*, 1923, III, p. 424.

9 M. Goldman, *Acting and Action in Shakespearean Tragedy*, 1985, pp. 9–11, argues that, 'When an actor appears before us, he appeals to us, above all, by communicating a promise of action'.

10 See the discussion of itinerant dramaturgy in D. Bevington, *From Mankind to Marlowe*, 1962.

11 Aristotle, *Poetics*, Ch. 4.

12 For the increase of court performances under the Stuarts see T.J. King, *Shakespearean Staging, 1599–1642*, 1971, p. 143, and for details of bad plague

years see G.E. Bentley, *The Profession of Player in Shakespeare's Time: 1590–1642*, 1982, p. 9 and p. 181.

13 See R. Hosley, 'The Gallery over the Stage in the Public Playhouse of Shakespeare's Time', *Shakespeare Quarterly*, VIII, 1957; and King, op. cit.

14 See G. Wickham, *Shakespeare's Dramatic Heritage*, 1969, p. 121f. and *Early English Stages*, [from 1959] *passim*.

15 Quoted in A. Gurr, *The Shakespearean Stage 1574–1642*, 1970, p. 89.

16 Chambers, op. cit., II, p. 365.

17 Studies of artifice in Shakespeare include, S.L. Bethell, *Shakespeare and the Popular Tradition*, 1944; J. Chang, 'Shakespeare's Dramatic Self-Consciousness on Stage and Film', *Iowa State Journal of Research*, 53, 3, 1979, pp. 207–12; and J.L. Styan, 'Changeable Taffeta: Shakespeare's Characters in Performance', in P. McGuire and D.A. Samuelson (eds), *Shakespeare: The Theatrical Dimension*, 1979.

2 The itinerant player and *Sir Thomas More*

1 D. Bevington, *From Mankind to Marlowe*, 1962.

2 A.M. Nagler, *A Sourcebook in Theatrical History*, 1952, p. 57.

3 See Bevington, op. cit., p. 72 and *passim*; G. Taylor, ' "We Happy Few", the 1600 abridgement of *Henry V*', in S. Wells and G. Taylor, *Studies in Henry V*, 1979; J. Limon, *Gentlemen of a Company: English Players in Central and Eastern Europe 1590–1660*, 1985; G.E. Bentley, *The Profession of Player in Shakespeare's Time: 1590–1642*, 1984, pp. 184–6.

4 E.K. Chambers, *The Elizabethan Stage*, 1923, I, p. 332.

5 I. Lancashire, *Dramatic Texts and Records of Britain: A Chronological Topography to 1558*, 1984, p. ix.

6 For the widespread espousal of continuity, see for instance, B. Hunnigher, *Origins of the Theater*, 1953; R. Southern, *Seven Ages of Theatre*, 1962; A. Nicoll, *Masks, Mimes and Miracles*, 1963; R. Weimann, *Shakespeare and the Popular Tradition in Theatre*, 1978; and J. Opland, *Anglo-Saxon Oral Poetry: A Study of the Traditions*, 1980. Popular studies take it as axiomatic.

7 See D. Wiles, *The Early Plays of Robin Hood*, 1981, pp. 35–6.

8 The earliest references all seem to be perambulatory (i.e. short journeys by amateurs): e.g. in South Yorkshire the clerks of Snaith performed before Edward II at Cowick in 1323 (Lancashire, op. cit., 583); and the clerks of Selby visited the Abbey there in 1398 (ibid., 1376). Lancashire favours a visit in 1360 (ibid., 1243) as the first example of itinerance, but the evidence suggests only a brief journey from a nearby parish to an Oxford college. W. Tydeman, *The Theatre in the Middle Ages*, 1978, p. 218, suggests the first clear evidence of itinerants lies in the distinction made in the town accounts of King's Lynn in 1370–1 between 'menstralles' and 'ludentes'. During the next fifty years it is the term 'lusores' however that most frequently occurs, apparently associated with municipal religious performances. Thereafter it begins to be joined by 'player'. There is some suggestion that a company with the livery of the Duke of Gloucester performed a nativity play at Exeter in 1430, and again that the Duke of Buckingham's players visited Canterbury in 1451 (Lancashire 633 and xxi), but the first

unambiguous example of itinerant players claiming household status seems to be a visit to Dover by 'players of my lord Arundell' in 1478 (Tydeman, op. cit., p. 219).

9 A. Cook, *The Privileged Playgoers of Shakespeare's London*, 1981, p. 99f.

10 *Shakespeare Association Facsimiles No. 10*, 1935, Part Two sig A3v.

11 Chambers, op. cit., II, p. 86.

12 M.C. Bradbrook, *The Rise of the Common Player*, 1962, p. 37.

13 I am grateful to David Wiles who made this point to me in correspondence.

14 See E.K. Chambers, *The Medieval Stage*, 1903, II, p. 181, who takes the view that 'inter-' means between two or more performers, and A.W. Pollard, *Miracle Plays, Moralities and Interludes*, 1927, p.lii, who regards the term as meaning between other entertainments. In support of the latter view, J.A.W. Bennet and G.V. Smithers, *Early Middle English Verse and Prose*, 1966, quote Gavin Douglas in *The Palace of Honour*: 'Greit was the preis, the feist royall to sene,/ At eis thay eit, with interludis betwene'.

15 Amydde the theatre, shrowdid in a tent,/ Ther cam out men gastful of her cheris,/ Disfigurid her facis with viseris,/ Pleying by signes in the peoples sight,/ That the poete songen hath on hight. (John Lydgate, *Troybook*, c. 1412–20.)

16 For a discussion of play as 'game' see J. Huizinga, *Homo Ludens*, 1949, and for the 'game' element in medieval drama, R. Axton, *European Drama of the Early Middle Ages*, 1974, *passim*, and V.A. Kolve, *The Play Called Corpus Christi*, 1966, p. 8f.

17 Limon, op. cit., pp. 1–3.

18 Chambers, op. cit., II, pp. 272–3.

19 Studies of doubling include W.J. Lawrence, *Pre-Restoration Studies*, 1927, Ch. III; T.W. Craik, *The Tudor Interlude*, 1958; R. Hosley, 'Was there a 1"Dramatic" Epilogue to The Taming of the Shrew?', *Studies in English Literature*, I, 2, 1961, pp. 17–34; Bevington, op. cit.; W.A. Ringler Jr, 'The Number of Actors in Shakespeare's Early Plays', in G.E. Bentley (ed.), *The Seventeenth Century Stage*, 1968; and S. Booth, 'Speculations on Doubling in Shakespeare's Plays', in P. McGuire and D. Samuelson (eds), *Shakespeare: the Theatre Dimension*, 1979. Lawrence describes doubling as 'gallery slavery' and Bevington sees it as burdensome. Craik and Ringler are concerned that it should be concealed. Hosley discusses its practical function, but only Booth recognizes that it multiplies the pleasures of impersonation.

20 On female marginality and its stage representation see C. Lenz etc. (eds), *The Woman's Part: Feminist Criticism of Shakespeare*, 1983; and L. de Bruyn, *Women and the Devil in Sixteenth-Century Literature*, 1979.

21 For evidence of early playhouse doubling see the 'plots' in W.W. Greg, *Dramatic Documents from the Elizabethan Playhouses*, 1931. For a speculative casting of Shakespeare's plays see Ringler, op. cit. For an extensive discussion of doubling in later cast lists see G.E. Bentley, *The Profession of Player in Shakespeare's Time 1590–1642*, 1984.

22 Ringler, op. cit., p. 129f.

23 S. McMillin, *The Elizabethan Theatre and "The Book of Sir Thomas More"*, 1987, p. 53f.

24 C. Chillingworth, 'Playwrights at Work: Henslowe's not Shakespeare's,

Book of Sir Thomas More', English Literary Renaissance, 10, 1980, pp. 439–79, has argued, in pushing the proposed date of composition back to 1603, that the original draft of the play was a collaboration by a syndicate whose working method can be traced in Henslowe's *Diary*; Munday making the fair copy and Heywood supervising the revision. More recently S. McMillan, op. cit., has argued for a ten-year gap between the original version, written for Strange's Men in 1592/3, but not performed then, and a subsequent revision for a smaller company in 1603, as part of Alleyn's return to the theatre with the Admiral's Men.

25 These texts are to be found in W.C. Hazlitt (ed.), *Dodsley's Old English Plays*, 4th edn, 1874, II, pp. 46–7, 81–5 and 269.

26 F.S. Boas, 'The Play Within the Play', in *Shakespeare and the Theatre*, 1927, notes the *Menaechmi* by Plautus as having been performed by the singing men of Wolsey's chapel in 1527, but no evidence of his having had a professional company.

27 J. Huizinga, *Homo Ludens*, 1949, p. 8.

28 *banquet*: a 'slight repast' [OED], perhaps a dessert of sweetmeats, fruit and wine. The main meal, the 'supper', is to be imagined just finishing in another room.

29 Of the imagined repertory, three plays are extant, one is described above, and one, *Dives and Lazarus*, is lost.

30 *folly waits on wit*: Erasmus wrote his *Encomium Moriae*, 'In Praise of Folly', in 1509, whilst on his journey to More, and puns on his friend's name in the title. See A.J. Krailsheimer, *The Continental Renaissance*, 1971, p. 387f. Whilst Folly is to be avoided, it is also part of our human nature.

31 *you shall not be gone*: The reason there appears to be a lack of consistency here is because Munday, having added a song in which Vanity comes on brazenly, now reverts to the pretended coyness of the original. *Offers* is a technical term to describe a kind of suspended animation in which the character is about to do something, but doesn't.

32 *8 angels*: P. Happe, *Tudor Interludes*, 1972, p. 418, explains: 'The player means that More could be expected to give them £3, £5, or £10. If an angel was worth 10s., they would have so far received £4, and the player is prepared to bet 12d. that this is £1 short'.

3 Evidence of players in Hamlet

1 See Ch. 8.

2 For further discussion of the Play Metaphor see particularly A. Righter, *Shakespeare and the Idea of the Play*, 1962; H. Weisinger, 'Theatrum Mundi: Illusion as Reality', *The Agony and the Triumph*, 1964; T. Stroup, *Microcosmos: The Shape of the Elizabethan Play*, 1965; and R. Egan, *Drama Within Drama*, 1975.

3 See F. Berry, *Shakespeare Inset*, 1965.

4 See F.S. Boas, 'The Play Within a Play', *Shakespeare and the Theatre*, 1927, p. 151; and A. Kernan, 'The great fair of the world and the ocean island', *The Revels History of Drama in English*, III. R.L. McGuire, 'The Play within

the Play in *I Henry IV*', *Shakespeare Quarterly*, 18, 1967, pp. 47-52, and P.A. Gottschalk, 'Hal and the "Play Extempore" in *I Henry IV*', *Texas Studies in English Literature and Language*, 15, 1974, pp. 605-14, take opposite views on the significance of the play-scene.

5 J. Huizinga, *Homo Ludens*, 1949.

6 I.-S. Ewbank, ' "These Pretty Devices": a study of Masques in Plays', in T. Spencer and S. Wells (eds), *A Book of Masques*, 1967, gives a catalogue from the plays of gatecrashing, rape, seductions, and abductions. The anonymous *Woodstock* shows Richard II using a masque to make away with his uncle the Protector. Henry IV subsequently banned 'disguisings' after they had been used in an attempt on his life by supporters of Richard.

7 R. Payne, *The Great God Pan*, 1952, pp. 293-4.

4 Kemp, clowns, and improvisation

1 Thomas Nashe in *Pierce Penniless*, 1592, tells a story of a foolish magistrate who beat the country people around him for laughing, and thus not respecting the Queen's livery, 'when Tarlton first peeped out his head'. Of Reade, a character in the Praeludium to *The Careless Shepherdess*, c. 1638, says 'I never saw Reade peeping through the Curtain,/ But ravishing joy entered into my heart'. For a discussion of *The Wits* frontispiece see R.A. Foakes, *Illustrations of the English Stage, 1580–1642*, 1985, pp. 159–61.

2 Being 'goosed' in popular parlance means to be tweaked between the legs from behind. Pretending such had been attempted on him was a regular piece of business of the late Eric Morecambe. It consisted of twitching the pelvis away from the hand of the celebrity victim, whilst turning to face them with mock affront, and thus suggesting in the timeless tradition of the fool that beneath all virtuous exteriors there is an animalistic sexuality, and that he, the fool, is an object of universal sexual attraction. Incidentally he also did the peeping through the curtain joke, and stage curtains were built into the TV set for the purpose.

3 See D. Wiles, *Shakespeare's Clowns*, 1987, p. 136f.

4 In the Praeludium to *The Careless Shepherdess* (c. 1638) the courtier and the Inns of Court man welcome the absence of a clown in the play to come. The countryman reluctantly stays, but the citizen takes his money back and goes off to see a play at the Red Bull or The Fortune where there will be a jig. A. Gurr, *Playgoing in Shakespeare's London*, 1987, p. 181, notes that it was alleged by Shirley in 1631 that tastes at the Cockpit were so conservative that jigs were still popular with the gentry.

5 R. Weimann, *Shakespeare and the Popular Tradition in the Theater*, 1978, p. 213.

6 ibid., p. 158 and p. 185f.

7 See C. Spencer (ed.), *Five Restoration Adaptations of Shakespeare*, 1965, p. 22. Tate's version of *King Lear*, omitting the Fool, held the stage from 1681 until Macready's production in 1838.

8 Martin Holmes, *Shakespeare and his Players*, 1972, p. 47.

9 See the list of entries from the *Stationers Register* quoted in C.R. Baskervill, *The Elizabethan Jig*, 1929, pp. 107–8.

10 Middleton and Rowley, *The Spanish Gypsy*, c. 1623, IV.ii. '. . . there is a way/ Which the Italians and the Frenchmen use,/ That is, on a word given, or some slight plot,/ The actors will extempore fashion out/ Scenes neat and witty'. Kyd makes a similar statement in *The Spanish Tragedy*, c. 1587, IV.i.163f., whilst in Jonson's *The Case is Altered*, II.vii.36, the Italian characters distinguish the plays of Utopia/England from their own as 'premeditated things'. L.M. Lea, *Italian Popular Comedy*, 1934, p.384, neatly distinguishes the received view of the two traditions: 'To a theme the Italians were expected to fit a plot, to the English a rhyme'.

11 D. Fenton, *The Extra-Dramatic Moment in Elizabethan Plays before 1616*, 1930, p. 18.

12 Kemp is mentioned by name in the Second Quarto text, presumably printed from Shakespeare's own manuscript. There is similar evidence for Dogberry in *Much Ado About Nothing*.

13 P. Davison, *Popular Appeal in English Drama to 1850*, 1982, p. 43f.

14 E.K. Chambers, *The Elizabethan Stage*, 1923, II, p. 326–7 and Wiles, op. cit., p. 41.

15 In 1602 a playbill was issued announcing that *England's Joy* would be performed by gentlemen and gentlewomen at The Swan. As much as two shillings was to be charged at the door. The perpetrator, one Vennar of Lincoln's Inn, subsequently claimed that only pursuit by bailiffs for debt prevented the performance, but the popular view was that he left as soon as he had collected the money. (Chambers, op. cit., III, p. 500). The bill is reprinted in W.W. Greg, *Dramatic Documents from Elizabethan Playhouses*, 1931.

16 The play touches on the vexed issue of why there were no women on the English stage, when they were common in other countries. Thomas Nashe in *Pierce Penniless* takes a similar view to Kemp, 'Our players are not as the players beyond sea, a sort of squirting bawdy comedians, that have whores and common courtesans to play women's parts, and forbear no immodest speech or unchaste action that may procure laughter'. Other travellers were less condemnatory. Fynes Moryson, *Itineraries*, 1617, said the improvisations of the women actors of Florence 'were full of wantonness, though not gross bawdry', and Thomas Coryat, *Crudities*, 1611, is even complimentary. He says of Venetian actresses, they performed 'with as a good a grace, action, gesture, and whatsoever convenient for a player, as ever I saw any masculine actor', and Sir Richard Wynn, in 1623, said of the Spanish that: 'The men are indifferent actors, but the women are very good, and become themselves far better than any I ever saw act those parts, and far handsomer than any women I saw; to say the truth, they are the only cause their plays are so much frequented' (J. Nichols, *Progresses etc. of James I*, 1828, III, p. 1118). Chambers, op. cit., I p. 371, reviews the evidence for women on the London stage, but the only unambiguous reference is by one Richard Maddox in 1583: 'went to the theatre to see a scurvy play set out all by one virgin, which there proved a fyemarten' [pine marten] 'without voice, so that we stayed not the matter'. His objection seems to be technical rather than moral.

5 Clown as justice: *The Mayor of Queenborough*

1 R.C. Bald (ed.), *Hengist, King of Kent*, 1938. For theories of its auspices, possibilities of collaboration, and its critical standing see S. Schoenbaum, *Middleton's Tragedies*, 1955; R.H. Barker, *Thomas Middleton*, 1958; D.M. Holmes, *The Art of Thomas Middleton*, 1970; J.F. McElroy, *Parody and Burlesque in the Tragi-Comedies of Thomas Middleton*, 1972; Margot Heinemann, *Puritanism and Theatre*, 1980 and G.E. Bentley, *The Jacobean and Caroline Stage*, 1941, IV, p. 883.

2 W. Willeford, *The Fool and his Sceptre*, 1969, p. 47.

3 *Whirligig* is glossed in the OED to include 'lively or irregular proceeding', 'a fantastical notion'. *Whibble* is an obsolete variation of Quibble. *Woodcock* is an easily-caught bird, and hence a dupe. The OED lists this as the only occurrence of *Carwigeon*, and hazards it as a variant of Carriwitchet, 'a quibble, conundrum or hoaxing question'. Harbage's *Annals*, Bentley and Bald all suggest that the titles are fictitious.

6 Attacks on the common player

1 The Induction to the anonymous *The Taming of a Shrew* (c. 1589), performed by Pembroke's Men amongst others, is not an exception to the general rule. What Anne Barton, *The Riverside Shakespeare*, 1974, p. 109, describes as evidence that the players are 'bunglers', is no more than the company clown, Sanders, going about his business, as he continues to do in the main play, where he likewise retains his own name.

2 P.J. Finkelpearl, 'John Marston's *Histrio-mastix* an Inns of Court Play: a Hypothesis', *Huntington Library Quarterly*, 29, 1966, pp. 223–34.

3 The most convenient collection of anti-theatre (as well as pro-theatre) material remains the extracts printed in E.K. Chambers, *The Elizabethan Stage* 1923, IV, Appendix C, Documents of Criticism. The pamphlets themselves are edited by A. Freeman in individual volumes collectively entitled *The English Stage, Attack and Defence 1577–1730*, New York, Garland Publishing, 1972.

4 W. Ringler, 'The First Phase of the Elizabethan Attack on the Stage, 1558–1579', *Huntington Library Quarterly*, 4, 1942, p. 407, shows that far from being a summary of contemporary abuse, this is modelled closely on the received scholastic tradition of attack and the patrist comments of Lactantius and St Cyprian.

5 A. Weirum, ' "Actors" and "Play-Acting" in Moralities', *Renaissance Drama*, 3, 1970, pp. 189–214.

6 There was some variance of opinion amongst contemporaries as to the scope of the term. George Withers, *Abuses Stript and Whipt*, 1613, argues that one could be a Puritan without being 'puritanical'. James I, Preface to *Basilikon Doron*, 1603, restricts it to 'that vile sect amongst the Anabaptists called the Family of Love'. See M. Heinemann, *Puritanism and Theatre*, 1980, p. 25 and pp. 77–8. It is in the more restricted sense that dramatists tend to use the term.

7 Heinemann, op. cit., p. 9f.

8 See R. Frazer, *The War Against Poetry*, 1970, p. 5, and Ringler, op. cit., p. 414.
9 Ringler argues that City control was initially only concerned with preventing abuses, not suppressing playing. It was only the vast expansion of the activity and the dangerous widening of the social basis consequent on the establishment of the theatres, he argues, that provoked citizen hostility (Ringler, op. cit., p. 394f.) Arthur Kinney, *Markets of Bawdrie: The Dramatic Criticism of Stephen Gosson*, 1974, likewise shows that Gosson's early objections were to abuses, and only later to mimesis itself.
10 John Earle, 'A Player', *Microcosmography*, 1628, observes rather more sympathetically, (and with a different pun): 'His life is not idle, for it is all action. . .'
11 D.S. Kastan, ' "Proud Majesty Made Subject": Shakespeare and the Majesty of Rule', *Shakespeare Quarterly*, 37, Winter 1986, 4, pp. 459–75, suggests there is an implicit threat to monarchy in its stage representation.
12 According to Henry Clifton's deposition of events at Blackfriars in 1600, his son was threatened with a whip if he was not obedient (Chambers, op. cit., II, p. 44).
13 Marston and Daniel became shareholders of the Chapel Children in 1603 and 1604 respectively. See M. Shapiro, *Children of the Revels*, 1977, p. 25.

7 *The Poetaster,* the 'War of the Theatres', and the Children

1 R.A. Small, *The Stage Quarrel between Ben Jonson and the so-called Poetasters*, 1899, and J.H. Penniman, *The War of The Theatres*, 1879.
2 Small, op. cit., pp. 3–7.
3 J.B. Leishman, *The Three Parnassus Plays*, 1949, p. 82f.
4 O.J. Campbell, *Comical Satyre and Shakespeare's 'Troilus and Cressida'*, 1938, p. 109.
5 Small, op. cit., p. 119.
6 See the discussion of a 'curiously Jonsonian dialogue between aspects of himself' in A. Barton, *Ben Jonson, Dramatist*, 1984, p. 297. She sees it most fully expressed in *The Magnetic Lady*.
7 Penniman, op. cit., p. 115 and Campbell, op. cit., p. 122. They probably misread Tucca's remark IV.vii.2166–7 as a reference to professional playing rather than, as is likely, an expression of his regret at having taken part in Ovid's masquerade.
8 A. Leggatt, *Ben Jonson: His Vision and Art*, 1981, p. 200.
9 J. Barish, *The Anti-Theatrical Prejudice*, 1981, p. 150 likewise perceives a 'delicate equilibrium' in Jonson's work, but is inclined to centre it on his ambivalence towards 'formal theatricalism'.
    I am aware that my reading here is very much out of step with most modern literary criticism which tends to see the play as a more general discussion about the qualities of a poet, and to accept Jonson on his own terms (as their titles indicate). See G.B. Jackson, *Vision and Judgement in Ben Jonson's Drama*, 1968, p. 29; G. Parfitt, *Ben Jonson: Public Poet and Private Man*, 1976, p. 51; P. Edwards, *Threshold of a Nation*, 1983, p. 147; R. Dutton, *Ben Jonson*, 1983, p. 142; A. Barton, op. cit., p. 81.

10 Of the seventy-eight performances recorded at court between 1558–76, forty-six were given by boys, of which twenty-one were by Paul's as against fifteen by the two Chapels Royal.

11 R. Gair, *The Children of Paul's*, 1982, p. 44f. This may have been helped by a reduction in their duties consequent on the abandonment of the Catholic liturgy.

12 See the discussion of Farrant's possible logistics in M.C. Bradbrook, *The Rise of the Common Player*, 1962, p. 222.

13 T. Lennam, *Sebastian Westcott, the Children of Paul's and 'The Marriage of Wit and Science'*, 1975, p. 35.

14 By 1606 the Chapel Children are said to have become 'Masters themselves', 'taking the risks and paying the syndicate for use of the hall' (E.K. Chambers, *The Elizabethan Stage*, 1923, II, p. 52) and attention is being drawn to the advancing age of their rivals, 'the Youths of Paul's, commonly called the children of Paul's . . .' (see M. Shapiro, *Children of the Revels*, 1977, p. 23). By 1608, the Chapel Children are being referred to as 'the players', and some of them are being sent to prison for giving offence in a *Byron* play. Keysar claimed in 1610 that of the 'eighteen or twenty persons' in the Chapel Company, 'all or most of them' had been together for ten years (Chambers, op. cit., II, p. 57).

15 Gair, op. cit., p. 118.

16 The social composition of Elizabethan theatres remains hotly disputed. A. Cook, *The Privileged Playgoers of Shakespeare's London*, 1981, countered Alfred Harbage's earlier studies by arguing for the dominance of the 'privileged classes' in both types of theatre. M. Butler, *Theatre and Crisis, 1632–42*, 1984, p. 298f., argues on the other hand, that London was not yet the magnet for gentry she suggests, and that 'the size of the ratio between population and theatre-capacity seems to point very strongly . . . towards inclusiveness rather than exclusiveness'. A. Gurr, *Playgoing in Shakespeare's London*, 1987, argues for a broader citizen base, and, most cogently, that the characteristics of audiences were subject to considerable variation. Shapiro, op. cit., p. 68, argues that the Children's Theatre audience would 'consist largely of aspirants to high aristocratic rank or those wishing to emulate the fashions of the upper nobility', but Gair, op. cit., p. 69f., suggests an audience often drawn from the immediate environs and with a broader social composition.

17 See for instance the assassination of Ferneze in *The Malcontent* II.v. 'whilst the song is singing', and Aurelia's use of music to indicate her heartlessness (IV.i.68f.). See also C. Kiefer, 'Music and Marston's *The Malcontent*', *Studies in Philology*, LI, 2, 1954, pp. 163–71. For the extent and quality of their music see the account of a performance at Blackfriars in 1602 attended by the Duke of Stettin-Pomerania, quoted by G.K. Hunter in his Revels edition of *The Malcontent*, p.lii.

18 G.E. Bentley, *The Seventeenth-century Stage*, Chicago, Chicago University Press, 1963, p. 3, cites Dekker's *The Gull's Hornbook* in support of his view that spectators sat on the stage in the public theatres. However Dekker's satire encompasses both types of theatre and alternates between the two. Bentley's chief argument, that they go by boat, could equally well refer to a journey along the north bank, especially as they are following horses.

19 The following bibliography emerges from the attacks, mainly by Richard Levin, on the theory developed by R.A. Foakes that Marston's *Antonio* plays are parodies of the adults: A. Caputi, *John Marston, Satirist*, 1961; R.A. Foakes, 'John Marston's Fantastical Plays: *Antonio and Mellida* and *Antonio's Revenge*, *Philological Quarterly*, XLI, 1962, pp. 229–39; D.L. Frost, *The School of Shakespeare*, 1968, pp. 181–3; E.J. Jensen, 'The Style of the Boy Actors', *Comparative Drama*, II, 1968, pp. 100–14; G.D. Kiremidjan, 'The Aesthetics of Parody', *Journal of Aesthetics and Art Criticism*, 28, 1969, pp. 231–42; R.A. Foakes, 'Tragedy at the Children's Theatre after 1600: a Challenge to the Adult Stage', in D. Galloway (ed.), *Elizabethan Theatre* II, 1970, p. 37f.; J.A. Lavin, 'The Elizabethan Theatre and the Inductive Method', in ibid., pp. 78–9; R.A. Foakes, *Shakespeare: The Dark Comedies to the Last Plays: from satire to celebration*, 1971; J. Reibetanz, 'Hieronimo in Decimosexto: A Private Theatre Burlesque', *Renaissance Drama* (New Series), 5, 1972, pp. 89–121; A. Kirsch, *Jacobean Dramatic Perspectives*, 1972; R. Levin, 'The New *New Inn* and the Proliferation of Good Bad Drama', *Essays in Criticism*, 2, 1972, pp. 41–7; R.A. Foakes, 'Mr Levin and "Good Bad Drama" ', *Essays in Criticism*, 22, 1974, pp. 327–9; R. Levin, 'The Proof of the Parody', *Essays in Criticism*, 24, 1974, pp.–312–16; M. Shapiro, *Children of the Revels*, 1977; p. 103f.; R.A. Foakes, 'On Marston, *The Malcontent* and *The Revenger's Tragedy*', in G. Hibbard (ed.), *Elizabethan Theatre*, VI, 1978, VI, pp. 59–75; R. Gair, op. cit.; K. Tucker, '*The Return from Parnassus Part II*: a Possible Key to the Acting Style of Marston's Plays', *American Notes and Queries*, 20, 1982, pp. 131–4; R. Levin, 'The Acting Style of the Children's Companies', to which Mr Tucker appended a reply, *American Notes and Queries*, 22, 1983, pp. 34–5; A. Blake, 'The Humour of the Children: John Marston's Plays in the Private Theatres, *Review of English Studies* (New Series), XXXVII, November 1987, No. 152, pp. 471–82.
20 Goethe on an all-male performance of Goldoni's *La Locandiera* in Rome in c. 1787, quoted in A.M. Nagler, *A Sourcebook in Theatrical History*, 1952, p. 433.
21 Quoted in G. Salgado, *Eyewitnesses of Shakespeare*, 1975, p. 30. See Jonson's Epigram CXX, *Epitaph on S.P.*, for a tribute to Pavy's effectiveness.
22 See U. Ellis-Fermor, *Jacobean Drama*, 1958, p. 100, who talks of 'a deeply inherent non-dramatic principle' in Jonson's work.
23 *Pyrgi*: a *pyrgus* was a tower-shaped dicebox with holes at the bottom. Herford and Simpson [Oxford edition 1922] explain: 'The gamester Tucca nicknames his pages *'pyrgi'* because he uses them to find out a likely lender; he throws a cast with them for this purpose.
24 101–9. An approximation of lines from *The Spanish Tragedy* II.i.
25 112–14. Not traced.
26 Although lines 115 and 130 are given for Histrio and Demetrius to speak together, I have delayed Demetrius' entrance, as being more effective, and allowing Jonson to lambast the players separately for ostentation and then beggarliness (as with Aesop later).
27 128–9. From Chapman's *The Blind Beggar of Alexandria*.
28 133–41. From *The Spanish Tragedy*. Given its popularity, in performance and parody, there may be a further joke in Tucca's not being able to place the

character (Lorenzo) or name the play, perhaps accompanied by a mime, as we might of Laughton's Quasimodo or Newton's Long John Silver.

29 144–6. From Peele's *The Battle of Alcazar*, IV.ii.
30 233–9. From *The Battle of Alcazar*.

8 University drama and *The Return from Parnassus*

1 See J.H. Hexter, 'The Education of the Aristocracy in the Renaissance', *Reappraisals of History*, 1961.
2 See H. Kearney, *Scholars and Gentlemen: Universities and Society in Pre-Industrial Britain, 1500–1700*, 1970, p. 23, and M.H. Curtis, 'The Alienated Intellectuals of Early Stuart England', *Past and Present*, 23, November 1962, pp. 25–40. Lord Chancellor Elsemere observed in 1611, 'I think we have . . . need for better living for learned men . . . for learning without living doth but breed traitors . . .'. Hobbes put it even more bluntly, 'The core of rebellion . . . are the universities'.
3 T.H. Vail Motter, *The School Drama in England*, 1929.
4 F.S. Boas, *University Drama in the Tudor Age*, 1914, p. 26.
5 For the most recent discussion of the Rainolds/Gager argument see J.W. Binns, 'Women or Transvestites on the Elizabethan Stage?: an Oxford Controversy', *Sixteenth Century Journal*, V, 1974, pp. 95–120.
6 J. Nichols, *Progresses etc of James I*, 1828, III, pp. 52–3.
7 Boas, op. cit., p. 317. For the continued decline of university drama in the seventeenth century, and the growing distaste for it, see G.C. Moore Smith, *College Plays Performed by the University of Cambridge*, 1923, p. 14f.
8 G. Wickham, *Early English Stages*, 1, p. 248, and R. Leacroft, *The Development of the English Playhouse*, 1973.
9 P.J. Finkelpearl, *John Marston of the Middle Temple*, 1969, p. 75.
10 Carey Conley, *First English Translators of the Classics*, 1927, quoted in Finkelpearl, op. cit., p. 20.
11 M.H. Curtis, *Oxford and Cambridge in Transition 1558–1642*, 1959, pp. 149–61; M.C. Bradbrook, *The Rise of the Common Player*, 1962, p. 271; G.Y. Gamble, 'Institutional drama: Elizabethan tragedy at the Inns of Court', 1969, unpublished PhD thesis, Stanford University, pp. 32f.
12 A. Harbage, *Shakespeare and the Rival Traditions*, 1952, p. 95; P. Sheavyn, *The Literary Profession in the Elizabethan Age*, revised 1967, p. 89f.; G.E. Bentley, *The Profession of Dramatist in Shakespeare's Time*, 1971, Ch. 5.
13 Views were mixed on the relative standing of professional and university performers. Brome in *The Antipodes*, 1636/7, II.i.16–20, scorns the latter, but at about the same time, when both had performed *The Royal Slave*, Archbishop Laud reported 'By all men's confession the players came short of the University actors' (G.E. Bentley, *The Jacobean and Caroline Stage*, 1941, III, p. 136).
14 For a survey of burlesques of the play see J. Reibetanz, 'Hieronimo in Decimosexto: A Private-Theatre Burlesque', *Renaissance Drama* (New Series), 5, 1972, pp. 89–121; and for university hostility to it, P. Glatzer, *The Complaint of the Poet: The Parnassus Plays*, 1977, p. 247.

15 David Wiles, *Shakespeare's Clowns*, 1987, pp. 35–42.
16 *Untruss*: reference to *Satiromastix or The untrussing of the Humorous Poet*; literally to unfasten the laces or 'points' that held up the hose.
17 *Worshipful Headsmen of the town/Know well what the horn meaneth*: implications of citizen cuckoldry, but perhaps also fleecing gallants. See C.G. Petter's New Mermaid edition of *Eastward Ho!*, 1973, p. 9.

9 *Histriomastix* and the Inns of Court

1 G.Y. Gamble, 'Institutional drama: Elizabethan tragedy at the Inns of Court', 1969, unpublished PhD, thesis, University of Stanford, p. 17.
2 P.J. Finkelpearl, *John Marston of the Middle Temple*, 1969, p. 12f.
3 See also M. Shapiro, *Children of the Revels*, 1977, p. 53; and Finkelpearl, op. cit., p. 27.
4 Gamble, op. cit., p. 95.
5 Edward Hall, *Chronicle*, p. 710, quoted by Gamble, op. cit., p. 96.
6 See L. Salingar, *Shakespeare and the Traditions of Comedy*, 1974, pp. 203–9, and M. Doran, *Endeavours of Art*, 1954, p. 167.
7 E.K. Chambers, *The Elizabethan Stage*, 1923, III; p. 348 and p. 514.
8 Gamble, op. cit., p. 5.
9 See R.C. Bald, 'Thomas Middleton, the Inner Temple Masque, or *Masque of Heroes* (1619)', in T.J.B. Spencer and S. Wells, *A Book of Masques*, 1967.
10 See B. Brown, *Law Sports at Gray's Inn* (1594); A. Wigfall Green, *The Inns of Court and Early English Drama*, 1931; and Finkelpearl, op. cit., *passim*.
11 Perhaps John Davies was cast in this role as 'Stradilax' in 1597/8, and one not altogether to his liking? (See Finkelpearl, op. cit., p. 54.)
12 See D. Bland, 'Inns of Court Nomenclature', *Notes and Queries*, 202, 1957, p. 49.
13 Green, op. cit., p. 94.
14 Finkelpearl, op. cit., p. 55.
15 Green, op. cit., p. 71.
16 Gamble op. cit., p. 90.
17 Green, op. cit., p. 137.
18 Compare for instance the rather comfortable view of Green (p. 53) of an unruffled 'comity subsisting between the crown and the Inns of Court . . .intensified by acts of friendship and gallantry', with Gamble's description (p. 19) of the efforts of the Inns to restrain 'incursions upon the common law by . . . royal prerogative'. M. Heinemann, *Puritanism and Theatre*, 1980, pp. 35–6, discusses the part played by the legal profession in the opposition movement, including the satire on projectors in the antimasques to *The Triumph of Peace*, itself supposed to be a restoration of 'comity'. See also Finkelpearl, op. cit., Ch. 5.
19 Stephen Gosson, *Plays Confuted in Five Actions etc.*, 1582.
20 See G.E. Bentley, *The Jacobean and Caroline Stage*, 1941, II, pp. 694–5.
21 There are strong parallels between the features satirized in Posthast and in the Balladino passage in *The Case is Altered*, whilst *A True Report of the Death and Martyrdom of Thomas Campion* echoes the satire on Posthast's extemporizing pretensions and links Munday with anti-player polemic, probably as

'Anglo-phile Eutheo'. Munday's identification suggests the possibility of the Duttons as the company being pilloried, for which there is further corroboration in verses written on them as a result of a fracas with Inns of Court men (Chambers, op. cit., II, pp. 98–9). If this were the case, then it would argue for a return to the earlier theory that the play was originally written c. 1580 by persons unknown, probably at the Inns, and subsequently revised by Marston c. 1599.

22 M.C. Bradbrook, 'Shakespeare and the Multiple Theatres of Jacobean London', in G. Hibbard (ed.), *Elizabethan Theatre VI*, 1978, p. 98f., suggests that *The Comedy of Timon* and *Tom a Lincoln* are other Inns of Court burlesques of the popular repertoire.

23 Chambers, op. cit., IV, p. 18.

24 *Canadoe*: a word not found elsewhere; it may be an unusual drink, but since Posthast is rhyming extempore, and badly, perhaps he converts the ending of Canary, a popular drink, to make it rhyme with 'bravado'. This would add further humour to their stupidity in repeating it. See The Praeludium to *The Careless Shepherdess*: '*Thrift*: Sir, I have heard 'um say, that Poets may/ Write without Ink rather than Wine. *Landlord*: And I/ Have heard that 'tis as hard to make a Play/Without Canary, as it is to make/ A Cheese without Rennet. . .'

25 *Ingle*: catamite. Also variant of 'angel'. Seems used here in the modern sense of theatrical 'angel', a patron or investor with a personal interest in the performer. Jonson uses it in the former sense in *Epicoene*, I.i. 23–31 and in the latter in *The Poetaster*, I.ii. 18. Not to be confused with INKLE.

26 *A Petronell* was a large pistol, named so because the butt end was held against the chest. *Sir Petronell Flash* was also a character in *Eastward Ho* (1605), addicted to gambling.

27 III. 183–6. Robert Greene, *Greene's Groatsworth of Wit* (written 1592 and published posthumously in 1596), urges a similar course of action: 'O that I might entreat your rare wits to be employed in more profitable courses: and let these Apes imitate your past excellence, and never more aquaint them with your admired inventions.'

28 *Proud Statute Rogues*: The title of the play seems a direct reference to the *Act for the punishment of Vagabonds* of 1572 and/or its revision in 1598. Both provided for whipping of players without a licence, the later version specifying that they shall 'be stripped naked from the middle upwards and shall be openly whipped until his or her body be bloody'. There is further provision in the latter for Rogues that 'appear to be dangerous to the inferior sort of People' to be banished out of the realm (as these players are), on pain of execution if they return.

29 *Ram Alley*, 1607–8, a Children's play, alleges (IV.i) that it is common policy with players: 'That one should be a notorious cuckold,/ If it be but for the better keeping/ The rest of his company together.'

30 *Humour*: play on the modern meaning in 1. 188, as against Gutt, 1. 187, who means someone with physiological peculiarities whose uncertain temper makes a good acting part. (See *As You Like It*, I.ii. 245, 'The Duke is humourous'.)

10 Apprentice drama and *The Hog Hath Lost his Pearl*

1 G.E. Bentley, *The Jacobean and Caroline Stage*, 1941, I, p. 161f. A. Gurr, *Playgoing in Shakespeare's London*, 1987, p. 170, explains the riot in terms of a response to Beeston's transferral of his company and plays from The Red Bull to the newly-built Cockpit and his raising of the prices of admission.

2 Bentley, op. cit., II, pp. 690–1.

3 See A. Cook, *The Privileged Playgoers of Shakespeare's London*, 1981, p. 221; and Gurr, op. cit., p. 52, who estimates that one in eight apprentices were of genteel origins, rising to nearly a third amongst goldsmiths.

4 Cook, op. cit., p. 46.

5 ibid., p. 47.

6 ibid., p. 65.

7 Printed with the play in W.C. Hazlitt, *Dodsley's Old English Plays*, 4th edn; 1875, XI, p. 425.

8 The first workhouse, also used in the early seventeenth century as a local prison. See G. Salgado, *The Elizabethan Underworld*, 1984, p. 183.

9 See L.W. Payne (ed.), *Hector of Germany*, 1904, p. 20.

10 Bentley, op. cit., I, p. 207 n. 4.

11 C.R. Baskervill, *The Elizabethan Jig and Related Song Drama*, 1929, pp. 437–72.

12 D. Wiles, *Shakespeare's Clowns*, 1987, p. 44.

13 Baskervill, op. cit., p. 116.

14 Meg of Westminster: one of a group of celebrated female transvestites, including Mary Ambree and Moll Frith, whose mixture of courage, prostitution, crime, and sexual ambiguity seems to have fascinated the Elizabethans; witness a prose work, *The Life and Pranks of Long Meg of Westminster*, c. 1582; a play about her in 1594–5, and mentioned in *Amends for Ladies*, 1611; references to Meg and Mary in *Satiromastix* II.i, 1601; they both appear silently in *The Fortunate Isles and their Union*, 1625; and in *The Roaring Girl*, c. 1607–8, Meg is contrasted with the heroine Moll, as using physical strength rather than wit (V.i.2). See also P. Gartenberg, 'Shakespeare's Roaring Girls', *Notes and Queries*, 27, 1980, 2, pp. 174–5.

15 *Garlic*: to be popular the jig should be as odiferous as possible. Garlic was often associated with the low-class audience; as Marston in *Jack Drum's Entertainment*, who implies that a visitor to the public theatres would be 'choked/ With the stench of Garlic' (V.106–7). A passage from *The World's Folly* talks of the stage at The Fortune 'behung with chains of garlic', presumably at a performance of *The Roaring Girl*, 'as an antidote against their own infectious breaths' (E.K. Chambers, *The Elizabethan Stage*, 1923, IV, p. 254). I see no evidence for inventing an actor called Garlic (Chambers, op. cit., II, p. 318).

11 Heywood, Massinger, and the defence of playing

1 Christopher Beeston, 'To my good friend and fellow, Thomas Heywood', one of the commendatory verses printed with the *Apology for Actors*.

2 See D. Klein, *The Elizabethan Dramatists as Critics*, 1963, pp. 92f.

3 Thomas Heywood, *An Apology for Actors*, 1612, edited by R.H. Perkinson, 1941, sig F1v.
4 Heywood, op. cit., sig G3r.
5 See P. Edwards and C. Gibson, *The Plays and Poems of Philip Massinger*, 1975, p. xxix.
6 M. Butler, 'Romans in Britain: *The Roman Actor* and the Early Stuart Classical Play', in D. Howard (ed.), *Philip Massinger: A Critical Reassessment*, 1985.

12 Ambiguities

1 For general discussions of attitudes to theatre and their ambiguities see J. Barish, *The Anti-theatrical Prejudice*, 1981, and W. Worthen *The Idea of the Actor*, 1984.
2 H. Granville-Barker, *Prefaces to Shakespeare*, 2nd Series, 1930.
3 Philip Stubbes, *Anatomy of Abuses*, 1583. For studies of anti-player charges of this nature see W.R. Davies, *Shakespeare's Boy Actors*, 1939, *passim*, and J.E. Teagarden, 'Reaction to the professional actor in Elizabethan London', 1957, unpublished PhD thesis, University of Florida, p. 43f.
4 L. Jardine, *Still Harping on Daughters*, 1985, p. 29, argues for the focusing of homosexual eroticism on the actors playing these roles. Sarah Maitland, *Vesta Tilley*, 1986, p. 102, makes a similar point in discussing how a woman would construct a cross-dressing act today.
5 For a discussion of the associations of *hungan* and actor, see D. Cole, *The Theatrical Event: A Mythos, A Vocabulary, A Perspective*, 1975, p. 33f.
6 See A. Righter, *Shakespeare and the Idea of the Play*, 1962, p. 148f.
7 Barish, op. cit., p. 147.
8 E.K. Chambers, *The Elizabethan Stage*, 1923, IV p. 218. W. Ringler, 'The First Phase of the Elizabethan Attack on the Stage, 1558-1579', *Huntington Library Quarterly*, 4, 1942, p. 409, suggests Gosson's own motives, as a failed playwright hired by the citizens, were suspect. A. Kinney, *Markets of Bawdrie*, 1974, p. 17, defends Gosson.
9 E.B. Partridge. 'Ben Jonson: The Makings of a Dramatist (1596-1602)', in J.R. Brown and B. Harris (eds), *Elizabethan Theatre*, 1966, p. 238.
10 R.B. Sharpe, *The Real War of the Theatres*, 1935, p. 135.
11 A. Covatta, *Thomas Middleton's City Comedies*, 1973, pp. 44-5.
12 Thomas Nashe, *Selected Works*, ed. S. Wells, 1964, p. 66; Thomas Heywood, *Apology for Actors*, sig D1r and sig G1r; and Thomas Randoph, *The Muses Looking Glass*, Dodsley, XI, p. 190.
13 Kinney, op. cit., p. 65, shows how much other polemicists borrowed from Gosson.
14 Modern critics seem uncertain (and inconsistent) in their treatment of these pamphlets. A. Cook, *The Privileged Playgoers of Shakespeare's London*, 1981, on the one hand acknowledges that Nashe 'may have been stretching a point' in suggesting that plays may distract the discontented from felonies or treason (p. 99), but continues to treat Greene's surely invented meeting with the player he mistakes for a gentleman as though it were genuine evidence (p. 121). A Gurr, *Playgoing in Shakespeare's London*, 1987, resists

Samuel Rowlands, who 'joked', he says, 'about gallants choosing between a play and a bawdy house' (p. 133). However he describes *Pierce Penniless* as 'sociological delving' (p.133) and uses the Grocer in *The Knight of the Burning Pestle* as evidence of how mush citizens spent at the theatre (p. 75).

15 M.C. Bradbrook, *The Rise of the Common Player*, 1962, p. 272, says of the *Parnassus* plays, 'the mixture of admiration, envy and scorn for the common stages cannot be reduced to final coherence.'

13 Conclusion

1 M.C. Bradbrook, *The Rise of the Common Player*, 1962, p. 265f.

2 ibid., p. 256.

3 M. Shapiro, *Children of the Revels*, 1977, p. 68f.

4 The first reference I have come across is in the 1545 proclamation of Henry VIII which provided that 'common players' could be impressed for the 'Fleet of Foot', although this may refer to gamblers. J. Cocke, *A Common Player*, 1615, restricts the term to a particular category of players: 'Yet in the general number of them, many may deserve a wise man's commendation: and therefore I did prefix an Epithet of "common", to distinguish the base and artless appendants of our city companies, which often times start away into rustical wanderers and then (like Proteus) start back again into the City number.'

5 E.K. Chambers, *The Elizabethan Stage*, 1923, II, p. 75.

6 Chambers, op. cit., pp. 43–4.

7 T. Cole and H. Chinoy (eds), *Actors on Acting*, revised edn, 1970, p. 40. For the participation of professionals in amateur performances see J.C. Coldeway, 'That Enterprising Property Player: Semi-Professional Drama in Sixteenth-Century England', *Theatre Notebook*, 31, 1977. pp. 5–12; and G. Wickham, *The Medieval Theatre*, 1974, p. 196.

8 R. Levin, *New Readings v. Old Plays*, 1979, and H. Hawkins, *Likeness of Truth*, 1972 and *The Devil's Party*, 1985, have done much to show the weakness of thematic and moralistic criticism.

9 S.R. Gardiner, 'The Political Element in Massinger', *Contemporary Review*, XXVIII, 1876, pp. 495–507; A.H. Cruikshank, *Philip Massinger*, 1920; T.A. Dunn, *Philip Massinger, Man and Playwright*, 1957, p. 131: 'He was a born moralist'. A.K. McIlwraith (ed.), *Five Stuart Tragedies*, 1953, xvii, suggests that at the centre of the play Massinger is posing the question: 'When will loyalty break?' For the recent rehabilitation see D. Howard (ed.), *Philip Massinger: A Critical Reassessment*, 1985, especially the essays by A. Barton and M. Butler.

10 Middleton's comedies for the adolescent troupe at St Paul's c. 1604–6, for instance, have been rendered all but unrecognizable by the weight of dour critical interpretation. *A Mad World, My Masters*, in which a likable young scapegrace uses comic stratagems to get hold of *his own* inheritance, apparently concerns 'the repudiation of sin' (D. Holmes, *The Art of Thomas Middleton*, 1970, p. 26), and 'an absolute condemnation of our inescapable sinfulness' (D. Farley-Hills, *The Comic in Renaissance Comedy*, 1981, p. 101). At the very least, the critics agree, the comedies 'shape character and

incident in order to bring alive the underlying social and moral issues. . .'
(B. Gibbons, *Jacobean City Comedy*, 1980, p.3).

11 M. Butler, *Theatre and Crisis 1632–42*, 1984, p. 281.

12 Howard in his own essay in the collection makes a questionable distinction
(p. 118) in suggesting that Massinger turned from psychological studies to
political ones because they could be more adequately represented by
straightforwardly good or evil characters.

13 Dunn, op. cit., p. 43f.

14 Kemble performed the Defence as a separate item in 1781, Macready in
1812, and Kean in 1822, and it was still being performed by Coleman in
1850. See P. Edwards and C. Gibson, *Plays and Poems of Philip Massinger*,
1975, pp. 10–12.

15 H. Wolfflin, *Principles of Art History*, trans. M.D. Hottinger, 1932, p. 166, 'A
characteristic of the multiple unity of the sixteenth century is that the
separate things in the picture are felt to be relatively equal in material
value'.

Appendix B: Henslowe's wardrobe inventory, c. 1602

1 Material woven with raised areas, which were cut and left as pile.

2 Patterns created by removing threads.

3 With red threads running across the top of it.

4 Either slashed longitudinally to reveal the garment or lining beneath, or
with pieces of material sewn on to give this effect. Also used of the trunk
hose decorated in this manner.

5 Pleated skirt appended to the doublet.

6 Rich embroidered cloth with gold thread on woof of silk.

7 The word 'hose' is used in this period not of stockings, but of padded trunks,
often attached to other leg-coverings. French hose are short, often puffed,
trunks, worn either with long stockings, or some additional close-fitting
thigh coverings, often called 'canions'. The term does not appear in these
lists, but scholars seem uncertain of the identity of 'scalins', and their
frequency here suggests they are the same as, or similar to, canions.

Bibliography

Allen, P.S., 'The Medieval Mimus', *Modern Philology*, VI, 1910, p. 329–44.

Armstrong, W., 'Shakespeare and the Acting of Edward Alleyn', in A. Nicoll, (ed.), *Shakespeare Survey 7*, Cambridge, Cambridge University Press, 1954.

Axton, R., *European Drama of the Early Middle Ages*, London, Hutchinson, 1974.

Baldwin, T.W., *The Organisation and Personnel of the Shakespearean Company*, Princeton, NJ, Princeton University Press, 1927.

Barber, C.L., *Shakespeare's Festive Comedy*, Princeton, NJ, Princeton University Press, 1959.

Barish, J., *The Anti-Theatrical Prejudice*, Berkeley, California University Press, 1981.

Barker, R.H., *Thomas Middleton*, Westport, Greenwood Press, 1958.

Barroll J. Leeds *et al.* (eds), *The Revels History of Drama in English*, III, London, Methuen, 1975.

Barton, A., *Ben Jonson, Dramatist*, Cambridge, Cambridge University Press, 1984.

Baskervill, C.R., *The Elizabethan Jig*, Chicago, Chicago University Press, 1929.

Beckerman, B., *Shakespeare and the Globe*, New York, Macmillan, 1962.

Bennet, J.A.W. and Smithers, G.V., *Early Middle English Verse and Prose*, Oxford, Clarendon Press, 1966.

Bentley, G.E., *The Jacobean and Caroline Stage*, Oxford, Oxford University Press, 1941.

Bentley, G.E., *The Seventeenth-century Stage*, Chicago, Chicago University Press, 1963.

Bentley, G.E., *The Profession of Dramatist in Shakespeare's Time: 1590–1642*, Princeton, NJ, Princeton University Press, 1971.

Bentley, G.E., *The Profession of Player in Shakespeare's Time: 1590–1642*, Princeton, NJ, Princeton University Press, 1984.

Berry, F., *Shakespeare Inset*, London, Routledge & Kegan Paul, 1965.

Berry, R., *Shakespeare and the Awareness of the Audience*, London, Macmillan, 1985.

Bethell, S.L., *Shakespeare and the Popular Tradition*, Westminster, King and Staples, 1944.

Bethell, S.L., 'Shakespeare's actors', *Review of English Studies*, New Series, I, 1950, pp. 193–205.

Bevington, D., *From Mankind to Marlowe*, Cambridge, Mass., Harvard University Press, 1962.

Bevington, D., *Tudor Drama and Politics*, Cambridge, Mass., Harvard University Press, 1969.

Bills, B.D., ' "The Suppression Theory" and the English Corpus Christi Play: a Re-Examination', *Theatre Journal*, 32, 1980, pp. 157–69.

Binns, J.W., 'Women or Transvestites on the Elizabethan Stage?: an Oxford Controversy', *Sixteenth-century Journal*, V, 1974, pp. 95–120.

Blake, A., 'The Humour of the Children: John Marston's Plays in the Private Theatres', *Review of English Studies*, New Series, XXXVII, 152, November 1987, pp. 471–82.

Bland, D., 'Interludes in Fifteenth-century Revels at Furnival's Inn', *Review of English Studies*, 3, 1952, pp. 263–8.

Bland, D., 'Inns of Court nomenclature', *Notes and Queries*, 202, 1957, p. 49.

Bland, D., 'A Checklist of Drama at the Inns of Court', *Research Opportunities in Renaissance Drama*, 9, 1966, pp. 47–61.

Boas, F.S., *University Drama in the Tudor Age*, Oxford, Oxford University Press, 1914.

Boas, F.S., 'The Play Within a Play', The Shakespeare Association, *Shakespeare and the Theatre*, Oxford, Oxford University Press, 1927.

Bodkin, M., *Archetypal Patterns in Poetry*, Oxford, Oxford University Press, 1934.

Bradbrook, M.C., *The Rise of the Common Player*, Cambridge, Cambridge University Press, 1962.

Brown, A., 'The Play within a Play: An Elizabethan Dramatic Device', *Essays and Studies*, 1960, pp. 36–48.

Brown, J.R., *Shakespeare's Dramatic Style*, London, Heinemann, 1970.

de Bruyn, L., *Women and the Devil in Sixteenth-Century Literature*, 1979.

Burns, E., *Theatricality*, London, Longmans, 1972.

Butler, M., *Theatre and Crisis, 1632–42*, Cambridge, Cambridge University Press, 1984.

Calderwood, J.L., *Shakespearean Metadrama*, Minnesota University Press, 1971.

Campbell, O.J., *Comical Satyre and Shakespeare's 'Troilus and Cressida'*, San Marino, Huntington Library Publications, 1938.

Caputi, A., *John Marston, Satirist*, Ithaca, Cornell University Press, 1961.

Chambers, E.K., *The Medieval Stage*, Oxford, Oxford University Press, 1903.

Chambers, E.K., *The Elizabethan Stage*, Oxford, Oxford University Press, 1923.

Chang, J., 'Shakespeare's Dramatic Self-Consciousness on Stage and Film', *Iowa Stage Journal of Research*, 53, 3, 1979, pp. 207–12.

Chillingworth, C., 'Playwrights at Work: Henslowe's not Shakespeare's *Book of Sir Thomas More*', *English Literary Renaissance*, 10, 1980, pp. 439–79.

Clopper, L.M., *Records of Early English Drama: Chester*, Manchester, Manchester University Press, 1979.

Coldeway, J.C., 'That Enterprising Property Player: Semi-Professional Drama in Sixteenth-Century England', *Theatre Notebook*, 31, 1977, pp. 5–12.

Cole, D., *The Theatrical Event: A Mythos, A Vocabulary, A Perspective*, Middleton Conn., Wesleyan University Press, 1974.

Cole, T. and Chinoy, H., *Actors on Acting*, 2nd edn, New York, Crown Publishers, 1970.

Cook, A., *The Privileged Playgoers of Shakespeare's London*, Princeton, NJ,

Princeton University Press, 1981.

Covatta, A., *Thomas Middleton's City Comedies*, Lewisburg University Press, 1973.

Craik, T.W., *The Tudor Interlude*, Leicester, Leicester University Press, 1958.

Cruikshank, A.H., *Philip Massinger*, Oxford, Blackwell, 1920.

Curtis, M.H., *Oxford and Cambridge in Transition 1558–1642*, Oxford, Clarendon Press, 1959.

Curtis, M.H., 'The Alienated Intellectuals of Early Stuart England', *Past and Present*, 23, November 1962, pp. 25–40.

David, R., 'Shakespeare and the Players', in P. Alexander (ed.), *Studies in Shakespeare*, Oxford, Oxford University Press, 1964.

Davies, W.R., *Shakespeare's Boy Actors*, London, Dent, 1939.

Davison, P., 'The Theme and Structure of the Roman Actor', *Aumla*, 19, 1962, pp. 39–56.

Davison, P., *Popular Appeal in English Drama to 1850*, New Jersey, Barnes & Noble, 1982.

Dawson, A.B., *Indirections: Shakespeare and the Art of Illusion*, Toronto, University of Toronto Press, 1978.

Doran, M., *Endeavours of Art*, Madison, Wisconsin University Press, 1954.

Dramaticus, 'The Players who Acted in *The Shoemaker's Holiday* etc.', *Shakespeare Society Papers*, 1849.

Dunkel, W.D., *The Dramatic Technique of Thomas Middleton in his Comedies of London Life*, New York, Russell & Russell, 1925.

Dunn, T.A., *Philip Massinger, Man and Playwright*, Edinburgh, T. Nelson, 1957.

Dutton, R., *Ben Jonson*, Cambridge, Cambridge University Press, 1983.

Edwards, P., *Threshold of a Nation*, Cambridge, Cambridge University Press, 1983.

Egan, R., *Drama Within Drama*, New York, Columbia University Press, 1975.

Eliot, T.S., *Selected Essays*, London, Faber & Faber, 1932.

Ellis-Fermor, U., *Jacobean Drama*, London, Methuen, 1958.

Farley-Hills, D., *The Comic in Renaissance Comedy*, London, Macmillan, 1981.

Fenton, D., *The Extra-Dramatic Moment in Elizabethan Plays before 1616*, Philadelphia, Philadelphia University Press, 1930.

Fiedler, L., 'The Defence of Illusion and the Creation of Myth', *English Institute Essays*, 1948, pp. 74–94.

Finkelpearl, P.J., 'John Marston's *Histrio-mastix* an Inns of Court Play: a Hypothesis', *Huntington Library Quarterly*, 29, 1966, pp. 223–34.

Finkelpearl, P.J., *John Marston of the Middle Temple*, Cambridge, Mass., Harvard University Press, 1969.

Foakes, R.A., 'The Player's Passion', *Essays and Studies* (New Series), VIII, 1954, pp. 62–77.

Foakes, R.A. and Ricketts, R.T. (eds), *Henslowe's Diary*, Cambridge, Cambridge University Press, 1961.

Foakes, R.A., 'John Marston's Fantastical Plays: *Antonio and Mellida* and *Antonio's Revenge*', *Philological Quarterly*, XLI, 1962, pp. 229–39.

Foakes, R.A., *Shakespeare: The Dark Comedies to the Last Plays: from satire to celebration*, London, Routledge & Kegan Paul, 1971.

Foakes, R.A., 'Mr Levin and "Good Bad Drama" ', *Essays in Criticism*, 22, 1974, pp. 327–9.

Foakes, R.A., *Illustrations of the English Stage, 1580–1642*, London, Scolar Press, 1985.

Frazer, R., *The War Against Poetry*, Princeton, NJ, Princeton University Press, 1970.

Frost, D.L., *The School of Shakespeare*, Cambridge, Cambridge University Press, 1968.

Frye, N., *A Natural Perspective*, New York, Harcourt, Brace & World, Inc., 1965.

Gair, R., *The Children of Paul's*, Cambridge, Cambridge University Press, 1982.

Galloway, D. (ed.), *Elizabethan Theatre*, II & III, Toronto, Macmillan, 1970 & 1973.

Gamble, G.Y., 'Institutional drama: Elizabethan tragedy at the Inns of Court', 1969, unpublished PhD thesis, Stanford University.

Gardiner, S.R., 'The Political Element in Massinger', *Contemporary Review*, XXVIII, 1876, p. 495–507.

Gartenberg, P., 'Shakespeare's Roaring Girls', *Notes and Queries*, 27, 2, 1980, pp. 174–5.

George, D., 'Pre-1642 Cast-lists and a New One for *The Maid's Tragedy*', *Theatre Notebook*, 31, 2, 1977, pp. 22–7.

Gibbons, B., *Jacobean City Comedy*, 2nd edn, London, Methuen, 1980.

Glatzer, P., *The Complaint of the Poet: The Parnassus Plays*, Salzburg, Salzburg University Press, 1977.

Goldman, M., *Shakespeare and the Energies of Drama*, Princeton, NJ, Princeton University Press, 1972.

Goldman, M., *Acting and Action in Shakespearean Tragedy*, Princeton, NJ, Princeton University Press, 1985.

Goldsmith, R., *Wise Fools in Shakespeare*, Liverpool, Liverpool University Press, 1974.

Goldstein, L., 'On the Transition from Formal to Naturalistic Acting on the Elizabethan and post-Elizabethan Stage', *Bulletin of the New York Public Library*, 62, 1958, pp. 330–49.

Gottschalk, P.A., 'Hal and the "Play Extempore" in *I Henry IV*', *Texas Studies in English Literature and Language*, 15, 1974, pp. 605–14.

Granville-Barker, H., *Prefaces to Shakespeare*, 2nd Series, London, Batsford, 1930.

Green, A.W., *The Inns of Court and Early English Drama*, New Haven, Yale University Press, 1931.

Greenfield, T., *The Induction in Elizabethan Drama*, Corvallis, Oregon University Press, 1969.

Greg, W.W., *Dramatic Documents from the Elizabethan Playhouses*, Oxford, Clarendon Press, 1931.

Gurr, A., 'Elizabethan Action', *Studies in Philology*, 63, 2, 1966, pp. 144–56.

Gurr, A., 'Who Strutted and Bellowed', in A. Nicoll (ed.), *Shakespeare Survey* 16, Cambridge, Cambridge University Press, 1970.

Gurr, A., *The Shakespearean Stage 1574–1642*, Cambridge, Cambridge University Press, 1970.

Gurr, A., *Playgoing in Shakespeare's London*, Cambridge, Cambridge University Press, 1987.

Habicht, W., 'Tree Properties in Elizabethan Theatre', *Renaissance Drama*, New Series, 4, 1972, pp. 69–92.

Harbage, A., *Shakespeare and the Rival Traditions*, Bloomington, Indiana University Press, 1952.

Harbage, A., *Annals of English Drama* (revised S. Schoenbaum), London, Methuen, 1964.

Hattaway, M., *Elizabethan Popular Theatre*, London, Routledge & Kegan Paul, 1982.

Hawkins, H., *Likeness of Truth in Elizabethan and Restoration Drama*, Oxford, Oxford University Press, 1972.

Hawkins, H., *The Devil's Party*, Oxford, Oxford University Press, 1985.

Heinemann, M., *Puritanism and Theatre*, Cambridge, Cambridge University Press, 1980.

Hibbard, G. (ed.), *Elizabethan Theatre*, VI & VII, Toronto, Macmillan, 1978 & 1980.

Hexter, J.H., 'The Education of the Aristocracy in the Renaissance', *Reappraisals of History*, 1961.

Hillebrand, H., *The Child Actors*, New York, Russell & Russell, 1926.

Hodges, C.W., *The Globe Restored*, 2nd edn, Oxford, Oxford University Press, 1964.

Holmes, D.M., *The Art of Thomas Middleton*, Oxford, Oxford University Press, 1970.

Holmes, M., *Shakespeare and his Players*, London, John Murray, 1972.

Homan, S., *When the Theatre turns to itself: The Aesthetic Metaphor in Shakespeare*, Lewisburg, Bucknell University Press, 1981.

Hosley, R., 'The Gallery over the Stage in the Public Playhouse of Shakespeare's Time', *Shakespeare Quarterly*, VIII, 1957.

Hosley, R., 'The Discovery Space in Shakespeare's Globe' in A. Nicoll (ed.), *Shakespeare Survey* 12, Cambridge, Cambridge University Press, 1959.

Hosley, R., 'Was there a "Dramatic" Epilogue to *The Taming of the Shrew*?', *Studies in English Literature*, i, 2, 1961, pp. 17–34.

Hosley, R., 'The Staging of the Scenes in *Antony and Cleopatra*', *University of Pennsylvania Library Chronicle*, 30, 1964, pp. 62–71.

Howard, D. (ed.), *Philip Massinger: A Critical Reassessment*, Cambridge, Cambridge University Press, 1985.

Huizinga, J., *Homo Ludens*, London, Routledge & Kegan Paul, 1949.

Hunnigher, B., *Origins of the Theater*, New York, Hill & Wang, 1953.

Ide, R.S., 'Elizabethan Revenge Tragedy and the Providential Play-Within-a-Play, *Iowa State Journal of Research*, 56, 1, 1981, pp. 91–6.

Ingram, W. (ed.), *Records of Early English Drama: Coventry*, Manchester, Manchester University Press, 1981.

Jackson, G.B., *Vision and Judgement in Ben Jonson's Drama*, New Haven, Yale University Press, 1968.

Jardine, L., *Still Harping on Daughters*, Brighton, Harvester Press, 1983.

Jensen, E.J., 'The Style of the Boy Actors', *Comparative Drama*, II, 1968, pp. 100–14.

Johnson, A. and Rogerson, M. (eds), *Records of Early English Drama: York*, Manchester, Manchester University Press, 1978.

Joseph, B., *Elizabethan Acting*, 2nd edn, Oxford, Oxford University Press, 1964.

Kastan, D.S., ' "Proud Majesty Made Subject": Shakespeare and the Majesty of Rule', *Shakespeare Quarterly*, 37, 4, Winter 1986, pp. 459–75.

Kay, W.D., 'Ben Jonson, Horace and The Poetomachia', unpublished dissertation, Princeton, NJ, University of Princeton, 1968.

Kearney, H., *Scholars and Gentlemen: Universities and Society in Pre-Industrial Britain, 1500–1700*, London, Faber, 1970.

Kernan, A., ' "John Marston's" Play *Histriomastix*', *Modern Language Quarterly*, XIX, 1958, pp. 134–40.

Kernan, A., 'The Court and the Public Theatre under Elizabeth and James', *Research Opportunities in Renaissance Drama*, 1980, pp. 15–19.

Kerrigan, J., 'Hieronimo, Hamlet and Remembrance', *Essays in Criticism*, 31, 2, April 1981, pp. 112–13.

Kiefer, C., 'Music and Marston's *The Malcontent*', *Studies in Philology*, LI, 2, 1954, pp. 163–71.

King, T.J., *Shakespearean Staging 1599–1642*, Cambridge, Mass., Harvard University Press, 1971.

Kinney, A., *Markets of Bawdrie: The Dramatic Criticism of Stephen Gosson*, Salzburg, Salzburg University Press, 1974.

Kiremidjan, G.D., 'The Aesthetics of Parody', *Journal of Aesthetics and Art Criticism*, 28, 1969, pp. 231–242.

Kirsch, A., *Jacobean Dramatic Perspectives*, Charlottesville, Virginia University Press, 1972.

Klein, D., *The Elizabethan Dramatists as Critics*, Westport, Greenwood Press, 1963.

Knights, L.C., *Drama and Society in the Age of Jonson*, London, Chatto & Windus, 1937.

Kolve, V.A., *The Play Called Corpus Christi*, California, Stanford University Press, 1966.

Krailsheimer, A.J., *The Continental Renaissance*, Harmondsworth, Penguin Books, 1971.

Lake, D., '*Histriomastix*: Linguistic Evidence of Authorship', *Notes and Queries*, April 1981, pp. 148–52.

Lancashire, I., *Dramatic Texts and Records of Britain: A Chronological Topography to 1558*, Cambridge, Cambridge University Press, 1984.

Laslett, P., *The World We Have Lost*, London, Methuen, 1965.

Lawrence, W.J., *Pre-Restoration Studies*, Cambridge, Mass., Harvard University Press, 1927.

Lea, L.M., *Italian Popular Comedy*, New York, Russell & Russell, 1934.

Leacroft, R., *The Development of the English Playhouse*, London, Methuen, 1973.

Leech, C., 'Shakespeare's Prologues and Epilogues', *Studies in Honour of T.W. Baldwin*, ed. D.C. Allen, 1958, pp. 150–64.

Leggatt, A., *Ben Jonson: His Vision and Art*, London, Methuen, 1981.

Leiblin, 'The Lesson of Feigning in *A Mad World, My Masters*', *Modern Language Studies*, 8, 1, 1977–8, pp. 23–32.

Lennam, T., *Sebastian Westcott, the Children of Paul's and the 'Marriage of Wit and Science'*, Toronto, Toronto University Press, 1975.

Lenz, C., etc., *The Woman's Part: Feminist Criticism of Shakespeare*, Urbana, Illinois University Press, 1983.

Levin, R., *The Multiple Plot in English Renaissance Drama*, Chicago, Chicago University Press, 1971.

Levin, R., 'The New *New Inn* and the Proliferation of Good Bad Drama', *Essays in Criticism*, 2, 1972, pp. 41–7.

Levin, R., 'The Proof of the Parody', *Essays in Criticism*, 24, 1974, pp. 312–16.

Levin, R., *New Readings v. Old Plays*, Chicago, Chicago University Press, 1979.

Levin, R., 'The Acting Style of the Children's Companies', *American Notes and Queries*, 22, 1983, pp. 34–5.

Limon, J., *Gentlemen of a Company: English Players in Central and Eastern Europe, 1590–1660*, Cambridge, Cambridge University Press, 1985.

McCollum, W.G., 'Formalism and Illusion in Shakespearean Drama 1585–1598', *Quarterly Journal of Speech*, 31, 1945, pp. 446–53.

McCullen, J.T., 'Madness and Isolation of Characters in Elizabethan and early Stuart Theatre', *Studies in Philology*, 48, 1951, pp. 206–18.

McElroy, J.F., *Parody and Burlesque in the Tragi-Comedies of Thomas Middleton*, Salzburg, Salzburg University Press, 1972.

McGuire, R.L., 'The Play within the Play in *I Henry IV*', *Shakespeare Quarterly*, 18, 1967, pp. 47–52.

McGuire, P. and Samuelson, D. (eds), *Shakespeare: the Theatre Dimension*, New York, AMS, 1979.

McMillin, S., *The Elizabethan Theatre and 'The Book of Sir Thomas More'*, Ithaca, Cornell University Press, 1987.

Maitland, S., *Vesta Tilley*, London, Virago Press, 1986.

Mehl, D., 'Forms and Function of the Play-Within-Play', in S. Schoenbaum (ed.), *Renaissance Drama*, 1965, pp. 41–61.

Mehl, D., *The Elizabethan Dumb Show*, London, Methuen, 1965.

Motter, T.H.V., *The School Drama in England*, London, Longmans, 1929.

Nagler, A.M., *A Sourcebook in Theatrical History*, New York, Dover, 1952.

Nelson, R., *Play Within Play*, New York, Da Capo Press, 1971.

Nichols, L., *Progresses etc. of James I*, 1828.

Nicoll, A., *The Development of Theatre*, London, Harrap, 1927.

Nicoll, A., *Masks, Mimes and Miracles*, New York, Cooper Square, 1963.

Ogilvy, J.D.A., '*Mimi, Scurrae, Histriones*: Entertainers of the Early Middle Ages', *Speculum*, 38, 1963, pp. 603–19.

Opland, J., *Anglo-Saxon Oral Poetry: A Study of the Traditions*, New Haven, Yale University Press, 1980.

Orgel, S. *The Illusion of Power*, Berkeley, California University Press, 1975.

Oz, A., 'The Doubling of Parts in Shakespearean Comedy', *New York Literary Forum*, 1980, pp. 175–82.

Parfitt, G., *Ben Jonson: Public Poet and Private Man*, London, Dent, 1976.

Parker, R.B., 'Middleton's Experiments with Comedy and Judgement', in J.R. Brown and B. Harris (eds) *Jacobean Theatre*, London, Arnold, 1960.

Partridge, E.B., 'Ben Jonson: The Makings of a Dramatist (1596–1602)', in J.R. Brown, and B. Harris (eds), *Elizabethan Theatre*, London, Arnold, 1966.

Paterson, M., 'The Stagecraft of the Revels Office during the Reign of Elizabeth', in C. Prouty (ed.), *Studies in Elizabethan Theatre*, Hamden, Conn., Shoestring Press, 1961.

Payne, R., *The Great God Pan*, New York, Hermitage House, 1952.

Penniman, J.H., *The War of the Theatres*, Boston, Ginn and Co., 1879.

Pollard, A.W., *Miracle Plays, Moralities and Interludes*, Oxford, Clarendon, 1927.

Potter, L. *et al.* (eds), *Revels History of Drama in English IV*, London, Methuen, 1981.

Reibetanz, J., 'Hieronimo in Decimosexto: A Private Theatre Burlesque', *Renaissance Drama*, New Series, 5, 1972, pp. 89–121.

Rhoads, H.G., *Wm. Hawkins' Apollo Shroving*, 1936.

Righter, A., *Shakespeare and the Idea of the Play*, London, Chatto & Windus, 1962.

Ringler, W., 'The First Phase of the Elizabethan Attack on the Stage, 1558–1579', *Huntington Library Quarterly*, 4, 1942, pp. 391–418.

Ross, L., 'The use of a 'fit-up' booth in *Othello*', *Shakespeare Quarterly*, 12, 1961, pp. 359–70.

Salgado, G., *Eyewitnesses of Shakespeare*, Brighton, Sussex University Press, 1975.

Salgado, G., *The Elizabethan Underworld*, Gloucester, Alan Sutton, 1984.

Salingar, L., 'The Decline of Tragedy', in B. Ford (ed.), *Pelican Guide to English Literature*, II, Harmondsworth, Penguin, 1955.

Salingar, L., *Shakespeare and the Traditions of Comedy*, Cambridge, Cambridge University Press, 1974.

Schoenbaum, S., *Middleton's Tragedies*, New York, Gordian Press, 1955.

Scott, M., *John Marston's Plays*, London, Macmillan, 1978.

Selden, S., *Theatre Double Game*, North Carolina University Press, 1969.

Shaar, C., 'They hang him in the arbour', *English Studies*, February 1966, pp. 27–8.

Shapiro, M., *Children of the Revels*, New York, Columbia University Press, 1977.

Sharpe, R.B., *The Real War of the Theatres*, Boston, D.C. Heath, 1935.

Shaw, J., 'The Staging of Parody and Parallels in *I Henry IV*', in K. Muir (ed.), *Shakespeare Survey, 20*, Cambridge, Cambridge University Press, 1967.

Sheavyn, P., *The Literary Profession in the Elizabethan Age*, 2nd edn, Manchester, Manchester University Press, 1967.

Slights, W., 'The Trickster Hero in Middleton's *A Mad World, My Masters*', *Comparative Drama*, 3, 1969, pp. 87–98.

Small, R.A., *The Stage Quarrel Between Ben Jonson and the so-called Poetasters*, 1899.

Smith, G.C.M., *College Plays Performed by the University of Cambridge*, Cambridge, Cambridge University Press, 1923.

Smith, J.L., 'They hang him in the arbour: a defence of the accepted text', *English Studies*, 47, October, 1966, pp. 372–3.

Spencer, C. (ed.), *Five Restoration Adaptations of Shakespeare*, Urbana, Illinois University Press, 1965.

Spencer, T. and Wells, S. (eds), *A Book of Masques*, Cambridge, Cambridge University Press, 1967.

Spivak, B., *Shakespeare and the Allegory of Evil*, New York, Columbia University Press, 1958.

Stone, L., 'The Educational Revolution in England 1560–1640', *Past and Present*, 28, July 1964.

Stone, L., *The Crisis of the Aristocracy 1558–1641*, Oxford, Oxford University Press, 1965.

Street, J.B., 'The Durability of Boy Actors', *Notes and Queries*, December 1973, pp. 461–5.

Stroup, T., *Microcosmos: The Shape of the Elizabethan Play*, Lexington, Kentucky University Press, 1965.

Taylor, G., ' "We Happy Few", the 1600 abridgement of *Henry V*', in S. Wells and G. Taylor, *Studies in Henry V*, Oxford, Clarendon Press, 1979.

Teagarden, J.E., 'Reaction to the professional actor in Elizabethan London', 1957, unpublished PhD thesis, University of Florida.

Thaler, A., 'The Travelling Players in Shakespeare's England', *Modern Philology*, XVII, 9, 1920, pp. 489–514.

Thaler, A., 'Doubling in Shakespeare', *Times Literary Supplement*, 13 February, 1930.

Thompson, A., '*The Taming of the Shrew* and *The Spanish Tragedy*', *Notes and Queries*, 31, 2, 1984, pp. 182–4.

Thomson, P., *Shakespeare's Theatre*, London, Routledge & Kegan Paul, 1983.

Tucker, K., '*The Return from Parnassus Part II*: a Possible Key to the Acting Style of Marston's Plays', *American Notes and Queries*, 20, 1982, pp. 131–4.

Turner, R.G., 'The Causal Induction in Some Elizabethan Plays', *Studies in Philology*, LX(2)i, 1962, pp. 183–90.

Tydeman, W., *The Theatre in the Middle Ages*, Cambridge, Cambridge University Press, 1978.

Van Laan, T., *Role Playing in Shakespeare*, Toronto, Toronto University Press, 1978.

Waith, E., 'The Staging of *Bartholomew Fair*', *Studies in English Literature*, 2, Spring 1962, pp. 181–96.

Weimann, R., *Shakespeare and the Popular Tradition in the Theater*, ed. R. Schwartz, Baltimore, Johns Hopkins University Press, 1978.

Weirum, A., ' "Actors" and "Play-Acting" in Moralities', *Renaissance Drama*, 3, 1970, pp. 189–214.

Weisinger, H., *The Agony and the Triumph*, East Lansing, Michigan State University Press, 1964.

Welsford, E., *The Fool*, London, Faber & Faber, 1935.

Wentersdorf, K.P., 'The Repertory and Size of Pembroke's Company', *Theatre Annual*, 33, 1977, pp. 75–85.

Wentersdorf, K.P., 'The Original Ending of The Taming of the Shrew: a reconsideration', *Studies of English Literature*, XVIII, Spring 1978, No.2, pp. 201–12.

Wickham, G., *Early English Stages*, London, Routledge & Kegan Paul, [from 1959].

Wickham, G., *Shakespeare's Dramatic Heritage*, London, Routledge, & Kegan Paul, 1969.

Wickham, G., *The Medieval Theatre*, London, Weidenfeld & Nicolson, 1974.

Wiles, D., *The Early Plays of Robin Hood*, London, D.S. Brewer, 1981.

Wiles, D., *Shakespeare's Clowns*, Cambridge, Cambridge University Press, 1987.

Willeford, W., *The Fool and his Sceptre*, Arnold, 1969.

Wolfflin, H., *Principles of Art History*, trans. M.D. Hottinger, London, G. Bell & Sons, 1932.

Wood, H., 'Shakespeare burlesqued by two fellow dramatists', *American Journal of Philology*, XVI, 3, 63, 1895.

Worthen, W., *The Idea of the Actor*, Princeton, NJ, Princeton University Press, 1984.

Index

Breughel 10
Brome, Richard 58, 65–7, 221, 251
Bryan, George 23
Burbage, Richard 18, 141–7, 217
Burghley, William Cecil, Lord 133
Bury St Edmunds Grammar School
129
Bussy D'Ambois 111
Butler, Martin 193–4, 221–2

Caesar's Revenge 138
Calfhill, James 135
Cambises 23, 24, 26, 231, 234–5
Campbell O. J. 103, 107
Cardinal, The 64
Careless Shepherdess, The 58, 253
Carleton, Sir Dudley 153
Case is Altered, The 102, 156, 208
Chamberlain's Men 28, 42, 58, 64,
66, 68, 77, 100, 105, 110, 128
Chambers, Sir Edmund 157
Chapman, George 191, 211
Charles I, King 7, 191, 222
Chaste Maid in Cheapside, A 189
Chester Banns 220
Chettle, Henry 187, 199, 213
children 43–4, 98–9, 111–27, 149,
214, 217–20
Children of the Chapel 93, 103, 135,
179, 220, 249
Christ Church, Oxford 214
Christ College, Cambridge 137,
Christian Terence movement 130
Christmas Prince, The 3, 136
Christmas Revels 151, 215
Christopherson, John 130
Cicero 190
Civil War 96, 154
City Comedy 112–13, 121, 256
Clare Hall, Cambridge 137
Clifton, Henry 220, 248
clowns 2, 27, 38, 52, 54–92, 141–6,
182, 224
Club Law 137
Clyomon and Clamydes 15
Cocke J. 97, 192
Cockpit, The 178, 254
Coleman, John 257
Comedy of Errors, The 151

commedia dell'arte 22, 66, 69–73,
108
commedia erudita 129–32, 218
Common Conditions 23, 25, 231, 236–7
common law 136, 153–4
Common Player, A 97
'common players' 106, 219, 256
'coney-catching' pamphlets 75, 138–
41, 211–13
Confessions 198
Conley, Carey 136
Cook, Ann 18
costumes 7–12, 24, 75, 98, 227–8, 257
Covatta, Antony 212
Cradle of Security, The 21, 24, 30, 229–
30
Curtain, The 68–9, 97, 180, 182, 220
curtains 8, 27, 56, 61, 245
Cynthia's Revels 102, 113, 117, 119,
209
Cyprian 199

Daniel, Samuel 248
Davies, Sir John 110, 136, 149, 211
Davison, Peter 68
Day, John 66, 68–9
Dekker, Thomas 10, 15, 101–11, 115,
210–12, 249–50
Deuteronomy 95, 132
Devil is an Ass, The 201
Devil Tavern 109
devils 5, 12, 24, 96
Dido 135
Disobedient Child, The 29
disparity of player and role 25–7,
116–17
Dr Faustus 5, 68
de Dominus, Marco Antonio 7
Donatus 190
doubling 24–8, 32–3, 243
Drama's Vindication, The 193
Drummond, William 102, 109
Duchess of Malfi, The 200
dumb shows 21–2, 44
Dutch Courtesan, The 190
Dutton, John and Lawrence 133, 253

Earle, John 198
Eastwood Ho! 179, 208, 252

INDEX

women actresses 26, 70–3, 246–7
Women Beware Women 50, 206
Worcester's Men 69
World Tossed at Tennis, The 12
Wotton, Sir Henry 179–80

Wright, James 222

York acting regulations 221
Your Five Gallants 74
Yuletide 214